BEING NUMEROUS

20|21

BEING NUMEROUS

Poetry and the

Ground of Social Life

Oren Izenberg

PRINCETON   UNIVERSITY   PRESS

PRINCETON   AND   OXFORD

Copyright 2011 © by Princeton University Press

Published by Princeton University Press, 41 William Street, Princeton, New Jersey 08540

In the United Kingdom: Princeton University Press, 6 Oxford Street, Woodstock, Oxfordshire OX20 1TW

press.princeton.edu

Cover art: Jason Salavon, *The Grand Unification Theory (Part Three: Every Second of "It's a Wonderful Life")*. Detail on front and on back.

All Rights Reserved

Library of Congress Cataloging-in-Publication Data

Izenberg, Oren.

  Being numerous : poetry and the ground of social life / Oren Izenberg.

    p. cm. — (20/21)

    Includes bibliographical references and index.

    ISBN 978-0-691-14483-2 (cloth : alk. paper) — ISBN 978-0-691-14866-3 (pbk. : alk. paper)   1. Poetry, modern—20th century—History and criticism—Theory, etc.   I. Title.

    PN1271.I94 2010

    809.1'04—dc22   2010020738

British Library Cataloging-in-Publication Data is available

This book has been composed in Helvetica Neue

Printed on acid-free paper. ∞

Printed in the United States of America

10 9 8 7 6 5 4 3 2 1

CONTENTS

ACKNOWLEDGMENTS

I owe my first debt of gratitude to my parents. My father, Gerald Izenberg, showed me by his example how to lead a life of the mind while being fully present to others. My mother, Ziva Izenberg, has always instructed me with her powerful good sense and her unshakable will. They are the most generous people I know. Together, they have encouraged and supported everything I have set out to do; this book is dedicated to them.

I went to the Johns Hopkins University to study with Allen Grossman, a decision that was rewarded beyond all expectation. For many years, in Baltimore, Lexington, and Chicago, Allen's immense learning and deep humanity—along with his powerful conviction that the work of poetry is intimately related to the work of being a person in the world—have shaped my sense of what it is to be a scholar and a teacher. His inimitable voice is in my ear when I read poems and when I write about them—may it always be so. If Allen was this work's first audience, Walter Benn Michaels was its second. Long afternoons spent working these ideas out in the pitched battle that is apparently his native idiom make up some of my best and most vivid memories of Hopkins. In recent years, Walter has been as generous in his friendship as he is merciless in argument; I am grateful for both.

Others have left their mark as well. Sharon Cameron showed me an unsparing intensity of attention to poems that I can only hope to approximate. John Guillory and Frances Ferguson, first as teachers and then later as colleagues, showed me how to follow an idea to its root. My fellow graduate students from those days formed an intellectual community that—though now flung far—continues to instruct and inspire me. Some of them—in particular, Scott Black, Abigail Cheever, Daniel Denecke, Andrew Franta, Joanna Klink, Larissa MacFarquhar, Stacey Margolis,

Dan McGee, Deak Nabers, Michael Szalay, Jane Thrailkill—will find that sentences they have spoken to me have made their way into this book.

At Harvard University, I was fortunate to be a part of a tremendous cohort of young faculty. My fellow Garden Level residents—Lynn Festa, Yunte Huang, John Picker, Leah Price, Sharmila Sen, Ann Wierda Rowland—made my time in Cambridge a happy one. Many other Harvard colleagues contributed to this book as well—special thanks to Forrest Gander, Jorie Graham, Barbara Johnson, Robert Kiely, and Peter Sacks.

Being Numerous was completed at the University of Chicago. There, Robert von Hallberg, by sheer force of personality and passionate devotion to literature and scholarship, created—for a time—a truly remarkable place to think and talk about poems. I am grateful to him, and to the rest of the faculty in the Program in Poetry and Poetics—Danielle Allen, Kelly Austin, Robert Bird, Bradin Cormack, Alison James, Liesl Olson, Mark Payne, Chicu Reddy, Jennifer Scappettone, Richard Strier, David Wray—for years of conversation about my work and theirs. Other Chicago colleagues have been generous friends and interlocutors; particular thanks go to Lauren Berlant, Suzanne Buffam, Sandra Macpherson, and Eric Slauter for personal and intellectual companionship. Jim Chandler and Françoise Meltzer made the Franke Institute for the Humanities—which generously supported part of a year's leave—an intellectually lively and productive place to be. I have also been tremendously fortunate in my students at Chicago. Joshua Kotin, Jenny Ludwig, Marta Napiorkowska, Kiki Petrosino, Andrew Rippeon, Michael Robbins, Dustin Simpson, and Michelle Taransky helped me to think through many of the arguments in this book in a memorable (to me) seminar on Radical Poetics. Throughout my years at the University, they, along with V. Joshua Adams, Stephanie Anderson, Joel Callahan, Michael Hansen, Billy Junker, Chalcey Wilding, and Johanna Winant have continued to teach me with their love for poems and for ideas.

Good conversation about poetry transcends the narrow confines of institution and discipline. Charles Altieri, Brett Bourbon, Steve Burt, Jeff Dolven, Roland Greene, Lyn Hejinian, Susan Howe, Sean McCann, Maureen McLane, Sianne Ngai, Marjorie Perloff, Ron Silliman, and Barrett Watten have all challenged me to think harder—through their writing, in their questioning, and sometimes by their opposition. Mark Canuel and the English Department at the University of Illinois at Chicago have provided an intellectual haven. Jennifer Ashton deserves special acknowledgment. She has read many of these pages many times, and I am thankful for her critical intelligence and for her steady friendship.

Audiences at Brown University, Williams College, and the Johns Hopkins University provided helpful responses to work in progress. Earlier versions of some of these chapters have appeared in several journals: thanks to the editors of *Critical Inquiry*, *Modernism/Modernity*, and *Modern Philology* for allowing me permission to reprint from them here. Thanks to Hanne Winarsky at Princeton University Press for believing in this book and shepherding it through to publication; to two anonymous readers for their insightful commentary and criticism; and to Ellen Foos and Jodi Beder for their exhaustive work on the manuscript. After their careful attention, any mistakes that remain are my own.

Above all, I am thankful to Sonya Rasminsky. Her intelligence, judgment, and nearly infinite patience have made this work possible. Her love and friendship make everything else possible. These pages are about the burdens and obligations of being a person. Sonya, together with our children, Toby and Miri, have taught me the joys.

INTRODUCTION

Poems, Poetry, Personhood

It is time to explain myself. Let us stand up.

BEING NUMEROUS ADDRESSES a set of interdependent problems in the history, theory, and politics of recent Anglo-American poetry. In it, I offer a challenge and an alternative to a nearly unanimous literary-historical consensus that would divide poetry into two warring camps—post-Romantic and postmodern; symbolist and constructivist; traditionalist and avant-garde—camps that would pit form against form on grounds at once aesthetic and ethical. Rather than choosing sides in this conflict or re-sorting the poems upon its field of battle, I argue that a more compelling history might begin by offering a revisionary account of what poetry is or can be. Poetry is not always and everywhere understood as a *literary* project aiming to produce a special kind of verbal artifact distinguished by its particular formal qualities or by its distinctive uses of language.[1] Nor is it always understood as an *aesthetic* project seeking to provoke or promote a special kind of experience—of transformative beauty, for example, or of imaginative freedom—in its readers.[2] Among the possible alternative ways of understanding poetry, I focus on the one that seems to me at once the most urgent and the one most fully obscured by our current taxonomies. For a certain type of modern poet, I will argue, "poetry" names an ontological project: a civilizational wish to reground the concept and the value of *the person*.

This shift of emphasis, from "poems" as objects or occasions for experience to "poetry" as an occasion for reestablishing or revealing the most basic unit of social life and for securing the most fundamental object of moral regard, has precedents and justifications in the long history of the theory of poetry:[3] in the ancient association of song with the most important forms of social recognition (Homer's κλέος ἄφθιτον, or "immortal fame," for example); or in the Romantic idea that the play of poetic imagination is constitutive of what it means to be human (Friedrich Schiller's "[der Mensch] ist nur da ganz Mensch, wo er spielt").[4] But the modern versions of these claims are altered and intensified to the extent that the need to reground personhood responds to history on another scale: to a set of civilizational crises that are at once theoretical (the desacralization or critique of the concept of the person) and devastatingly real. These include the upheavals of decolonization and nation formation, the levelings of consumer culture, "the end of history," and above all, genocide and the specter of total annihilation. In discussions centered on writers from a range of historical moments, formal traditions, and political orientations (William Butler Yeats, George Oppen, Frank O'Hara, and the Language poets), I identify a tradition of poets for whom our century's extreme failures to value persons adequately—or even to perceive persons as persons— issue to poetry a reconstructive philosophical imperative that is greater than any imperative to art; indeed, it is hostile to art *as such*.

But why should art and personhood come to seem opposed to each other? As both Classical and Romantic examples attest, it would seem rather more common to regard them as two moments in the project of self-fashioning or soul- making (what might, in a more technical or skeptical idiom, be called "subject formation"). When we describe a poem as having a "speaker," or as giving "voice" to a person, we are not *assuming* anything about what a person is. Rather, we are taking the artifice of voice in the poem to offer something like a model or a theory of the person, or even a pedagogy of personhood. In its orchestrations of perception, conception, and affect, a poem elaborates upon or expands the possibilities of what a person can see, think, and feel. Through its constructive work with the sound and matter of language, the poem gives shape to the concept of the person who can think, say, and make *these things*.[5] Likewise, it has often seemed intuitive to see poems as fostering recognition and solidarity between persons. As public objects, poems strive to make their ideas or conceptions of personhood perceptible and durable—if not always immediately legible—to others. In their scoring of the voice, or in their stretching of the word beyond or beneath the horizons of ordinary speech, they produce opportunities for readers and hearers to extend and expand their sympathies, and to identify even the most baroque utterance or repulsive sentiment as the testimony of a fellow mind.

But if poetry has seemed well—even powerfully—suited to redress failures of human sociability, it has also been understood to be profoundly implicated in them. The accounts of personhood made available to sense by poetry's vivid presence are burdened with art's limits. The work of art in John Ashbery's "Self-Portrait in a Convex Mirror" may be the means by which "[t]he soul establishes itself"; but the "secret" of the soul made manifest in art is "that the soul is not a soul / Has no secret, is small, and it fits / Its hollow perfectly: its room, our moment of attention." In their economy of means and their requirements of closure, even the most expansive poems can be felt to reproduce—and to make palatable or attractive— the bounded scope and restricted application of the concepts that they make available.

Similar problems accrue to the poem conceived as an occasion for sympathy. As objectifications of thought or voice destined for the eyes and ears of others, poems are dependent on the capacities of their readers for attention and perception, interest or pleasure. As a result of this dependency, works of verbal art may seem to emphasize, not the autonomy or dignity of the other of whom they tell, but rather the sense in which persons *themselves* are dependent upon the perceptions and inclinations of others for survival. Hannah Arendt begins *The Life of the Mind* with this very thought: "Nothing and nobody exists in this world whose very being does not presuppose a *spectator*."[6] Not to be beheld is not to exist; thus, when Sappho declares poetry's cultural function to supply the privilege of value-bearing personhood in the form of eternal perceptibility, she does so precisely by way of withdrawing that privilege in contempt:

> When you lie dead there will be no memory of you,
> No one missing you afterward, for you have no part
> in the roses of Pieria. Unnoticed in the house of Hades
> too, you'll wander, flittering after faded corpses.[7]

For Ashbery's "Daffy Duck in Hollywood," it is not just the immortalization of life but life itself that is afflicted with a dependency upon the attention of another: "I have / Only my intermittent life in your thoughts to live. . . . Everything / Depends on whether somebody reminds you of me." In some serious sense, we are all animated figures, for whom much (perhaps it is everything) depends upon whether we seem sufficiently like "somebody" to be worthy of having our claims credited or to be granted justice.

In the face of a century of emergencies, some poets come to see the relation between art's power and its limits, not as a simple fact, as Arendt sees it; not as a point of privilege, as Sappho understands it; and not as an occasion for the witty performance of regret and evasion, as Ashbery treats it; rather, they see the requirements of closure and perceptibility as an intolerable burden and an affront to human dignity. For such poets, the poetic response to crises of human value entails reimagining the object of the art—a task that they perform as a sort of sacrifice. The effort to evade the limits and dependencies of the person—once they are understood to be inseparable from the form and substance of the poem itself— results in a conception of art with a conflicted and attenuated relation to both substance and form. The poets I am *most* interested to describe throughout this book will thus resist their own will to formal mastery, shy away from the sensory richness of their own strongest work, and undermine the conceptual particularity and moral exemplarity of their poetic vision. At the extremes, they long, threaten, or enjoin themselves to do away with poetry altogether. More precisely, they strive to conceive of or even produce a "poetry" without poems; as though the problems with what philosophy calls "person-concepts"—our definitions of and attempts to give an account of personhood—could be addressed by subverting or destroying the very medium that bears them.

Thus, what begins as an argument about the contours of recent literary history opens into a reconsideration of the nature or status of the literary artifact and of the role that poetry can play in social thought. The poets I will discuss here cannot be recruited into the war of kinds I describe at the outset without obscuring their deepest commitments. Nor can their choice of styles be understood to be part of an ethical or political project aimed at expanding the sphere of attention or social sympathy. For these poets, and for others of their kind, *no* style could be adequately capacious to convey the limitless value of the person; no poem that had to be perceived in order to live could produce confidence, beyond skepticism or error, that a valued life was present.

But what is the alternative—in poetry, for personhood—to style and to perceptibility, to appearance and phenomenology? Against a poetics of poems that enters deeply into the texture of the experience of persons (whether as representation of that experience or occasion for it), the poets I will describe here seek ways to make their poetic thinking yield accounts of personhood that are at once *minimal*—placing as few restrictions as possible upon the legitimate forms a person can take—and *universal*—tolerating no exemptions or exclusions. Finally, they will also demand that our concepts of personhood identify something *real*: not political fictions we could come to inhabit together, or pragmatic ways of speaking we might come to share, but a ground on which the idea of a "we" might stand. This poetry, I argue, is an important site for the articulation of a new humanism: it seeks a reconstructive response to the great crises of social agreement and recognition in the twentieth century.

I. Two Kinds

"There are two kinds of poets, just as there are two kinds of blondes," opines Oliver Wendell Holmes's unnamed Author in *The Autocrat of the Breakfast-Table*.[8] The choice offered to the residents of an imaginary New England boardinghouse in the pages of the *Atlantic Monthly* in 1858—between

"NEGATIVE or WASHED" and "POSITIVE or STAINED"—has justly been treated with less seriousness than some other, better known attempts to divide poetry in two: Plato's account of the passion-driven and imitative poet (banished) and the properly devotional and moral poet (welcome), for example; or Schiller's classification of poets and stages of culture as "naïve" and immediate or reflectively "sentimental."[9] Nevertheless, it is Holmes's slighter and more superficial taxonomy that seems apt for our present moment. Like his Author, the authors of our histories of poetry in the twentieth century—and now the twenty-first—have divided the art into two jealous and irreconcilable kinds. And like the distinction between "negative" and "washed" or "positive" and "stained," our distinctions and descriptions begin with the promising technical sheen of analysis, but they quickly devolve into fashions.

> "[Movement of curiosity among our ladies at table. - Please to tell us about those blondes, said the schoolmistress.]"[10]

The first of these poetic kinds has been defined through its traditionalist lineage: its modernism is continuous with Romanticism in its faith in the power of art—and in the modes of consciousness and powers of mind that poetic forms access or promote—to redeem or remake the self and history, even as it casts a cold eye on the Romantic celebration of naturalized subjectivity as history's highest achievement.[11] Rooted in W. B. Yeats's symbolism and his dream- and spirit- haunted atavisms, this version of Modernism encompasses T. S. Eliot both in his religious strivings and in the avowed classicism of his art; it takes in Wallace Stevens's ornate beauties as well as his supreme fictions. Postmodernists like Robert Lowell, Elizabeth Bishop, and Sylvia Plath are, in their turn, skeptical of modernism's totalizing forms of artistic mastery; newly receptive, too, to the human particularity and social situatedness of the poetic speaker. But even in his ironic deflations of aesthetic or imaginative heroism, a poet like Lowell never wholly breaks with the modernist conception of the poetic vocation, and never relinquishes the elevated ambition to transform the merely empirical person into the valued person by poetic modes of speech and thought.[12]

> We are poor passing facts,
> Warned by that to give
> each figure in the photograph
> his living name.[13]

Contemporary champions in this line may be found wherever poets understand themselves to be the inheritors of a single art as of an unbroken thought. Such poets understand poetry's ageless continuity as an ally or fellow-fighter; a supplement to the limits and contingencies of the human mind. Frank Bidart's appeal to the great makers of the past—his plea for a transformative intensification of self that would differentiate him from a mere creature of instinct—marks him out as a poet of this sort:

> Not bird not badger not beaver not bee
> Many creatures must
> make, but only one must seek
> within itself what to make
>
> . . .
>
> Teach me, masters who by making were
> remade, your art.[14]

The second kind of poet, less thoroughly canonized but more comprehensively theorized, is conceived as the inheritor of a paradoxical "avant-garde tradition." This tradition, too, lays some claim to the energies of Romanticism (here, in its most revolutionary aspects). But its repeated promises of originality and continual discoveries of discontinuity are more securely grounded in modernist experiments: Gertrude Stein's "beginning again and again";[15] Ezra Pound's epic of assemblage, "containing" history by constructing it; the open-eyed immanence of William Carlos Williams's "clarity, outline of leaf."[16] The privileging of unending novelty, constructivist experiment, and unadorned sight justifies an explosion of mid-century movements and schools, united (if at all) in valuing difference and in busily seeking for continual change. Something of the formal, conceptual, and geographic range of this moment is on display at mid-century in Donald Allen's anthology *The New American Poetry 1945–1960,* which opened so many poets' eyes to the varieties of American poetic innovation with transformative results. The century's end saw a consolidation of these experimental energies around the work of the American avant-garde school known as the Language poets; and it is this movement, more than any other, that continues to give formal and theoretical shape to the poetic present, whether as positive influence or troubled inheritance.

This "alternative" tradition pits a thoroughgoing skepticism about the representational powers of language and the coherence of selves against a theoretical optimism about the constructive possibilities of language and its capacity to remake selves or to release them from conceptual fetters. Contemporary poets in its line take the poem as an occasion not so much for self-discovery as for the disassembly and reassembly of persons—often in the same act or moment, as in Rae Armantrout's self-theorizing performance of a speaker's always unfinished work of manifestation:

> A moment is everything
> one person
> (see below)

takes in simultaneously
though some
or much of what
a creature feels
may not reach
conscious awareness
and only a small part
(or none) of this
will be carried forward
to the next instant.[17]

These are, I have suggested, familiar stories—even overfamiliar. The narratives I have been elaborating are well enough entrenched in our present conversation about poetry that they seem to lie on the very surfaces of poems, so that we can sort confidently between Bidart's poem and Armantrout's—and, it would some-times seem, any others—by gestalt.[18] Indeed, part of the intuitiveness, force, and durability of the split stems from precisely this kind of impressionism. But in fact, the analytic categories underwriting and justifying the division vary substantially from critic to critic. Marjorie Perloff, for example, has most recently cast the op-position as between a dominant "expressivist paradigm" that takes poetry as a "*vehicle*" for "thoughts and feelings" that originate in selves prior to language, and a "constructivism" that takes language as "the site of meaning making."[19] Harold Bloom, characteristically uncompromising, elaborates the criteria of a great tradition in terms derived from the Romantic line he favors—"aesthetic splendor, intellec-tual power, wisdom"—but does not countenance the existence of an alternative to greatness. Rather, he conceives of the split as the division between "poetry" and "non-poetry."[20] Others, continuing the Whitmanian tradition of equating "the free growth of metrical laws" with political freedom, or endorsing Eliot's conflation of his impulse to conserve literary traditions with his impulse to uphold traditional institutions ("classicist in literature, royalist in politics, and Anglo-Catholic in reli-gion") have taken the difference between wisdom and invention, splendor and disruption to be political in design or effect, and map the difference between tradi-tion and experiment onto a difference between right and left.[21]

Rachel Blau DuPlessis provides a vivid example of the multiplicity of grounds upon which our history currently stands in her definition of objectivism, which, as she writes,

usefully designates a general aesthetic position in modern and contemporary poetry encompassing work based, generally, on "the real," on history, not myth, on empiricism not projection, on the discrete not the unified, on vernacular prosodies not traditional poetic rhetoric, on "imagism" not "symbolism" or "sur-realism," and on particulars with a dynamic relation to universals.[22]

This description of a specific poetic movement produces the full effect of the two-tradition model in microcosm. The terms it proposes are both useful and forceful: they do pick out recognizable elements both in poems that we know and in ones that we might discover. But the poetic position described here is unstable because the terms used to define it are heterogeneous in kind. Sometimes they evoke literary-historical movements ("imagism" vs. "symbolism"); sometimes they seem to reflect formal or functional commitments that transcend the boundaries of schools and histories ("discrete" vs. "unified" or "vernacular" vs. "rhetorical"); and sometimes they suggest philosophical commitments with strong ideological implications but no necessary aesthetic dimension ("history" vs. "myth" or "empiricism" vs. "projection"). Still, despite the various or shifting or incommensurable terms in which the division is described or conceptualized, the critical champions of each side do achieve virtual unanimity about the *fact* of the split, and an impressive (if imperfect) consensus about which poet belongs to whom.

This book began in my dissatisfaction with this state of affairs—one which has, despite the fact that others have begun to share that dissatisfaction, shown few signs of disappearing.[23] The need to make navigable or usable the dense field of the past century's poetry has resulted in a sorting engine so efficient that it has reproduced itself as orthodoxy not just in criticism—where it has leapt from the conclusion of an argument to its unexamined premise[24]—but even in the work of poets themselves. What began as a description of the art has been adopted by the artist as an obligation; the poet's felt need to find a productive community and a usable past has turned into the demand to pick a side; and style has become less a way of solving artistic problems than a declaration of allegiance.[25] As a general rule, critical and poetic partisans, bent on consolidating, celebrating, claiming, or extending one tradition, take note of the other only long enough to deride—and too often such derision is a reflexive reaction rather than an analytic one.

There are a number of ways to go about criticizing this view of the poetic field. Certainly any literary history so powerfully streamlined courts criticism for the poverty or indelicacy of its distinctions. Many of the kinds of poetry written in the last hundred years fit only uneasily or tendentiously into this binary of tradition and experiment. Poetries that draw from the wellsprings of neglected experiences, from oral literatures, or from traditions that originate beyond Europe and the Americas, for example, may appear both traditional and innovative at once, as the ideology of authenticity may offer possibilities of renewal to a cultural sphere unfamiliar with the sound of marginalized voices. The critical movement to recover the rich tradition of poetry by women is one notable instance of the complex interplay in which authenticity is itself a kind of experiment;[26] similar dynamics are at work in the hard-to-classify case of Afro-Modernism in the first half of the century, or of Asian American poetry in the second.[27] From an even broader vantage, the sheer volume and multiplicity of poetries in the last hundred years in America produces a cacophony of voices that resist categorization almost entirely—a fact elevated to a principle by the two-volume Library of America offering *American Poetry: The Twentieth Century,* a collection that "organizes" some two hundred poets, versifiers, and lyricists by mere chronology, so that the Dadaist provocation of Baroness Elsa von Freytag-Loringhoven stands next to the vernacular formalism of Robert Frost, and Lightnin' Hopkins's "Death Bells" accompany May Sarton's decorous music.[28]

Critics have also (usually implicitly) qualified the two-tradition narrative by paying rigorous attention to the multiple aspects or moments to be found within a single poet's work. Such intensely particularizing scrutiny can make a poet seem *sui generis*, a school or industry unto himself. Pound is an exemplary figure in this vein. Considered for their monumental stature as an archive of formal inventions, his *Cantos* are, as Basil Bunting declared them, the Alps of the modernist poetic landscape—inimitable, inevitable, demanding harrowing passage. Considered in terms of his totalizing ambitions and wretched politics, Pound is the queen of spades in the game of literary history—the card nobody wants. John Ashbery is uncategorizable in another (more slippery, less agonistic) sense. In his endless productivity and insistent changefulness he seems to belong to every category we can imagine or desire. Our jack of diamonds, he is claimed at one moment for the tradition of Stevens and at the next for the tradition of Stein.

The split between kinds, so clear in theory, may not be so clear in the actual conduct of literary life, where relations between poets often reveal themselves with the force of surprise. When Robert Lowell and Allen Ginsberg read together at St. Mark's in 1977, the *New York Times* attested to the collision of two species: the "tense ruddy history-ridden New England Brahmin" on the one hand and a "bearded Paterson-East Side Hasid guru" on the other.[29] Yet Lowell the Brahmin attests to his shared genealogy with Ginsberg the Hasid ("Actually, we're from two ends of the William Carlos Williams spectrum"), and confirms (though somewhat grudgingly) Ginsberg's influence in his letters. Poets may also deliberately *strive* to overcome divisions and sequestrations that they feel as overly constraining.[30] Moxley's choice of poetic dedications and homages (to Keats, to Oppen), along with her polemically broad courting of dictions, forms, and influences, hone her book's dedication "to my contemporaries" into a pointed rebuke to the burdensome allegiances that the contemporary demands of the emerging poet.

I have some sympathies with all of these qualifications, projects of recovery and pluralization, and angles of revision and self-expansion. But none of them describes the course this book has taken. While I, too, had hoped to dissolve the distinctions that seem to have cut poets of whatever kind off from fully half of their art, I have come to think that our analytic divisions need to be intensified instead. Thus, as it happens, *Being Numerous* does argue for the existence of yet another distinction within modern and contemporary poetry. But because the division I have in mind will prove to be more fully grounded in poets' philosophical (indeed, their ontological) commitments rather than their strictly formal or ideological ones, it cuts across the current lines drawn according to style and politics. And because it arises from the intuitions of a certain kind of poet about the most fundamental questions—not just about the nature of literary artifacts, but about the human nature of their makers and readers—it results in a poetic taxonomy that is, if less total in scope, more absolute in nature.

. . .

Symptoms of this absoluteness may be found in the depths of poetic incomprehension. Though Yeats and Pound actually shared a physical home at Stone Cottage as well as metaphysical and occult sources, the older poet's bewilderment in the face of the younger's attempt to explain the structure of the *Cantos*—and of history—is as complete as his admiration:

> He has scribbled on the back of an envelope certain sets of letters that represent emotions or archetypal events—I cannot find any adequate definition—A B C D and then J K L M, and then each set of letters repeated, and then A B C D inverted and this repeated, and then a new element X Y Z, then certain letters that never recur, and then all sorts of combinations of X Y Z and J K L M and A B C D and D C B A, and all set whirling together.[31]

Wider still is the gulf between Pound and Stevens, who shared no affections and barely a common alphabet, and whose quarrels never even rose to the level of mutual misunderstanding. They appear hardly to have read each other's work at all.[32]

Misunderstanding is translated into the next generation of poets as a kind of willful indifference. George Oppen's letters over a half-century and his copious notebooks and "daybooks" are full of news of the literary world, but they reveal the horizon of that world to have been quite close.[33] "Four men in Pound's generation wrote poetry," Oppen proclaims, "Perhaps an equal number since."[34] The so-called Objectivist poets like Louis Zukofsky, Carl Rakosi, and Charles Reznikoff are Oppen's constant interests and interlocutors, while the poets most often understood as the central figures of that generation—Randall Jarrell, John Berryman, Sylvia Plath, or Robert Lowell—hardly even appear as worthy topics of conversation. The exception in this case outdoes the rule; Oppen's slighting mention of Elizabeth Bishop, as the author of "the silliest line ever written,"[35] produces even more effectively than silence a near total erasure of the work. Bishop herself similarly erases half the poetic world in her own elegant and voluminous correspondence; one would look in vain for the barest mention of any poet calling himself an objectivist.[36]

Incomprehension, indifference, and erasure are symptomatic of something important that lies beneath the shrillness of our present acrimony. If the latter is best understood as a competition for limited resources of publication and the dwindling stocks of honor and prestige available to poetry of any kind in our culture,[37] the more complete separation looks less like a clash of tribal styles and more like two entirely different practices only accidentally going by the same name. I believe Harold Bloom has captured something of this all-or-nothing distinction in his insistence on characterizing recent poetic history as the contest between "poetry" and "non-poetry." While lesser poetry might, for a time, triumph over the greater in some period's sensibility (such may be the case, according to Bloom, with T. S. Eliot and Ezra Pound, "the Cowley and Cleveland of this age"[38]), poetry cannot be in genuine competition with non-poetry. Perhaps one could mistake the ersatz for the real thing; but such a mistake would be categorical, an error of reason rather than a lapse of judgment. I would like to suggest (very much against the spirit of his intention) that we read Bloom's categorical claims in a register that is neither merely dismissive nor even fundamentally evaluative, but rather as genuinely and usefully taxonomic. This is to say that the idea of "non-poetry"—an art that does not merely lack aesthetic "splendor" in some degree, but that instead negates the very idea of aesthesis as the privilege and destination of poetry—captures something important about the formal features of an as-yet-undefined poetic kind. It also, I will soon argue, suggests something quite precise about the characteristic intentions of certain "non-poets" with respect to the objects and purposes of their art.

But for the moment, I would simply note that this difference between conceptions of the poem lies behind another fact that has been hard for readers interested in the innovative poetry of the twentieth century to acknowledge. The lack of what might be called poetic realization results in work that can be hard to love, or even to like. So variously fragmented, occulted, difficult, and silent; so assertively trivial, boring, or aleatory are the types of poetry on the "experimental" side of the critical divide, that critics who champion the work have gone to great didactic and theoretical lengths to imagine, explain, justify, and market alternative species of pleasure and interest to compensate for the loss of traditional aesthetics. Such justifications include "the fascination with what's difficult," the penetration of the veil of the esoteric, the masochistic pleasures of derangement, the politicized shock of estrangement, the tranquilizing or meditative dwelling in the ambient.[39]

This pointed catalogue may read like a judgment of taste, or a way of casting my lot with a particular family of poetic styles through descriptive abuse. But my goal here and throughout is not to refuse any sort of pleasure or interest no matter how recondite; nor is it to uphold "traditional" aesthetic standards in relation to poems that do not seek them. Still less do I mean for a new poetic taxonomy to proscribe aesthetic choices for contemporary artists in the way of the old one (though I may hope that my argument opens some compelling possibilities for writing). Rather, my point will be to show that the *a priori* conviction that all poetic projects imagine the crucial relation to poetry to be a relation to an object—an object of labor, of perception, of interpretation—is an unwarranted assumption; even a sort of fetishism. If many of the poems I gravitate to in this book appear to be in various ways silent—strange, broken, or otherwise unforthcoming with any of the pleasures we expect and demand of well-made things—it is because they are deliberately made in such a way as to present problems for reception, problems for which *none* of our vocabularies of response (traditional or innovative, aesthetic, affective, constructivist, pragmatic) are appropriate. An insistence upon the centrality or even the reality of the poem is not consistent with what every poet means by undertaking poetry. Let there be as many kinds of pleasure and interest as can be conceived; the frequency with which we can encounter "non-poetry" as a literary fact should, if we attend to it, point us in the direction of a deficiency not just with the ways poetic history has been described, but with the ways that poetry itself has been conceived. Stated most simply: The persistent production of non-poems asks that we entertain the notion that *what the poet intends by means of poetry is not always the poem.*

II. Poetry in the General Sense

Of course, poets do intend their poems. The idea of the poem as the product of great and focused labor will be familiar to anyone who has ever tried to write one. It is a notion as deeply ingrained in the tradition as its opposite, the ideal of full-throated ease that work on the poem paradoxically strives to approximate:

> I said: 'A line will take us hours maybe;
> Yet if it does not seem a moment's thought,
> Our stitching and unstitching has been naught. . . .'

But just what is it—besides the appearance of effortless spontaneity—that a poet intends by his painstaking work on the line? And what is the benefit for the reader of what the poet, also in "Adam's Curse," calls the "idle trade" of working *through* the line, whether in "beautiful old books," or (as some more avant-garde poet might prefer it) in the estranging and new?

The question of how to relate the distinctive forms and phenomenologies of poems to the intentions of their makers and the effects upon their readers has been the central problematic for poetic criticism in the last half-century. W. K. Wimsatt, in "*The Verbal Icon*," provides the canonical instance of the New Critical way of handling—which is to say, exacerbating—the problem:

> [P]oems are taken by the critic not as abstract or intentional, but in what might be called solid, or artifactual, dimensions. The verbal object will be viewed by

the critic in a kind of stereoscopic perspective that makes it look somewhat like a physical object. The poet himself is taken as artist, not as intender, but as accomplisher.[40]

Much of the poetic criticism that has followed in the wake of the New Criticism has been concerned to theorize ways to reconcile the "artifactual" solidity of the poem that Wimsatt argues for here—an objectification that licenses the heightened attention to form and pattern that we call "close reading"—with a concern with the shaping influences of history. Thus, Theodor Adorno begins his 1957 essay "On Lyric Poetry and Society" by imagining a hypothetical listener's anxious—one might say Wimsattian—concern that the critic's attempt to relate a lyric to society does worse than merely misconstrue the poem; it "does not *see* it at all." The properly dialectical reading that would allay such anxieties, Adorno goes on to explain, will resist taking the poem for the wrong sort of thing—"objects with which to demonstrate sociological theses"—only if it respects the objecthood of poems in the right sense: only if, that is, "the social element in [poems] is shown to reveal something essential about the basis of their quality."[41] "Material," as Adorno puts it in *Aesthetic Theory,* "is always historical."[42] Despite his resistance to the ideology of modernist claims to self-sufficiency, Adorno's poem, like Wimsatt's, manifests itself as solid and artifactual, walled off in the enclosure of its forms, autonomous and functionless. But, Adorno argues, the "basis" of that peculiar quality of autonomy is the social world that the work refuses: or, as he puts it, "the demand that the lyric word be virginal is itself social in nature."[43] Adorno's artifactual lyric is the manifest negation of sociality—all its modes of talk, its restrictive notions of causality, its reductive spheres of concern—and it is this negation that will prove in his analysis to be the very mode of art's social engagement.

Between the object as masterful accomplishment and the object as masterful refusal there lies a range of other possibilities. Adorno's preservation of formalism as the crucial category for even the most historically inclined reader has itself been preserved in one sense by critics who treat the poem's formal or artifactual nature as a reactionary withdrawal from history. It has been honored in a still more capacious sense by historicist critics who share Adorno's view of form as the site of the poem's contact with history, but subtract his insistence on negation or refusal as the only properly poetic mode of historical engagement.[44] Rather than offering some new angle on the familiar question of how to render the apparent rift between aesthetic object and its social intentions merely apparent, however, I would first like to consider alternatives to the original premise: not just to Adorno's claim that the poem of modernity is distinguished by a heightened kind of formalization or objectification, but to the more general claim that the primary way to do justice to poetry as poetry is "to see it at all." Or, more capaciously, to consider it in its phenomenal modes: in the music of its language, the vividness of its figures, the force of its rhetoric, even the disposition of its words across the surface of the page.

This reconsideration, too, has a basis as much in intuitions that arise from the making of poems as from central texts of poetic theory. First the intuition: I have already suggested that anyone who writes a poem will be familiar with the feeling of laborious "ease" that goes into its realization. But now I would like to suggest that the poet undertaking to enter poetry will also recognize a feeling of deep and sometimes troubling disjunction between the work he or she does on the poem on the one hand—both the formal work on the way to what Wimsatt calls the poem's "accomplishment," and the signifying work on the way to communicating or constructing meaning—and the poet's intentions *for* poetry on the other. In "To Some I Have Talked With by the Fire," the poem Yeats chose as the dedication to his 1906 *Poetical Works,* the poet subtly attests to the disjunction by contrasting the effortful labor of poetic making with the effortless and intransitive "brimming" of the heart with dreams:

> While I wrought out these fitful Danaan rhymes,
> My heart would brim with dreams about the times
> When we bent down above the fading coals
> And talked of the dark folk who live in souls
> Of passionate men, like bats in the dead trees.

The oblique relation in this poem between the work of making rhymes and the heart's dreaming—actions that are represented as simultaneous, but one not obviously causing or caused by the other—suggests a separation between the work of poetic making and the poet's generative vision. This vision is of an ever-deepening set of communal relations. It begins with shared talk among equals, but within that conversation arise thoughts of still more elemental collectivities: "dark folk"; "wayward twilight companies"; and finally, an "embattled flaming multitude." This last image of communal life or collective action arises seemingly of its own volition; description of the "multitude" dilates to take over the present scene of the poem, breaking the frame of retrospective mediations (talking within dreaming within writing) in which it is nested:

> Who rise, wing above wing, flame above flame,
> And, like a storm, cry the Ineffable Name,
> And with the clashing of their sword-blades make
> A rapturous music, till the morning break
> And the white hush end all but the loud beat
> Of their long wings, the flash of their white feet.

This multitude has its own "rapturous music," which, though the poem may speak of it, cannot be identified with its own "fitful" rhymes; it beats out a loud and regular rhythm that cannot be heard in the strangely patterned pentameter of the lines that house it.

This separation between verse form and vision reappears in the next poem in the volume as an oblique disrelation between the formal features of poetry and what they reveal to their reader: *"Because to him who ponders well / My rhymes more than their rhyming tell."* Just as what a rhyme "tells" is not quite the same as what it says or means, so too the reader's good work of "pondering" is not quite the same as her reading or hearing. And like the white hush that ends all talk and all music, the unspoken truth of what is "told" and "pondered" exceeds anything that might be meant through poems or read in them.

Lest this be thought the sort of idea that would appeal only to a Neo-Platonist, we can find similar intuitions in poets of an anti-metaphysical temper. William Carlos Williams's account of Marianne Moore in *Spring and All*, for example, elaborates his strangely disembodied concept of poetry by means of tautology:

> I believe in the main that Marianne Moore is of all American writers most constantly a poet—not because her lines are invariably full of imagery they are not . . . and not because she clips her work into certain shapes . . . but I believe she is most constantly a poet in her work because the purpose of her work is invariably from the source from which poetry starts—that it is constantly from the purpose of poetry. And that it actually possesses this characteristic, as of that origin, to a more distinguishable degree when it eschews verse rhythms than when it does not. It has the purpose of poetry written into it and therefore it is poetry. (230)

This feeling of disjunction between the poem's variable "shapes" and its singular "purpose" (as well as the sense of a close relation between its "purpose" and its "origin") indexes, in the poet who has it, a different account of what a poet is, and of what the poet intends. And what the poet intends is not just the poem (the "accomplishment" of the object); not just something *by* the poem (that it mean something, convey or construct that meaning). Instead—or in addition—the poet intends something through or by *poetry*.[45] Allen Grossman, combining Yeats's intuition about poetry's aspiration to vision with Williams's insight about the "most constant poet's" indifference to forms, puts the matter more succinctly, if more polemically: "The true poet says: I *DO* the best I can. I also *KNOW* better. And assuredly knowing better IS closer to poetry than the 'poem' and more justifiably convincing."[46]

Perhaps the most powerful theorization of this idea of poetry—as a knowing better that "convinces," as a "purpose" that abides with poems but is not identical with them—may be found in Percy Shelley's "Defense of Poetry." Shelley famously begins his treatise by distinguishing between poetry "in a restricted sense" and poetry "in a general sense."[47] Poetry in the restricted sense encompasses the triumphs of language that we most often associate with the poem as an aesthetic object. Shelley singles out "metrical language"—"a certain uniform and harmonious recurrence of sound"—for special praise and consideration (484); but it would be entirely consistent with his argument to expand the category to admit a more capacious formalism: rhyme, figuration, the intense forms of poetic closure and enclosure—all the qualities that those who identify poetry with its forms take to be essential.

Poetry in the general sense, on the other hand, is defined as "the expression of the imagination," in *whatever* form that expression might take. Thus, Shelley argues, Plato and Bacon, Herodotus, Plutarch, and Livy are all in this general sense poets, authors of "highest wisdom, pleasure, virtue, and glory" (506). Religions and laws, perhaps even more so than verses and rhymes, are in this general sense "poetry." But if Shelley's point is that a particular kind of linguistic mastery is only one "expression" of poetry (though perhaps an important one), and that philosophy, true science, history, and sovereignty are equally to be attributed to the same origin, then the word "expression" seems a misleading way to describe the relation that he has in mind. Or rather, "expression" is here being used in a peculiar way, to denote not a semantic relation but a genetic and logical one. This is the sense of the term in which the nature of a thing is "expressed" by external tokens, as a phenotype expresses a genotype, or as "the excellence of beauty in Jesus was expressed."

The subordination or secondariness that Shelley attributes to the component materials of the poem—its "language," "color," or "form"—extends as well to the full material *fact* of the poem, which turns, in the *Defense,* from substance to shadow—"the most glorious poetry that has ever been communicated to the world is probably a feeble shadow of the original conception of the poet"—and from end to echo: "when composition begins, inspiration is already on the decline" (504). Even the *Defense*'s description of what it means to be a *stylist* is less bound to formal mastery (or its absence) than to the poet's possession of some other more vital force. Consider the pointed abstraction of Shelley's "stylistic" appreciation of Dante:

His very words are instinct with spirit; each is as a spark, a burning atom of inextinguishable thought; and many yet lie covered in the ashes of their birth, and pregnant with a lightning which has yet found no conductor. All high poetry is infinite; it is as the first acorn, which contained all oaks potentially. (500)

The disproportion between the fleeting illumination of the word-spark and the "inextinguishable" burning of the thought it somehow contains; the overleaping of the moment of change between a poem "pregnant" with a charge that cannot be conducted and the envisioned release of its lightning; the relation (which is equally a disrelation) between the material "acorn" of the poem and its infinitely generative potential: poetry, considered through these figures, is something like a *cause*—

"Language, color, form, and religious and civil habits of action, are all the instruments and materials of poetry; they may be called poetry by that figure of speech which considers the effect as a synonym of the cause." But the account of "cause" that Shelley has in mind is *formal,* in the Aristotelian sense in which "the form is the account of the essence."

Thus, for Shelley, the reason why "A man cannot say, 'I will compose poetry'" (503) is because "poetry" is not a species of composition. I would call special attention here to Shelley's choice of the term "conception" here, with its dual connotation of mentality and natality. "Poetry in a general sense" is both a power of the mind, a faculty, and a natal privilege that is coextensive with our nature as persons. Or, as Shelley puts it out the outset of the *Defense,* poetry is "connate with the origin of man" (480). Considered in the general sense, "poetry" is not so much the expression of the imagination as a revelation that imagination is the fundamental and value-bearing aspect of our nature. To treat poetry as a faculty—as the definitive human faculty—is to make it both descriptive and normative—to treat it as an ontological claim with moral significance. To "intend" this kind of poetry is to intend not something that we make or something that we mean, but something that we are. Maureen McLane has aptly described this aspect of Shelley's romanticism (and Romanticism more generally) as a sort of lyric anthropology, emerging less as a rejection of the human sciences' categorizations of human nature than as a competing version of them. "To define poetry via the human faculty of the imagination was not only to give it, as Coleridge desired, a philosophical foundation: such a definition also gave poetry an anthropological foundation. Poetry is defined, in fact, as the discourse of the species."[48]

If our dominant accounts of poetry have been in the broadest sense empiricist and phenomenological—centrally concerned with the *fact* of the poem, as a made thing and an object of experience—then the kind of poet Shelley asks us to consider might be called *rationalist.* (It might equally be called *intuitionist.*[49]) Such a poet understands "poetry" not as a kind of object, performance, or practice but as intending a *knowledge* or *capacity*—constitutive of what it is to be a person. What the poet of poetry in the general sense intends—insofar as he intends poetry—is not to produce that class of objects we call poems, but to reveal, exemplify, or make manifest a potential or "power" that minimally distinguishes what a person is.[50]

III. The Person

What conception of person is at stake in a poetic project defended in this way? And what possible purposes could "personhood" considered at this level of abstraction be answerable to? Sharon Cameron begins her recent study of literary impersonality by defining the term against which the writers she will consider mount their complex and various projects of negation, resistance, or extinction:

> The word *person* confers status . . . value, even equality; it establishes intelligibility within a political and legal system, indicating a being having legal rights or representing others' rights. . . . It does not, however, presume anything of substance.[51]

For Cameron—as for many scholars of personhood in literature, law, and anthropology—"person" is regarded primarily in its aspect as an honorific term or an ascriptive concept. Following the Hobbesian notion that "the definition of a person . . . is what we agree to treat as a person" (viii), such a view locates the sources of normative personhood in our linguistic and behavioral conventions and our social agreements; and, more powerfully, in the institutions that embody those conventions and give them extension and force. Whether the personhood in question is national, identified with the privileges and obligations of citizenship, or global, embodied in the uncertainly located legal domain of human rights, such contingent constructions or "agreements" about what will count as a person are in equal measures powerful and fragile—bound up with the problems of sovereignty and the hazards of identification and recognition.[52]

It is obviously not true, however, that all accounts of "the word *person*" presume "nothing of substance." In the theological context of the term's origin, and quite differently, in the context of modern and contemporary philosophy, many of the most important debates around personhood have been directly concerned with metaphysics and ontology—with the specification and description of properties that uniquely constitute persons, distinguish them from other kinds of beings, and determine their persistence across time. Where the substantive tradition in theology posited immaterial substances like souls, more recent philosophy has emphasized the unique organization of organic matter that frames the human animal or the human brain, as well as psychological desiderata like language, reflexive awareness, and memory, and faculties like reason and will.

What I take Cameron to be saying, then, is that while it is theoretically possible to distinguish between substantive and descriptive accounts of personhood and normative or ethical claims that are mounted upon them, the two have been difficult to tease apart in practice.[53] The Boethian definition—the first to attribute personhood to human rather than divine beings—is an early case in point: "*Person is an individual substance of rational nature . . . He is the highest of the material beings, endowed with particular dignity and rights.*" So too is the nominally secularized version of this claim found in Kant's *Groundwork*: "rational beings are called persons inasmuch as their nature already marks them out as ends in themselves"[54]—a rationality that gives them an incontrovertible "dignity" rather than a "price." Personhood is most frequently a portmanteau concept that bridges the gap between the "material nature" that we possess and the "particular dignity" we would assert—between fact and value—holding together physical, psychological, and moral aspects.[55] It is this uncertain and variable relation between the substantive and the normative—between claims about the criteria of personhood and the acts of interpretation and legislation that determine the just conduct of our lives as persons—that has provided such rich material for our histories of personhood, and indeed for skeptical critique of the concept as it has been deployed in anthropology and law.

I will here be more concerned to frame the problem in a different and somewhat more abstract way. The general problem of criteria in our thinking is prior to the problem of evidence in our legislating. Criteria are the means by which we subsume the objects of our experience under concepts; they determine what we can recognize and count as evidence. The philosophical tradition most engaged with the question of the criteriological judgments by which we learn what our concepts of *persons* are in highly particularized moments of perception is that of Ludwig Wittgenstein and his inheritors. I will thus be spending some time with that tradition in this chapter and throughout the book; I will also want to suggest also that this philosophical tradition's phenomenological or quasi-phenomenological approach to the problem of persons most closely resembles the mode of address adopted by some of our most troublingly original poets, though philosophic and poetic accounts grasp the problem for different reasons and to quite different ends.

I begin with a crucial but little noted moment of a much commented on section from the fourth chapter of Stanley Cavell's *The Claim of Reason*.[56] In this chapter, Cavell is concerned to argue that there are limits to conceiving the project of Wittgenstein's later philosophy as a complete disarming of skepticism. Though Cavell acknowledges one central Wittgensteinian claim—it is indeed impossible to sanely and consistently embrace skepticism about reality of the external world—nevertheless, he goes on to argue, we have no equivalent protection in the conduct of life from "the radical doubt of the existence of others" (477). A kernel of such doubt haunts even our most intimate relations beyond correction or philosophical purgation. Cavell denies that we can ever achieve certainty that we are in the presence of another person; he nonetheless shares in Wittgenstein's resistance to the traditional skeptical idea that our failure to achieve certainty is an epistemic problem: a failure to discover the real substance behind the substantive term "person." To put this another way, Cavell denies that his ineradicable core of skepticism is the same as a failure to perceive or to know the *personhood* of persons:

> To speak sensibly of seeing or treating or taking persons as persons—or of seeing or treating or taking a (human) body as giving expression to a (human) soul—will similarly presuppose that there is some competing way in which persons—or bodies—may be seen or treated or taken. (372)

Cavell considers and rejects a number of possible options for such a competing way—a person might be regarded a king, he proposes, or, more appallingly, as a thing. But in neither of these cases, he argues, have we failed to see persons. A king, of course, is a person, even if he is in some sense more than a person as well. And though Cavell concedes that it is common to *talk* about slaves as less than persons or even as non-persons; he insists that such talk is true only in a limited sense. It is true, for example, that chattel slavery operates by withholding much of the status that accrues to the *legal person*. But this concession to usage is not a philosophical concession: for Cavell argues that the specific forms of legally sanctioned brutality and exchange that constitute chattel slavery do not require that the slaveholder really mean his own skeptical words about the personhood of slaves. Indeed, he goes on to say, such words "cannot really be meant" (372), and such claims, though they can be acted upon and enforced, elaborated as reasons or embraced as justifications, cannot really be believed. Rather, "[w]hat he really believes is not that slaves are not human beings but that some human beings are slaves" (375). Or again, "He means, indefinitely, that there are *kinds* of humans."

Cavell's talk about slavery is not in any important way an argument about slavery as an institution.[57] Rather, he is taking the slaveholder as an extreme example of what it is like for a person to engage the problem of determining the presence of another mind and to fail. But such failures show us something about the actual conditions of success. For failing to treat a slave as a person is not, on Cavell's account, a failure of *knowledge* about what another is. (This is the force of calling his meaning "indefinite"—it is not based on substantive considerations or definitions.) And because our knowledge of persons is not knowledge of something lying behind or within the body we encounter, no amount of knowledge about the nature of persons or even of souls would correct it. What afflicts and deforms the slaveholder is, rather, a refusal to act on another form of knowledge that he possesses—the knowledge that is built into the very structure of his stance toward another, even when that stance is most brutal and unjust.

To distinguish between these two conceptions of "knowledge," Cavell substitutes the idea of *acknowledgment* for knowledge and *avoidance* for ignorance. It is avoidance of the other that constitutes the tragedy lurking within our ordinary relations to other persons.

> What is implied is that it is essential to knowing that something is human that we sometimes experience it as such, and sometimes do not, or fail to; that certain alterations of our consciousness take place, and sometimes not, in the face of it. Or in the presence of a memory of it. The memory, perhaps in a dream, may run across the mind, like a rabbit across a landscape, forcing an exclamation from me, perhaps in the form of a name. (Cp. Investigations, p. 197 and cp. Yeats's "A Deep Sworn Vow") (379)

How are we to understand Cavell's casual certitude that philosophy and poetry are engaged in the same problem? For certitude is what is implied by the parenthetical and unelucidated injunction to "compare" Yeats's poem "A Deep-sworn Vow" to the Wittgensteinian idea of person-seeing as aspect seeing. Here are the relevant passages to which Cavell directs us. First Wittgenstein:

> I look at an animal and am asked: what do you see? I answer: "a rabbit."—I see a landscape; suddenly a rabbit runs past. I exclaim "a rabbit!"[58]

And alongside it, for comparison, the Yeats:

> Others because you did not keep
> That deep-sworn vow have been friends of mine;
> Yet always when I look death in the face,
> When I clamber to the heights of sleep,
> Or when I grow excited with wine,
> Suddenly I meet your face.

In this section of *Philosophical Investigations*, Wittgenstein is offering an alternative to the idea that seeing is mere blank perception posing a sort of question to which we match our answering concepts. The exclamation, in its immediacy (it is as if it were forced from us, Wittgenstein says), is a kind of redemption of perception from emptiness. It speaks to the way our perceiving is already rich with knowing— our seeing is part sight, part thought.

By the same token, perceptions in poetry (like our perceptions of poems themselves) are charged with the knowledge that we bear as inhabitants of a shared world. If we were to supply the reading of Yeats's poem that Cavell intimates through the comparison, it would look something like this: The revelatory disclosure of the beloved's face at the poem's end represents a moment of acknowledgment after a duration of avoidance. The speaker's stance toward the beloved may change, has changed—in the forgetting or denial that comes with anger, betrayal, or distraction. But the recovery of the beloved's image in memory or dream is not a new access of certainty about her nature. It is a self-recovery of his inclination to see her person—to see her soul upon her face—that takes place against a backdrop of the beloved already being present to him as a person.

As I shall argue more fully in the next chapter, however, this is to get Yeats's poem quite wrong—both as an argument and as an artifact. The urgency that drives the attenuated syntax of "A Deep-sworn Vow" toward its final sudden revelation is not a recognition of the tragic failures of recognition embedded in ordinary life, but rather an extreme form of skepticism motivated by metaphysical terror. Yeats is haunted by the threat that meaningful personhood might be unattainable—a threat that is both intimate and political, and against which he marshals a deep—and deeply absurd—metaphysics. Accordingly, the image of the beloved that Yeats wishes to recover in sleep or in death is not an aspect, not a way of taking the person. It is an *origin*—a template of meaningful personhood given countenance in Yeats's lyric. To encounter this face is precisely to encounter the substance of what allows a person to count as a person.

If the *total* skepticism requiring such an extreme metaphysical antidote is a philosophical error, as Cavell insists it is, it is nonetheless an error to which a poet like Yeats commits his fullest acts of imagining. Yeats belongs to a tradition of poetry written under conditions of historical and philosophical extremity, in which skepticism about other minds is experienced and approached as a *real* danger, and in response to which poets formulate what I might call an ontological wish for accounts of personhood not susceptible to loss or risk. If the value of the person is dependent on the acknowledgment of others, whether by an individual's acts of recognition or by a state's, then that value will only be as generously distributed as our institutions permit, and only as durable as our sympathies allow.

As both the risks and the consequences of such failures or refusals of acknowlededgment increase, so too does the demand for foundational rather than relational concepts of personhood. The twentieth-century poets I will describe here, facing what they perceive as even greater threats to social cohesion, meaningful life, and even social survival, confront an additional demand that Shelley's Platonism evades: the sense that any account of persons that could serve as a legitimate ground for social life would have to take its orientation from something *real*. This is, in effect, to demand that their person-concepts be valid within a world understood in secular terms—that they be compatible with its metaphysics—and perhaps even with its physics. If that should prove impossible, then a poet must wrestle with the consequences of refusing those terms. As we shall see, such tensions between materialist and idealist accounts will lead Yeats to unite the perfection of the soul with the eugenic engineering of the body; it will lead the Language poets to invest their Shelleyan hope for a utopian "uncommunity" in a restrictive species concept like language itself.

The elaboration of the substantive criteria of personhood, however, may court the opposite danger—that of drawing of invidious distinctions and boundaries that exclude as-yet unrecognized kinds from moral consideration. This is why what I have called "rationalism" in poetry cannot be a commitment to reason as such. As a person-concept, reason has, notoriously, a *reality* problem, having been declared to be limited or defective (incapable of grounding the claims on its behalf), multiple (coming in different and competing forms and flavors), historical (a contingent rather than absolute basis for valuing), or merely fictional. But it also has what we might call a distribution problem; for even if reason was everything we could hope for, we have also shown great inventiveness in finding various disfavored groups either deficient or wholly lacking in it. Thus poets I describe will arrive by various routes at accounts of personhood that are distinctly *thin* or minimal, positing predicates it would be difficult to imagine withholding of anyone, modes of attention that push off the moment of decision as long as possible—and then longer.

The poetry I describe is in search of some real quality on the basis of which persons can be said to be *a priori* associated—to *be* and to be *numerous*—rather than a practice of association through the channels of reading, circulation, conversation, or sympathy. In so doing, it posits a distinction between "subjects" and "persons": if subjects (as poems conceive of them) are understood to possess qualities (voices, histories, features, bodies, genders, attachments, as well as rights and obligations, etc.), the persons intended by the poetic principle are defined by their possession of *value*—the sheer potential to be integrated into whatever social system. In their need to discover personhood as something substantial and yet abstract, distinguishing yet universal, the poets of poetry "in the general sense" find themselves on the horns of the dilemma formulated by two competing camps of critics of the Enlightenment in the wake of the brutal crises in the twentieth century:

> For the first, who might loosely be grouped as premodern, the Enlightenment is too thin, besotted by relativism, and incapable of searching and finding the good; a betrayal of traditional philosophy and theology. . . . By contrast, for the second set, who loosely may be grouped as postmodern, the Enlightenment and its legacy is too thick, characterized by the *hubris* of imposing a master narrative which artificially values only particular and limited aspects of human capacities and sensations and is marked by stereotypes and prejudices that remain unexamined. In this accounting, its universalism is a pretense and its ideas are instruments of power and domination.[59]

The fundamental questions with which poets must struggle—and they remain in many ways unresolved in the poetic tradition I will describe—are:

(1) Where—in what aspect, faculty or capacity—are we to ground the concept of person, such that all persons may be judged to possess it?

(2) How can *any* quality (no matter how widely distributed) constitute or articulate a sufficient *demand* for recognition or value?

(3) How do we reconcile the desire for a universal conception of personhood with the manifold forms of particularity brought to bear by actual poems?

It is to this last question that I now turn.

IV. The Noem

There is something troubling about the degree to which Shelley's account of poetry "in its general sense" is at odds with his own particular poetic practice. Whether we hold with Wordsworth that Shelley was among the first of his contemporaries "in workmanship of style,"[60] or with Pound that Shelley is the author of "one of the rottenest poems ever written,"[61] there is no denying that Shelley is a maker of poems in the "restricted sense." But there is also no avoiding the disproportion between the aesthetic mastery that his work displays on the one hand—the result of sustained effort directed at the realization of the artwork—and the forms of self-distinction and world-transformation that he describes as arising from song on the other.

> The breath whose might I have invoked in song
> Descends on me; my spirit's bark is driven,
> Far from the shore, far from the trembling throng
> Whose sails were never to the tempest given;
> The massy earth and spherèd skies are riven!

Here, in his great elegy "Adonais," the breath of song is transmuted into storm; the lightning that figures poetry's shattering effect is not (as in Shelley's Dante) contained in embryo within the pregnant word, but conducted from heaven to earth. And if in "Adonais" the storm invoked by song is said (merely!) to bring about the transformation of the spirit, in "The Mask of Anarchy" the storm released by words promises (in some future time) to bring about the transformation of the world:

> "And these words shall then become
> Like Oppression's thundered doom
> Ringing through each heart and brain,
> Heard again—again—again—

> "Rise like Lions after slumber
> In unvanquishable number—
> Shake your chains to earth like dew
> Which in sleep had fallen on you—
> Ye are many—they are few."

What Shelley famously promises is the legislation of the world by means of poetry. What he prophesies is the poetic production of free beings. What he fails to provide is a theory of mediation adequate to either task. The "burning atom" of the poem-in-potential could never give rise to such explosive effects without some way to release its energy. "Poetry" may be the historical custodian of a humanizing project, in which persons will arise "in unvanquishable number"; but *poems* are a singularly unpromising means to pursue it.[62]

  If one were in search of a term of art for a poetry that promises the kind of wholesale transformation of self and world that *actual* poems by their limited nature make impossible, one could do worse than Bloom's "non-poetry." But how—and here is the question that turns the distinction back in the direction of the revisionary taxonomic project I began by proposing—can we think of "non-poetry" as naming a poetic *kind*? Once a particular poetic oak has sprung from its all-potentiating seed, how will we recognize a poem as belonging to "poetry in the general sense" rather than in the restricted sense? If actual poems inevitably tell things "in confidence," reaching some audiences, repelling or foreclosing others, then what kind of mediation is the "true" non-poem? And, turning forward upon the largest horizon that I have claimed for this work in poetry, how could such a "kind," built as it seems to be on the negation of mediation itself, bear on the problem of thinking through the foundations of social relation—of being numerous?

In considering these questions I would like to turn briefly to a poet who lies somewhat beyond the linguistic and geographic boundaries that delimit the inquiry of this book: Paul Celan. I say "somewhat," because Celan has been taken up quite explicitly as an exemplary figure by and for Anglophone poets in the second half of the century in a way that makes him seem central to the division I have been describing and contesting. Celan's appeal has seemed at once formal and ethical. His reception has foregrounded both the idea that his poems are motivated by or answerable to the most brutal instances of dehumanization in the twentieth century, and the idea that his difficult poems present the problem of regrounding the shattered relation between persons precisely as a problem in "translation" or interpretation. Celan, in other words, makes the labor of intersubjectivity seem like a problem particularly well suited to a verbal art.[63]

In his 1967 poem "Weggebeizt," Celan compares the process of poetic making with the process of paring away dross or excess (as by acid on a printer's plate or by the natural forces of erosion) to reveal something significant that remains.

> Etched away from
> the ray-shot wind of your language
> the garish talk of rubbed-
> off experience—the hundred-
> tongued pseudo-
> poem, the noem.[64]

> Weggebeizt vom
> Strahlenwind deiner Sprache
> das bunte Gerede des An-
> erlebten—das hundert-
> züngige Mein-
> gedicht, das Genicht.

Michael Hamburger's translation has been decisive for Celan's English-language readers in calling special attention to the doubleness of the term *"Mein- / gedicht"* in the poem's opening stanza. Divided at once formally (by enjambment) and semantically (by its dueling etymologies), the term suggests that for Celan, the poems (*Gedichte)* in question are at once his creation and (therefore) *false*.[65] For Celan, writing in the language of a nation that was the source of his pain and in the genre whose beauties had become a source of shame, the idea that making and falsifying would take place in the same breath arose out of the particulars of his own experience. And yet the pairing of poetry and perjury is not meant to be specific to this poet alone; Celan takes it to reflect a general cultural condition in which the sensual pleasures of lyric aesthetics are in danger of being disallowed. On this account (familiar to us, as to Celan himself, from Adorno's notorious critique of poetry "after Auschwitz"), poetry, rather than forging the artifice by which personal pain can be made public, creates more opportunities for divisive individuation, misunderstanding, and misrecognition in a world in which persons are lost to us. "Don't come with *poiein* and the like," Celan writes to Hans Bender, in a 1960 letter otherwise extolling the individuated craft or "handiwork" of making poems; "I suspect that this word, with all its nearness and distance, meant something quite different from its current context." In the context in which Celan wrote, no mere making could suffice to address a world emptied of persons and denuded of care: "We live under dark skies, and there are few humans [*Menschen*]. This is probably why there are also so few poems."[66] The wish embedded in a poem like "Weggebeizt" is that there might be an alternative to *poiein,* to the making that Anne Carson has called the "imprecise perjury of the verbal art,"[67] and with it, an alternative mode of relation undarkened by mendacity and loss.

But if Celan's poem seeks to sort between an ideal of truth and the falsifying forms of expression, then it is not clear on which side of the divide between the true and the false the neologism that ends the first stanza—"*das Genicht*"—is meant to fall. In particular, it is not clear from the syntax of this stanza whether "*Genicht*" (felicitously translated by Hamburger as "noem") is meant to stand in *apposition* to the "*Mein-Gedicht*" or in *opposition* to it.[68] If the former, then "noem" is merely another name for the forked and mendacious talk with which art speaks. As one of the several things from which *something else* (as yet unnamed) is etched away, the "noem" is false precisely for its origin in experience—which the poem regards as secondary or impoverished ("rubbed-off")—and for its reception *as* experience, with its subjective and therefore multifarious ("hundred-tongued") interpretations and misinterpretations. Such a poem offers poetry as a problem to which there is no apparent solution or alternative.

If, however, the "noem" is regarded as the withheld grammatical subject of the attenuated sentence that forms the poem's first stanza, then we might understand it instead as that which *is* etched away. It would then be allied, not with the "garish" speech with which the poem begins, not with the "pseudo-poem" of which it is the negation, but with the *Atemkristall,* or "breathcrystal," with which the poem ends:

> Deep
> in Time's crevasse
> by
> the alveolate ice
> waits, a crystal of breath,
> your irreversible
> witness.

> Tief
> in der Zeitenschrunde,
> beim
> Wabeneis
> wartet, ein Atemkristall,
> dein unumstößliches
> Zeugnis.

A crystal, in its mute austerity, determinate singularity, and formal fixity, serves as a rebuke or alternative to all that is garish, multiple, and evanescent about mere "talk." And though (as the compound noun itself suggests) a "breathcrystal" is somehow compounded of breath, it does not, like a "ray-shot wind," eddy or shift according to the rise or fall of the living heat that generates it. Rather, an *Atem-kristall*, like every crystalline form, is held in an unchanging lattice or structure.

If we take the notion of the "noem" to be carved out in opposition to the "pseudo-poem," then perhaps we might imagine that a "breathcrystal," too, requires "etching," some process of paring and polishing to create its facets and angles out of a more ordinary substance. And, indeed, Celan's "breathcrystal" does appear only at the endpoint of the poem's process of selection and ordering: it seems to be the climax of a narrative, or figural journey, that conducts us (through the middle stanza) along a "path" or "way" (*"Weg"*) carved through "human-shaped snow" (*"menschen- / gestaltigen Schnee"*). That the snow has a human shape could suggest that perhaps it is a path a human has shaped, a way into the world made by his will and his labor. That the snow is "penitents' snow" (*"den Büßerschnee"*) might propose that there be a redemptive route that a person could travel, a figure he could cut, that would constitute a redeemed form of human making (*"poein"* or perhaps "the like") free from the shadowed world in which other persons are scarce or inaccessible.

But this sense of narrative progress or subjective *Bildung* would be deceptive. As Celan—aficionado of crystallography and glaciology—would certainly have known, the procession of cowled figures that make up the formation that we call "penitent snow" is a configuration of glacial ice that results from the different rates of melting and evaporation in snow on sunlit surfaces at very cold temperatures (figure I.1). By the same token, a crystal is neither "etched" by human hands nor cut by human tools. Rather, it is formed by processes of nucleation and attraction that govern matter at the most elemental level.

This is in part merely to state the obvious: that a breathcrystal is not an *art* object. A crystallization of vapor into ice, that is, may in a sense be *expressed*, or precipitate out of the human breath; but it does not *express* anything internal to the person. The *Atemkristal* is the sort of object that is, one might say, only incidentally an object for our perception. But neither is the breathcrystal a *brute* object like a stone—its symmetry, its perfection, and its origin in breath must also be to the point. The crystal's *resemblance* to an art object speaks to its curious intentional relation to the principle of its origin. Expressing nothing, it stands as the "expression" of the general laws that structure the world in which particular crystals reside.

Celan's identification of the poem with this curious sort of object—the kind of objects that subordinate their phenomenologies to the laws that give rise to them—should determine the way we navigate this poem as a shape, or a narrative. Though it appears at the end of the poem, the idea of an *Atemkristall* does not seem to be intended by the poem as a kind of insight, nor does it arise as an epiphanic leap—unforeseeable but justified—out of the progress of the poem's composition. Rather, the breathcrystal is characterized as that which "waits," lying "Deep / in Time's crevasse." Considered temporally, this is to say that it pre-exists the human measures that a poem counts; considered spatially, we might say it is located outside or beneath the conceptual frame that the poem occupies or charts. Rather than standing as the endpoint of a "way" (wayward, penitent, imperfect, prone to misdirection or loss), or appearing as the emblem of a communicative channel opened between individuated subjects, the *Atemkristall*—though it never quite appears—is a kind of argument that there exist forces of attraction that draw all things together and that are (under ideal circumstances) irresistible and perfecting.

These two possible accounts of the "*Genicht*"—first, as a sort of objectified epistemic prize, a truth grasped at the end of a difficult journey through individuating experience (a life that is "human shaped"); second, as not quite an object but (like the "breathcrystal") the expression of a timeless and dimensionless principle that governs the formation of objects through a force of attraction—lead us back to the consideration of the "noem" as a poetic kind. If the "non-poem" were to be understood primarily as a kind of art object, it might be precisely the sort of difficult object that Celan has been most commonly understood to make: indeed, the sort of object that Celan sometimes presented himself as making, as in his famous speech "*Der Meridian*": "The poem wants to reach an Other, it needs this Other, *it needs an Over-against*. It seeks it out, speaks toward it."[69] It is the interest of what

Figure I.1. Snow penitents. Photo © Dirk Sigmund, Dreamstime.com.

Celan calls an "encounter" that justifies all of the hermeneutic journeying, the laborious decoding of syntax, neologism, pun, arcane allusion, and figuration that make his poems difficult and particular. As Susan Stewart has argued, "The particularity of Celan's art demands an inexhaustible and universalizing labor of attention and semantic judgments, as task for the present and for the future."[70]

If, on the other hand, a "noem" is only *secondarily* an object for our perception, then our relation to it might not be a process of decoding or translation, but a relation of some other sort. The history of phenomenology offers us a term for that relation as a refused alternative. In the first, foundational section of his *Logical Investigations,* Husserl distinguishes between the *bedeutsamen Zeichen,* or "meaningful sign," and what he calls an "indication sign" (*Anzeichen*). Husserl ultimately wishes to leave aside a consideration of mere indications (what he also calls *Hinweisen,* or "hints") in favor of the phenomenology of *Ausdrücke* ("expressions") that will be his central concern.[71] It is nonetheless the *Anzeichen* that has seemed most useful to me in understanding the relation between the kind of object a "non-poem" is and how it stands in relation to meaning. For as Husserl explains it, the *Anzeichen* is a sign that motivates the belief in the reality of some state of affairs *without itself expressing that state of affairs.* And while his initial examples of indication signs make them look something like C. S. Pierce's indexical signs—smoke is the index of fire—the real force of an indication sign for Husserl, as for Celan, is that it motivates our confidence in the existence of an intending mind. The sign is not a communication, but it *tells.* More like smoke *signals* than smoke, but finally more like the syntax of a signal than its message, the indication sign tells of the person who stands behind the signs as principle of origin by which they may be taken as signs at all.[72]

It is here that the connection between "poetry" and what I have been calling "personhood" becomes more legible. If a poem is understood as an expression— which is to say, among other things, as an object that one must *interpret*, then the social relation that we are imagining taking place by means of poems is that of communication and, one hopes, understanding. "Empathic projection is to other minds what seeing is to material objects," Cavell suggests (*The Claim of Reason*, 425). In the case of reading poetry, to "see" the poem and to "project" the person behind it are not merely analogical, but identical acts. The relation to another conducted by means of such seeing and projecting is, because ungrounded, dependent on the exercise of the senses and the projections of feelings, in principle fallible, reversible, or even refusable.[73]

One could fail to embark upon a journey of understanding; one could get lost; one could turn around midway, as in Rilke's tragedy of reversals and misrecognitions in "Orpheus. Eurydice. Hermes.":

> And when without warning
> the god stopped her and with pain in his cry

spoke the words: He has turned around—,
she grasped nothing and said softly: *Who?*[74]

But such reversibility of relations between persons is precisely what "Weggebeizt" sets out—in full consciousness of its undeniability—to deny. The "breathcrystal" at the poem's end is explicitly placed parallel to "irreversible witness"—the sort of relation that, because it is premised upon a structural law rather than a contingent fact, cannot be gainsaid. Celan gives the impossible object a name: the *Genicht,* or "non-poem," that lies in wait, cold and austere. And in the shaping of the actual poem he gives notional or conceptual shape to the relation between the object and the form of solidarity it promises. That relation is neither identity (the breathcrystal is not itself "irreversible witness") nor metaphor (the breathcrystal is not *like* irreversible witness), but indication: the breathcrystal is the sort of object that motivates belief in the fundamental forces of attraction that structure it and that bind human lives, though as an object it is not itself "human shaped."

V. A History Containing Poetry

Being Numerous is a historical book. It seeks to retell a portion of the history of twentieth-century poetry on changed conceptual grounds, and to describe the consequences for poetry of a philosophical concern with personhood that emerges with a new intensity and a heightened self-consciousness in an era of unprecedented historical violence. As I have already begun to show, deemphasizing one taxonomic opposition—between the traditionalist poet and the avant-garde poet—in favor of another—the poet whose primary constructive investments are in the making of poems and the poet whose primary conceptual investments lie in the direction of persons—will require me to make some counterintuitive claims about the ontology of poems and of persons, to forward arguments about the oblique relation of poetic intentionality to the realized work of verbal art, and to offer some revisionary accounts of how we ought to go about linking thoughts about poetry to thoughts about social life and to political desires. To put it another way, *Being Numerous* is also a theoretical book.

From the perspective of our dominant modes of literary criticism, these two impulses might appear to be at odds with one another. The theoretical disposition upon which our present historicism rests is relentlessly nominalist and localist. What counts as a responsible historicist reading requires the elaboration of evermore-finely differentiated micro-histories of literary genres and functions; it involves situating literary work within richly articulated networks of symbolic and discursive practices; it demands close-up description of the material form of the literary artifact and an aerial charting of the channels of production, circulation, and reception. Perhaps nothing has seemed a riper target for this project of con-textualization and de-idealization than the idea of poetry itself. Thus, in her recent brief for what she calls a "historical poetics," Yopie Prins celebrates the achieve-ments of critics who would bring externalist historicism into the idealist heart of the poetic. In order for this critical renovation to be complete, Prins explains, "critics working in historical poetics would need to develop different approaches to differ-ent centuries, taking into account generic shifts in the production and circulation of poetry and insisting on the cultural specificity of poetic genres."[75]

Perhaps the most fully realized example of such a critic thus far is Virginia Jack-son, who, in her careful work on Emily Dickinson, inveighs against the modern retro-projection of the reifying category of lyric upon the incommensurable com-municative practices, personal relations, generic conventions, and discourse com-munities that make up the life led in proximity to poetry:

> [T]he overlapping or incongruous details, seasons, public and private histories, battles and pets, sex scandals and insect remnants, books, newspapers and all sorts of familiar letters that surrounded the lines later published as a Dickinson lyric could not be said to be what the lines are "about" . . . . the stories that could be unfolded from them may or may not have been relevant to the lines' potentially miscellaneous subjects (and objects) in the past. Once the lines were published and received as a lyric, these several and severally dated subjects and objects and their several stories faded from view, since the poem's referent would thereafter be understood as the subject herself—suspended, lyrically, in place and time.[76]

What is most striking about this impulse toward specificity (and what makes Dick-inson paradigmatic for historical poetics) is that it results not so much in a herme-neutic "approach" specific to Dickinson's century (or to any more finely parsed moment), nor in an account of poetic genre that belongs to her cultural context, but rather in an account of poetic making so fully particularized that only descrip-tion will do it justice. "[T]he difficulty of reading Dickinson' manuscripts," Jackson argues, "is that even in their fragmentary extant forms, they provide so much con-text that individual lyrics become practically illegible" (38).

Certainly, in light of this historicism's emphasis on poetry's "illegible" particularity and the "incongruous" miscellany of the persons who make them, any talk about "poetry in the general sense," or about a poet's commitment to abstract and highly noncontingent conceptions of personhood, starts to look suspiciously—indeed, symptomatically—ahistorical. It will look particularly suspicious if, as is the case in this book, the exposition is not, in any strict sense of the word, a *narrative* history of those contrary commitments and concerns. That is, while the poets I discuss do follow in rough chronological sequence, their work is not obvi-ously describable in terms of influence or inheritance; nor do their vocations seem subject to the same immediate cultural and political pressures any more than they seem subject to the same personal ones. Frank O'Hara may speak a language that is distinctively of New York, but his poetry, formed amidst mid-century artistic coteries and queer culture, bears little relation to George Oppen's "A Language of New York," born of the poet's aesthetic and ethical struggles with the radical American left. Yeats's role as a poet-senator, enmeshed first with the intense cultural politics of the Gaelic Revival and then the fractured practical politics of the Irish Free State, is not precisely parallel to the situation of the American Language poet seeking abroad for models and theories of an effectual solidarity within a highly professionalized literary economy at the end of the Cold War.

On principle, then, I agree there may be as many kinds of poem as there are tones that a socially situated person can sound, or arguments a worldly actor can entertain. There may be as many kinds of poetry as there are shapes that the living hand can form or modes of reflection that the furnished mind can undertake. But as the case studies that follow will show, reading in the history of the theory of poetry may benefit from a less straitened sense of what counts as a context and a more capacious view of what constitutes a moment. Poetry, perhaps not alone, but to a high degree among the arts, dwells in multiple temporalities.[77] Poetic responses to contingency are influenced by noncontingent entailments of the medium; the fact that a poem is a made thing that is heard, read, or seen motivates its perennial interest in problems of voice and address, substance and its perception. Such concerns are not just critical fantasies about or impositions upon poems, but common objects of poets' own conscious deliberation—whatever forms those deliberations take. On a different account of necessity (historical rather than material), a poet's view of the contemporary is refracted by shared terms and concerns that make up the long history of the art. Thus even the narrowest and most personal concern with self-manifestation may be pulled into generality by the gravity of poetry's historical obligation to the project of immortalization. The history of poetry's self-idealizations is not necessarily itself idealist.

Just as we need to preserve a sense of what it can mean to attend to concerns that are internal to the art, so too we need to maintain a full sense of how poets may be influenced by events external to it. Poetry's shape is determined by the material conditions that bear upon its makers and immediate audiences, but also by the intellectual and philosophical cultures whose scope is wider and whose pace of change is more gradual. In the case of the poets I consider in *Being Numerous,* the long history of intensifying skepticism toward the Enlightenment project is far from being a thing apart from or in addition to a poet's "private history"; the terror of skepticism about persons afflicts even the most intimate personal affections. By the same token, a century of unprecedented and escalating historical violence is a context pervasive enough that it can make a poet's silence *legible,* rather than "practically illegible."

The story that *Being Numerous* tells tries to keep hold of all of these dimensions of poetic practice, from the most personal to the global. Its chapters constitute not a *narrative* of a poetic tradition, but a set of limit cases that define its parameters and concerns. The poets I discuss are deeply and variously immersed in the idioms of their personal lives, local concerns, generic histories, and yet from within those "overlapping and incongruous" contexts, they each confront broadly shared cultural phenomena—the unprecedented historical threats to personhood that begin to be felt even before World War I combining with and exacerbating a secular and skeptical philosophical culture that emphasizes the contingency of human value. The radically different barriers to acceptance or comprehension that these poets present to readers—their moral or conceptual incoherence, their silence, triviality, boredom, or indifference—these are not indicators of incommensurable projects, but rather indexes of their convergence, out of idiosyncrasy, upon a shared account of poetry and of personhood: one that is deliberately hostile not just to "social contingency" and "public reading" but to *all* contingency and to *any* reading. Such an account may cross the distinct strands that make up the history of poetry without transcending history itself. Indeed, I will go further to say that a historicism that begins by assuming that generic variation and difference as *prima facie* evidence of methodological rigor cannot *help* but fail to perceive the existence of a tradition of poetic thinking in which the insistence upon difference (between poets, verse genres, as indeed between one person and another) is the very problem in need of a solution. The fervor of micro-historicism has a moral cast that exceeds the requirements of descriptive accuracy.

To say this, of course, raises a question about the normative stakes of my own argument. There are, this book will acknowledge, poets of the poem, for whom the social imaginary of the poem is that of the human journey toward understanding. I will be centrally concerned with describing another tradition, and another kind of poet; one whose drive to secure the universality of personhood will often seem to deprive poems (in the ordinary, restricted sense) of everything that we hold most dear about them: the way they negotiate the work of being a particular person embedded in a world of particulars; the way they allow us to enter very deeply into the texture of experience; the way they facilitate (or trouble) understanding by replaying experience in slow motion, by recasting it in durable materials, or by turning it inside out for observation; the way they create public analogues for private imaginings.

I am sympathetic to those who regard this turning away from particularity as a loss to poetry. Perhaps it is loss to politics as well, though not all of my poets have thought so; one of the things my book will show is that a commitment to abstract conceptions of personhood may turn out be as compatible with a democratic politics as with a fascist one, and that a poet may have a deeply realized social vision with hardly any political ideals to speak of, or else with deeply self-defeating ones. In describing another relation to poetry, and making the case for its interest and value, I will argue that there are compensations for such losses. A radical poetics, this book will argue, is not radical for its political commitments but for its pre-political or ontological commitments. The attempt to make the person appear anew as a value-bearing fact—as the necessary ground of social life—is a conceptual precursor to any effective politics, to any subsequent account of justice. In place of the myriad pleasures—aesthetic, intellectual, and moral—of the poem, the poet of "poetry" offers a drama in which the pleasures of object creation or perception, the search for self-possession, the particularized scene of valuing, the self-shattering or self-fortifying experience of love of another or of the world, all fall away, leaving in their place something else; a conviction (as George Oppen puts it) "That they are there"; an ontological confidence in the presence of other minds, in the meaning of being numerous. The history of this poetry in the twentieth century has been a history of pursuing this confidence and of negotiating its price.

. . .

I begin with a poet who is incontestably a maker of poems, and who regarded the mastery of art the highest of possible achievements—William Butler Yeats.

> The intellect of man is forced to choose
> Perfection of the life, or of the work

Faced with what he called "The Choice" between rival perfections, Yeats is most often understood to have chosen the second. His life was (as he characterized the lives of all poets) a "bundle of accident and incoherence": passionate attachments alongside destructive loves, noble political aspirations coupled to appalling political judgments, artistic genius feeding on occult foolishness. His work—"these masterful images, because complete"—placed him first among the moderns for successive generations of readers and critics.

My first chapter takes up both the philosophical origins and the political urgencies of Yeats's demand for "perfection" and "completeness." Despite the poet's own claims—his consciousness of poetic labor, his lifelong project of revision, his metrical sophistication and his care for the minutest details of publication and print—the perfection of the work of *art* mattered to him just insofar as it could actually be imagined as a means to realize the perfection of life. And not just the life of the artist—reborn in art as "something intended, complete"—but of all life. Yeats's early and abiding commitment to the esoteric roots of symbolism and his late interest in eugenic science both addressed the local project of forging a counterfactual identity. The poems of Yeats's middle period (*Responsibilities* and particularly *The Wild Swans at Coole*) imagine a tool—a bone, a poem, a man—bridging the gap between the perfected Ireland he conceived of and the degraded one he perceived.

Philosophically speaking, however, the idea of Great Mind that Yeats drew from Neoplatonism, ceremonial magic, and Theosophy could be squared only uneasily with the bounded concerns of his nationalism. Historically speaking, Yeats perceived "mere anarchy" to have been loosed not just on a divided Ireland but on "the world." Under such internal and external pressures, Yeats begins to imagine that art itself could be not just the nation's but the world's schoolroom; that the origin of the image—poem, painting, even the well-chosen picture on a coin—in primal and universal sources of being might have a transformative effect upon the spirit *and* body, remaking all persons in the image of their collective origins: "Bring the soul of man to God / make him fill the cradles right."

The poet's increasingly radical vision of aesthetic education, the shifting mechanisms by which he imagined it might work (sometimes by rational pedagogy, sometimes by magical transformation), and the ever-expanding horizon in which he envisioned its unifying effects (national, global, or metaphysical), placed conflicting and impossible demands on Yeats's actual poems. These demands are manifest as specific kinds of difficulty or "badness" (arcane symbol systems, uncontrolled rhetoric, fantasies of purifying violence), but also as formal *strangeness*: contortions of syntax and dead-ends of rhyme that strain to bend social speech and warp lived time to make another world apparent.

At the end of Yeats's career, both poetry and politics run aground on his extreme commitment to personhood. To be adequately universal is to renounce the heroism of human particularity; to be adequately general poetically is to renounce mastery, "to chaunt a tongue men do not know." But from his own conflicts and vacillations between poems and poetry, individual persons and universal personhood, Yeats produces for modernism and its successors the conflict that would be parceled out between poets of different kinds.

Renunciation lies at the heart of my second chapter. The 25-year silence at the center of George Oppen's poetic career was driven in part by his early choice of left-political activism over art. But for Oppen, class conflict in the 1930s was only a precursor to the more dire failures of sympathy and recognition that he would witness in World War II. In the context of total war, silence was not an alternative to art but an artistic solution—perhaps the only one suitable to the extremity of that history. Oppen's return to poetry was contingent upon his conceptualization of the rigorous charity of his silence—its refusal to model in speech and thought the kind of person who will count—and his discovery of a way to make such silence audible.

The chapter centers on the figure of Robinson Crusoe, who appears in Oppen's 1968 sequence *Of Being Numerous,* and who also figures importantly in other poetry and philosophy of the period. Crusoe is the paradigm of the person at once doomed to act out constrained and deformed versions of the social even in his solitude (as in Marx's reading), and to voice that constraint in the sociability and pathos of his *tone* (as in Elizabeth Bishop's "Crusoe in England"). For Oppen (as, I will suggest, for Saul Kripke's Wittgenstein), Crusoe is a radical isolate whose silence raises the question of how to recognize the morally salient presence of something or someone whose responses are so different from our own as to appear inhuman. Oppen's deliberate uncertainty about whether it is by listening or looking, feeling or thinking that we will come to value what needs valuing may sometimes look like a kind of intense skepticism about the senses and faculties—but his commitment to a poetics of silent attentiveness is a kind of faith in the human capacity for moral curiosity.

For both Yeats and Oppen, commitments to the moral seriousness of generality and abstraction create problems for the idea of poetic mastery, and indeed for the very idea of a poem. (Oppen: "Because I am not silent, the poems are bad."). In my third chapter, I turn to a poet whose problem is a specificity bordering on triviality. Whether criticized for his absence of technique and narrow frame of reference, or celebrated for his unadorned inclusion of everyday life, Frank O'Hara's "I do this, I do that" poems are best known for their loquacious over-particularity. Even loving O'Hara, as so many do, presents at once an aesthetic problem—Why should we care about the expression of such slight catalogues of likes and dislikes? What *reasons* can we give to our attachment to an ungeneralizable particular?—and an ethical problem—Why should we commit ourselves to a world in which the value of the person seems dependent on the vicissitudes of taste? Against sociologically inflected readings that take the poet's tastes as the symptomatic product of a consumer culture in which taste is all, or else (more optimistically) that take taste to carve out an alternative coterie whose affections oppose dominant social structures, I argue that O'Hara's dependence on preference does not *restrict* the extension of his poetry all. Rather, by *totalizing* the scene of judgment—by treating the whole world as a magnification of the art world—O'Hara dramatizes the consequence for social life of using a single scale—not taste, but *love*—to determine the value of a thing, regardless of what sort of thing it is. O'Hara understands "poetry" less as a collection of objects that appear than as a *medium* in which persons, things, or actions can appear. In his effort to respect both the particularity *and* the abstraction of his loves, he reimagines a world in which any kind of person has the potential to be valued, whether or not any particular person happens to value him.

These first three chapters of the book are part of the project of literary-historical revision I announced at the outset. They allow us to see connections between poets like Yeats and Oppen who lie on opposite sides of the apparent divide between tradition and experiment. They also seek to reinterpret the meaning of the experiments undertaken by Oppen and O'Hara—poets who have been recruited by our contemporary avant-gardes to provide a history and justification for their own exclusive vision of legitimate poetic practice—and so challenge the legitimacy of divisions made, in part, in the names of those predecessor poets. In my fourth chapter, I take up one of those contemporary avant-gardes directly. I take seriously something that the Language poets of the 1970s and '80s (and many of their successors) often said that they wanted—a sense of themselves as engaged in a communal and even political practice *by means of poetry.* The poets' own attempts to theorize and to practice this poetics of community may be compelling as desires, but their analyses and poems are hobbled by simultaneous and contradictory commitments to absolute constraint and absolute freedom. Examining the theory and practice of collaboration in the joint-authored book *Leningrad,* I argue that the account of the person implicit in the generative linguistics that the poets deplore—rather than in the poststructural linguistics that they have tended to embrace—provides something very close to what they have felt themselves to be looking for. A Chomskyan account of poetry as interested in highlighting the distinction between grammar and utterance both "saves the appearances" of many Language poems and is compatible with the intensity of the poets' valuation of linguistic innovation over convention. More importantly, the Chomskyan account of language as a capacity for an endlessly productive freedom grounds a conception of personhood that the constraints and determinations of grammatical, conceptual, and political systems cannot reach.

One of the methodological difficulties that this book presents is the question of what will count as evidence, or, to put it somewhat differently, what will count as a reading of a poem. Just as it is the case that a general account of personhood cannot be derived by averaging the qualities of any number of persons, so too an argument for a poetic tradition's being a tradition of "non-poems" cannot be derived solely by reading any number of poems. Poems, like persons, are always going about some business of their own, which in the moment seems much more urgent—and certainly more specifiable—than the business of being instances of what they generally, abstractly, essentially are. If the particular business of individual persons is what we mean by *living,* then the specification of the business of poems is what we generally mean by *reading.* My final chapter is thus an experiment in reading and in living. It tells a story of a reader (myself) who sought to read a poem with another person, but at a distance—"together apart." Where the preceding chapters describe the production of "indifferent" poems—poems that seek to put us off their phenomenal features, by poets who go about trying to take themselves, and us, *out of the moment*—this chapter describes the way that reading poems together may promote an attitude of indifference toward the specificity of *any* poem in the greater interest of solidarity with other persons. Taking up debates about collective intentionality within contemporary social philosophy, I propose an alternative to models of poetic community built around conversation, interpretation, or translation. Writing myself into the history of poetic intentions I describe, I also argue for the interest and value (if not necessarily the truth) of a theory of collective intentions that is crucially *internalist*: it conceives of the ability of forming intentions for partnership-in-action whether or not one has a partner—indeed, whether or not anyone else in the world exists. The ability to recover—by reading poems—a conviction in even the solitary person's innate and "primitive" capacity to formulate "we-intentions" may, I suggest, have a transformative effect on one's felt capacities for relationship, and reorient the person toward a shared world. The question that the poets in this tradition pose to social thought is of the most fundamental kind: not how to distribute fairly the privileges of identity, but how to secure the *ground* of identity; not just of how to do things with persons, but how to know that a person is there at all.

White Thin Bone

Yeatsian Personhood

> But first, Hippias, refresh my memory: Are you
> and I one, or are you two and I two?

A T LEAST FOUR DECADES of major American critical theorists, Daniel O'Hara writes in his 1987 essay "Yeats in Theory," were "essentially Yeatsian."[1] R. P. Blackmur solidified his sense of poetic form upon the work of the still-living artist whom he declared "our one indubitable major poet";[2] Northrop Frye's synoptic impulses and syncretic diagrams were decisively shaped by Yeats's gyres and wheels;[3] Harold Bloom's theory of influence generalized the transactions between Yeats and his Romantic precursors;[4] Paul de Man's early work on the types of Yeatsian figuration (the only part of his doctoral dissertation he chose to preserve and publish) predicts his later deconstructive distinction between "semiology" and "rhetoric."[5] But what distinguishes the "essentially" Yeatsian critic from the accidental Yeatsian who takes up the poet as a representative case in point, even early on in the development of a critical method or the formalization of an interpretive system? On O'Hara's account, the distinction is not just a matter of priority but of causality. That is, it is precisely the attempt to grapple with the "sublime" of Yeats's imaginative power in all its totalizing idiosyncrasy—"excited, passionate, fantastical"[6]—that provokes the critic into a rival systematization of imaginative power, and into offering passionate rationalization as a way for all readers.

"Rather than authoring 'Yeats,' then," O'Hara contends, "their chosen poet has authored and—paradoxically if not perversely—authorized them."[7]

It is, as O'Hara acknowledges, an "extravagant" claim.[8] It is also, in its very extravagance, one that the poet would have approved of. Yeats himself attributed extravagant causal powers to poetry, though the pathways of causation he imagined were often occult, and his avowed beliefs—themselves sometimes perverse—could be fogged by symbolism or qualified by the defensive rhetoric of supposition:

> A little lyric evokes an emotion, and this emotion gathers others about it and melts into their being in the making of some great epic; and at last, needing an always less delicate body, or symbol, as it grows more powerful, it flows out, with all it has gathered, among the blind instincts of daily life, where it moves a power within powers, as one sees ring within ring in the stem of an old tree. This is maybe what Arthur O'Shaughnessy meant when he made his poets say they had built Nineveh with their sighing; and I am certainly never sure, when I hear of some war, or of some religious excitement, or of some new manufacture, or of anything else that fills the ear of the world, that it has not all happened because of something that a boy piped in Thessaly.[9]

Some battles really do begin with song. O'Hara has provided an impressive roster of critics whose first or foundational work grapples with the poet; and many others might be counted one with Blackmur, Bloom, and Paul de Man.[10] For my purposes I would emphasize two more: Helen Vendler and Marjorie Perloff, the critics most often and powerfully associated with opposing poles of the divided poetic history I describe in the introduction, both began with books devoted to Yeats. The two careers begin in consensus: what gives Yeats pride of place for each is the poet's incomparable achievement as an architect of forms and a master of sound; and for each, the performances and prerequisites of such mastery are the primary objects of critical attention. Perloff's *Rhyme and Meaning in the Poetry of Yeats* is an exhaustive study of the semantics of Yeats's rhyming over the entire course of his career.[11] Vendler's *A Vision and the Later Plays* dwells at length upon the mysteries of the poet's visionary system, but does so in order to justify its contributory work to the making of strong poems—the aesthetic objects that warrant our real attention.[12] After these inaugural projects, the two scholars would veer in dramatically different directions. In 1990, Marjorie Perloff argued that it was precisely Yeats's organicist commitment to traditional forms that reined in the avant-gardist impulse toward "external ordering systems" implicit in his numerological designs, declaring (in a statement that describes the trajectory of her own learning as much as the course of poetic history) that "the future would lie with Khlebnikov and Pound."[13] For Vendler, meanwhile, Yeats was the future as well as the past. Her 2007 *Our Secret Discipline: Yeats and Lyric Form* fulfills the promise that the early work tendered to the poems with a book exhaustively devoted to the premise that "Yeats's style was the most important of his qualities, since it was what would make the poems last."[14]

To begin with Yeats, then, is to return to the primal scene of poetry's division into "two kinds," each projecting its own canon and its own ideology of style. In the spirit of Yeatsian extravagance, however, I would go further, and suggest that in beginning with Yeats we are returning not just to the occasion of a division invented by critics, but to a crucial moment of its conceptualization and intensification by the poet himself. To see this, though, we must view that division once again, not as a conflict between rival conceptions of form ("organic" vs. "external"), but rather as Yeats himself saw it: as a conflict between rival conceptions of poetry. The first: that poetry is most crucially an art in which "words alone are certain good," and where the reality that one most desires is that of artifice, whose formal perfection outlasts and outshines "dusty deeds" and "Grey Truth." The second: that song is at best secondary to the will to discover the perfection of persons and to make it unrefusable—or, as Yeats puts it in "Under Ben Bulben" (1939), "indomitable":

> Sing the lords and ladies gay
> That were beaten into the clay
> Through seven heroic centuries;
> Cast your mind on other days
> That we in coming days may be
> Still the indomitable Irishry.

Like the relation between Danaan rhymes and the brimming heart in "To Some I Have Talked With by the Fire," the relation between singing and whatever cognitive action Yeats intends by the injunction to "cast your mind" is loosely associative rather than strongly causal. Stronger, though still difficult to parse, is the asserted relation between this obscure casting of mind and a possible future in which some strong "we" will be identifiable, brought into concert, and freed of constraint. The difficulty is a difficulty of agency and of temporality. In the most straightforward sense, the poem's appeal to "other days" and to "coming days" might well seem intended as a corrective rebuke to the *present* days—a continuation and extension of the poet's admonition to Irish poets to "learn your trade" and to cultivate an appropriately placed contempt for the "now":

> Scorn the sort now growing up
> All out of shape from toe to top,
> Their unremembering hearts and heads
> Base-born products of base beds.

> ("Under Ben Bulben")

But this reading does not quite do justice to the syntax. For the speaker, despite his scorn for the base inhabitants of the present, also wishes to construe the indomitable future he desires as the continuation of the moment rather than a correction of it—"we" are meant to be "*still* the indomitable Irishry" rather than "again." The poem, that is, imagines that there could be some act of mind in which an image of a perfected state (whether past or to come—but certainly "other") might change "us"—not as a reader is changed by what she reads, but as the stroke of a pen changes a poem into the poem it was all along. If "Under Ben Bulben" cultivates uncertainty about the present condition of the "Irishry" by making them seem "now" deformed and "still" indomitable, it also raises questions about the nature of the Irish poet's "trade" by making it seem at once indispensable in bringing about change ("Sing whatever is well-made") and at the same time irrelevant—since in or through the poem the desired change can be understood to have been already accomplished. Just what then is the poet being enjoined to do?

According to O'Hara, what makes Yeats particularly provoking to the theorist— indeed what enjoins the theorist to theorize—is that the poet requires us to "confront the question of literature's status and effect" ("Yeats in Theory," 350). But the simplicity of O'Hara's conjunction belies the difficulty of the thought. Yeats is the maker of a uniquely intense tension that results from trying to *bind* the "status" of the poetic artifact—the object of Yeats's laborious craft—to an extreme vision of an "effect" which both does and does not seem to flow from poetry. In "Under Ben Bulben," as in the passage I cite above from Yeats's 1900 essay "The Symbolism of Poetry," this tension is expressed as a complex figure uniting the vision of poetry sponsored by the figure of Orpheus—a poetry in which the mortal singer achieves eternal knowledge of the self and its nature by virtue of his access to the sources of wisdom, which are atemporal and unchanging—with the effectual vision sponsored by Amphion, who intervenes in history, building the city-state of Thebes with the power of his lyre.[15] The extreme demand of self-knowledge and world-transformation that Yeats places upon actual poems taxes the poet's imagination of what a poem is, driving him to produce extreme figures of poetic mediation, and to conceive extreme and paradoxical theories of poetic agency.

My argument will proceed through three stages. First, I will endeavor to explain why such an excessive account of poetic agency might have appeared necessary in Yeats's historical situation; why, that is, more conventional (as well as more obviously nationalist) ways of imagining collective identity formation through literature would not serve in the Irish case. The details of the Irish national situation are, of course, highly complex and particular—and well studied. But sketching them out once again will reveal why Yeats regarded Ireland's peculiarity as paradigmatic in at least one sense: the internal contradictions of modern Irish politics highlight the ways in which any image of what a person is or should be—whether that image is offered by poet or statesman—produces division and conflict as often as it enables identification and fellowship.

Second, I will provide an account of how Yeats's alternative project of unification in the face of such complexity is supposed to work. The philosophical traditions at stake here are even more intensely idiosyncratic than the details of Irish politics, requiring a brief detour through two of the Yeatsian traditions that modern interpreters have found the least credible and creditable: the esoteric, which dominated the early part of Yeats's career, and the eugenic, which compelled him toward that career's end. Yeats declared Blake "a too literal realist of the imagination, as others are of nature"; here, as is so often the case with Yeats, the poet was at war with elements of his own thinking. For Yeats's interest in hereditarian biology represents both a literalization and a naturalization of the ontological claims implicit in the former interest in spirit. Insofar as poetry is understood to create the community it imagines, it serves less a nationalizing function than a *personmaking* function, re-creating contingent selves in the image of their essential natures. Many recent critics have been eager to point out the racialist dimensions of this project—and of course it is true that Yeats's commitments to the "rule of kindred" are eugenic commitments, and that his vision of a perfected Ireland is frequently an ethno-nationalist one. But I will argue that the ontology of Yeatsian personmaking, in which "All dreams of the soul / End in a beautiful man's or woman's body" ("The Phases of the Moon")—operates at a level both more abstract and more universal than that of race, and that its implications cannot be (and in Yeats's mind were not) limited to the boundaries of nation. The atavistic universalism of his essentialism cannot be reduced to the politics of fascism.

As extravagant as Yeats's account of poetic agency is, it is not as eccentric as it may at first appear. Versions of it survive, not only in the work of modern mystics who would simply affirm Yeats's claims about the magical powers of poetic form, but also in the work of skeptical and secular critics, for whom essentialist accounts of identity are anathema. They survive, that is, not in the sense that a secular critic like Edward Said believes that Yeats's poems transform physical persons after archetypes, but in the sense that strong arguments in defense of national-cultural identity—or indeed collective identity of any kind—cannot and do not take place without recourse to anti-empirical terms. In the absence of a religious system in which such terms can be credited, the transcendental supplement to empirical identity is at once sustained and stigmatized by being given the *name* "poetry." What Yeats came to understand better than more recent and more enlightened theorists of identity is that to imagine a poem—or indeed any cultural artifact—serving the function of identity formation requires some theory of agency adequate to the task, and a theory of subjectivity susceptible to such agency.[16] The problem of identity formation by cultural means raises a thorny problem of mediation for which the idea of a "political aesthetic" is a sort of conceptual patch. If collective identities are to be more than mere fictions or political strategies, then *something* like Yeatsian poetic eugenics is required to assemble the many minds under the auspices of the whole. Beginning his account of symbolic pedagogy in a material culture of reading and response, Yeats elaborates a vision in which "reception" changes minds until they are capable of transformative action, and in which mere perception can give rise to beautiful offspring.

Toward the end of his life, Yeats came to regard the attempt to conceive of a causal link between poetic form and collective life as destructive rather than sustaining. The third part of my argument finds Yeats in explicit rebellion, not against his universalist conception of personhood, which he never fully abandoned, but against his own will to poetic mastery. To put it another way, Yeats's career ends by dividing the actuality of his poems from his desire for "poetry in the general sense." This is the division—forged in the particulars of history, but cut loose from history by its own extremity—that Yeats bequeathed to his poetic successors.

I. A Deep-sworn Vow

In 1919, writing from Thoor Ballylee, the newly renovated ancient Norman tower that would serve as his primary poetic symbol of an Irish Ireland, W. B. Yeats posed the great riddle of "the unit of social life" in the form of a dream:[17]

> To take but one straw from a haystack, I have known a dream to pass through a whole house—I can never blind myself to the implications of that fact—but what I do not know is whether it so passed because all were under one roof, or because all shared certain general interests, or because all had various degrees of affection for one another. (*Explorations*, 278)

To abstract once again the haystack from the straw: the fundamental question raised by Yeats's experience of a commutable dream—the dream experienced as the expression, not of an individual psyche but of a totality bounded by "a whole house"—is the question of the ground of collectivity. To put that question more precisely, in the terms that will matter both to Yeats and to this study as a whole: What is the nature of and sufficient condition for collective life such that many persons may be said to be *of one mind*; such that (in Yeats's favored terms) they may dream the same dream?

Yeats proposes three figurative answers to this riddle. Each finds echo and elaboration in the discourses surrounding the then-urgent question of Irish national consolidation, and each appeals to Yeats in particular moments and moods. The first—that "all were under one roof"—is the answer given in various ways by United Irishmen, Home Rulers, Parnellites, and other parliamentary reformers. In its appeal to a community that is constructed by being given a formal limit (here imagined as an architectural form), it represents something like a political nationalism. For the political nationalist, the nation is the sum of individuals who have consented to enter into a form of governance and who remain within the limits of its sovereignty. While the scope of national sovereignty is not itself purely contractual—it is constrained by accidents of history and geography, for example—the nation so constructed is (in theory) voluntarist, rationalist, and cosmopolitan. Insofar as a political nationalism imagines an ideal collective entity, then, that entity is the modern state divested of its bureaucratic excesses and remodeled after the *polis*. Insofar as the state confers an identity upon its constituents, that identity is the product of rational education, and is therefore (theoretically) reproducible and transferable.[18] The common dream of this kind of community derives from the common concerns and experiences of liberal citizenship.

The second possible principle of unity—that of "shared general interests"—should certainly in Yeats's thought be understood to specify the interests of the Anglo-Irish Ascendancy, of which the poet was a celebrant if not precisely a member. "Interest" here may be understood in two ways. The Ascendancy, separated from the rising middle class by genealogy, economics, and religion, could indeed be said (albeit "generally") to be of one mind about the preservation of its class and status interests—the colonial hierarchy some version of which had been in place since the defeat of Hugh O'Neill at Kinsale in 1601. But for Yeats, another conception of "interest" seems plausibly at stake. The Ascendancy as Yeats imagined it was not the "classed" nobility of modern Ireland, but an anachronistic, Romantic conception of aristocracy requiring no institutional recognition and manifesting no material interest other than that of a timeless "universal class."[19] The "shared interests" of such dreamers might, by various rationales, be labeled Irish; but "Irish" such as these would have as much in common with the idealized Italian nobility of the sixteenth century as with the Irish middle classes of the twentieth. Community, on this account, inheres in the aristocratic personality that is the foundation of a nation's life rather than its product.

This leaves us with Yeats's third principle of affiliation—a relation of "affection" that is apparently neither the result of rational choice, nor quite the registration of an existing or imagined aristocratic form of life, yet which still seems to account for the common possessions of certain souls. This principle, seemingly the most mysterious, is not for all that to be discounted. For if the Yeats of the political meditations and exhortations of *If I Were Four and Twenty* affects a reluctance to stake himself upon a single principle that might account for the shared life of dreams, the Yeats of the poems in the contemporaneous collection *The Wild Swans at Coole* has no qualms about privileging an occult and oneiric affection above all other forms of relationship:

> Others because you did not keep
> That deep-sworn vow have been friends of mine;
> Yet always when I look death in the face,
> When I clamber to the heights of sleep,
> Or when I grow excited with wine,
> Suddenly I meet your face.

("A Deep-sworn Vow")

In the introduction I discussed Stanley Cavell's interest in this poem as an extraordinary representation validating an ordinary experience: the ubiquitous drama of the forgetting and remembering that thwart and haunt our everyday perceptions of other persons. A more fully elaborated reading of the poem's commitment to this understanding of the ordinary would take in not just the narrative sequencing of perception and recollection, but the poem's tone and the unfolding of its syntax. The speaker of the poem seems firmly situated in a community of civil associations and rational affections—recorded here thematically as "friendship," and registered stylistically in the elegant simplicity of his diction, in the fine balance between the prosodies of poetry and of talk. Indeed, one of the notable triumphs of this poem is the ease with which it bears its formal constraints across the divide between poetic elevation and natural speech, producing an enormously plausible imitation of ordinary language without compromising any traditional lyric virtue. Thus, R. P. Blackmur would hold up this poem as a paradigm not just of Yeats's artistic mastery, but of the sociability of poetic art itself: "Perhaps all poetry should be read as this poem is read," he writes, "and no poem greatly valued that cannot be so read."[20]

Blackmur initially cites "A Deep-sworn Vow" in order to oppose it to that *other* sort of Yeats poem: a poem like "All Souls' Night" (1921) or "The Phases of the Moon" (1919), or even the famous "The Second Coming" (1920), none of which, he argues, can be properly understood without reference to the esoteric tradition of *magic*: "an insight, a group of ideas, and a faith, with the discipline that flows from them, which taken together form a view of life most readers cannot share, and which, furthermore, most readers feel as repugnant, or sterile, or simply inconsequential" (147). And though Blackmur ultimately means to argue that Yeats used magic as a valid form of thought that can be *made* consequential, he also acknowledges that the poems that depend most heavily upon it are fundamentally cut off from readers. "Magic has a tradition," he goes on to say, "but it is secret, not public" (155). "A Deep-sworn Vow" represents for Blackmur an alternative poetic of ease. In the lucidity of its diction and its emotional generality, it strikes the sensibility with its bare immediacy (with what Blackmur calls "bare emotion without mood"); at that moment the burden of interpretation is lifted, the implied audience extended without limit.

And yet despite the universality and intensity of its emotion and the manifest comprehensibility of its language, there remains a persistent and disfiguring strangeness about this poem. It is not just as an artifact of lyric economy that the names of friends are omitted or that the grounds of the speaker's "community" of friendship are left unspoken. These names, along with the distinguishing qualities that make them available for identification as "A portion of my mind and life," can be named—as they *would* be named in "In Memory of Major Robert Gregory" (written a year later but published in the same volume): the learned Lionel Johnson; John Synge, "passionate and simple"; the "muscular" and "solid" George Pollexfen. In the pointed compression of this lyric utterance, the friendships in this poem are made to owe their existence less to any internal solidarities than to a prior cataclysm—the beloved's betrayal of the "deep-sworn vow." Unwinding the sense of what Denis Donoghue has called a "remarkably truculent piece of syntax," we find that the "you" whom the speaker addresses may be grammatically subordinate but is definitionally dominant. "Others" may be the ostensible subject; but unlike subjects, these others are not others-in-themselves, with their own talents and distinctions. They are merely "others because you did not keep."[21]

This dependency of all other relationships upon the apparently faithless "you" is more than a way of registering the difference between friendship and erotic love— even with their very great difference of intensity, risk, and depth of commitment. The hierarchy of relationships is underwritten by a deeper commitment to a hierarchy of conceptions of reality—one that accounts for both the truculence of the syntax and the depth of the deep-sworn vow. This commitment is evident in the poem's competing temporalities. We might, for example, think of the poem as constructing a narrative that takes in a time past, in which love was had, and vows were made; and a time sometime after, when vows were broken. This second moment in past time is followed by a duration, continuing at least up to the moment we are overhearing (the present perfect progressive "have been" leads us up to the present of utterance time, but is uncertain about the future). In stark contrast to this narrative of progression, the poem marks repetitive time of actions that are "always" undertaken. These include experiences that are plausible candidates to take an adverb of temporality like "always," such as sleep; others in which the sense of "always" is torqued, but not beyond acceptability, to mean something like "each time" (as in the case of drunkenness). But they also include events for which "always" seems singularly inappropriate—like Death. Indeed, Death is the paradigmatic element of the set; for in the poetic tradition as Yeats received it, wine, sleep, and death are *not* ways of freeing the individual mind into recollection or of releasing the unconscious memory. What is recalled with their aid is not of the same order as the narratable past; the image recovered at the height of sleep or in the *veritas* of wine is not the impress an actual event makes in the tablet of a developing psyche. Wine, sleep, and death are, rather, techniques of ecstasy, anamnetic techniques that reveal—as in a passion—the template or origin of the self in that great collective resource that Yeats called Great Mind or Great Memory. The face of the beloved is the image of this origin, recoverable only with the aid of supplements to conscious perception.

Thus, if the *narrative* of the poem (its sequence and its syntax) produces the opposition "Others/your face" as the familiar opposition between reality and desire, the anamnetic structure of the poem rewrites this as the opposition between contingent and essential identities—as the opposition between *myself-as-I-am-defined-by-"Others"* and *"myself"-as-I-am-prior-to-social-life-altogether*. "Friendship," on this account, is the domain of character; like character, it may be genuine or feigned, profound or passing, but will in any case always be a contingent affiliation. In a world defined by such contingencies, the lover's revealed passion will always appear to be irrational: not because it persists in spite of the experience of betrayal, but because it attaches the highest commitments of the person to an image that does not originate in experience.

The poem's commitment to this impersonal and anti-empirical conception of identity is most clearly articulated in the disposition of the rhyme—or rather, in the discovery that this exemplary poem is self-canceling in one crucial aspect; for "face" and "face" do not rhyme, they merely repeat. Yeatsian repetition characteristically accompanies and echoes a recurrent thematic of individual extinction—the emptying out of the person whose life is marked out as narratable by the incremental differences between one word, one choice, one sound and another.[22] To look death in the face and discover no difference between it and the face of this particular beloved is to view oneself not as a distinct individual, not as the sum of one's differentiating history, but as the repetition and perfection of an original intention that is not purely one's own. By the same token, the self's "choice" to commit itself to a future—"deep-sworn vow"—is not a contractual or even a willed one. It is, instead, a covenant of identity—and as such, evinces a peculiar temporality, a claim that is, as the poem proclaims, both "always" and "sudden." *Sudden*, because the covenant may be ratified at a punctual moment, and it may be so betrayed. *Always*, because a covenant is an acknowledgment of what one always is and has been, rather than an assumption of an obligation to become—and thus the sort of agreement that could never be broken. In this, the vow seems to work very much like the syntax of the poem itself—strained slowly to the point of breaking by the evolving contingencies of actual speaking about actual events, and yet abruptly recuperated into completion when confronted by the image of the reality of the self.[23]

The belief or discovery that one's origins and destiny may be discerned in the countenance of another is not simply an explanation for the persistence of unrequited individual affections—it is the justification for passionate collective affiliations of many kinds. Maude Gonne's particular "betrayal" (the ostensible subject of this poem) was her choice of marriage vows with John ("Foxy Jack") MacBride over the earlier promise of "spiritual marriage" with Yeats (which Yeats had envisioned in a dream in 1898 and imposed on Gonne soon after).[24] But it was also her choice of MacBride's form of extremist nationalism—a populist politics unregulated by higher principle—over the politics of spiritual self-knowledge that Yeats understood to be fundamental to an authentic nationalism. This choice, too, has a distinctive style—one that can be heard in a late poem like "The Statues" (1939)

> When Pearse summoned Cuchulain to his side,
> What stalked through the Post Office? What intellect,
> What calculation, number, measurement, replied?
> We Irish, born into that ancient sect
> But thrown upon this filthy modern tide
> And by its formless spawning fury wrecked,
> Climb to our proper dark, that we may trace
> The lineaments of a plummet-measured face.

"The Statues" is one of those highly esoteric works to which Blackmur refers. Although it conceives of itself as a defense of form, its ideology of form is quite different than that of "A Deep-sworn Vow." In this poem, the rigorous constructive principles that are said to underlie the powerful figures of Phidian statuary ("calculations that look but casual flesh") do not simply contradict the shapelessness and confusion of the present; rather, the formal rigor of the Greeks is unleashed upon the living present as the principle driving revolutionary consciousness. (Harold Bloom has aptly called this fantasy of art's corrective force "Pythagorean Fascism."[25]) In an ironic counterpoint to this fantasy of the power of order, the poem itself is written in a warped *ottava rima* and a barely controlled rhetorical mode, as if to demonstrate that the Greek synthesis between form and agency is no longer available to the artist in the present; that neither decorous form nor the perfection of speech are compatible with the *power* of art. Despite these differences in manifest form, however, I would emphasize this poem's deep structural similarity to the more decorous "A Deep-sworn Vow." Here too, Yeats devalues the domain of individual "character" (which the titular statues are said to "lack"); here, too, the discovery of an ideal countenance unavailable to ordinary sense (a "plummet-measured face" achieved through an ecstatic ascent to a "proper dark") images the rediscovery of a self that knows its destiny and can act upon it. In this case, the face that appears is not the face of the beloved, but that of a heroic figure from the mythic past, and the identity that is recovered from the wreckage of a "form-less" and contingent modernity is not a personal or erotic destiny but the destiny of "we Irish" conceived as an "ancient sect."

The appropriation of a topos of religious and erotic poetry as a prerequisite for the great and tragic assertion of Irish identity is surely a kind of mysticism—but it is not *merely* mysticism. The introduction of ontological sentiments learned from the poetic tradition into what appears to be a political discourse does not trans-form politics from action into mere contemplation. Padraic Pearse's "Ghosts" (1915) evokes the literary language of spirits to justify the coming insurrection:

> Here be ghosts that I have raised this Christmastide, ghosts of dead men that have bequeathed a trust to us living men. Ghosts are troublesome things, in a house or in a family, as we knew even before Ibsen taught us. There is only one way to appease a ghost. You must do the thing it asks you. The ghosts of a nation sometimes ask very big things and they must be appeased, whatever the cost.[26]

Pearse's trope is repeated and fulfilled in the "Proclamation of the Irish Republic" issued on the eve of the Easter Uprising:

> Irishmen and Irishwomen! In the name of God and of the dead generations from which she receives her old tradition of nationhood, Ireland, through us, sum-mons her children to her flag, and strikes for her freedom.[27]

We might, at this point, be inclined to assign a name to that mysterious affection that underwrites a conception of nationhood as "old tradition," ordained by God, maintained across generations, sustained by symbols: the name of cultural nation-alism. Countering the rationalist or voluntarist Kantian tradition with the tradition of Herder, Fichte, Hegel, and Mazzini, the cultural nationalist views nationhood as an essential characteristic of both places and persons; a "genius" through which natural nations express themselves in languages, literatures, and institutions. Al-though such thinking is obviously not uniquely or even originally Irish, Ireland is one of cultural nationalism's most dramatic early successes: in the period in which the intra-Irish conflict that followed the death of Parnell had rendered consensus or parliamentarian politics virtually impracticable (or so Yeats maintained), it was the cultural nationalist movement—spurred on by the Gaelic revivalists—that fueled the passionate insurgency that would result in the establishment of the Irish Free State in 1922. Pearse's sentimental politics of martyrdom and blood sacrifice—learned, in part, from his literary education—obeys that peculiar poetic temporality that identifies political desires, not with some identity to be contracted in the future, but with one deriving from a timeless past.

Edward Said, in his account of what poetry has to offer politics, has thus sug-gested that Yeats's greatest contribution to the nationalist project was *precisely* an orientation toward the past.[28] Announcing Yeats as an "indisputably great *national* poet who during a period of anti-imperialist resistance articulates the experiences, the aspirations, and the restorative vision of a people suffering under the dominion of an offshore power" (265–66), Said celebrates "the drama of Yeats's accomplishment in restoring a suppressed history and rejoining a nation to it" (286). This concise formulation, however, collapses what are, for Yeats, two separate processes. The first—"restoration"—encompasses the anthropological and ethnographic work of Yeats's early research into Irish folklore, a part of the collaborative archival work of the Revival in unearthing ancient customs, folk traditions, and languages that lie beneath the projected ground of empire.[29] "Rejoining," on the other hand, presents a more complicated problem—a *pedagogical* problem whose difficulties Yeats perceived with greater clarity and explicitness than Said does. Certainly no account of the pedagogical project of Irish cultural nationalism would be complete without an acknowledgment of Yeats's contributions to the movement. Yeats's early folkloric work fueled the enthusiasm for things Celtic both at home and abroad; his Irish literary theater served as a vehicle for the dissemination of nationalist ideology; and the reach of his poetic influence has distinguished Ireland as the birthplace of literary modernism.[30] But any account of Yeats's social thought must take note of the fact that for Yeats, nationalism and its educational requirements came second: second in terms of his own development, and second in terms of his philosophical commitments. What came first in both senses was his commitment to what he called "magic" in the famous 1901 essay of that name:

> I believe in the practice and philosophy of what we have agreed to call magic, in what I must call the evocation of spirits, though I do not know what they are, in the power of creating magical illusions, in the visions of truth in the depths of the mind when the eyes are closed; and I believe in three doctrines, which have, as I think, been handed down from early times, and been the foundation of nearly all magical practices. These doctrines are:—
>
> 1. That the borders of our minds are forever shifting, and that many minds can flow into one another, as it were, and create or reveal a single mind, a single energy.
> 2. That the borders of our memories are as shifting, and that our memories are a part of one great memory, the memory of Nature herself.
> 3. That this great mind and great memory can be evoked by symbols. (*Essays and Introductions*, 28)

This, too, is a discourse of pedagogy and of communal life—but it is not (or at any rate, not in any obvious way) a *national* one. Like "The Statues," Yeats's unorthodox revision of the Nicene Creed in "Magic" provides a vivid example of the sort of statement that has proved most troublesome to those critics who, in an effort to recover or decode Yeats's esoteric interests as political interests, have sought to substitute a discourse of cultural nationalism for the often obscure language of his poetic intentions.

Perhaps the most common response to the troubling combination of credulity and opacity in Yeats's matter-of-fact assertion of belief and in his methodical enumeration of mystical doctrines has been to ignore it—and the many other statements like it—entirely. Michael North, although he has written what is among the most nuanced discussions of Yeats's "political aesthetic"[31] (and despite the twofold promise of the term "political aesthetic"), makes little mention of the complex farrago of Theosophy, kabbalah, ceremonial magic, and Rosicrucianism Richard Ellmann has charmingly termed "Esoteric Yeatsism" (after the influential philosophical pamphlet "Esoteric Buddhism").[32] North's reasoning in this omission seems to bear some resemblance to the commonsense decoding advocated by the New Critics: Yeats's beliefs, the argument goes, may have been necessary for him to write the poems, but they are not necessary for us to understand them. But where the New Critic relied on the self-contained structure of the iconic poem and the ideal competence of a language speaker as sufficient context to divine the meaning of a poem, North relies on the equally self-contained structure of a "culture" defined in socioeconomic terms and the idealized competence of a political theorist—neither of which readily admits the relevance of claims about "the evocation of spirits."[33]

By recalling the primacy of magic in Yeats's thought, however, I am suggesting that Yeats cannot be thought simply another contributor (however influential) to the collaborative project of imagining a national culture in any ordinary sense. Yeats, as a synoptic interpreter of the idealist poetic tradition for modernity, was rather the inventor of a new technology for the creation and consolidation of identity as such in which poetry would play a vital role—one that was not, in any recognizable sense of the word, cultural, nor, in any meaningful sense of the word, national. In adopting the term "technology," I also mean to emphasize the inadequacy of the notion that Yeats's poetry was intended as a pedagogical tool or a vehicle for disseminating ideology. In the conflict between an identity that is historical—contingent and empirical—and one that is essential—necessary and ideal—"A Deep-sworn Vow" insists upon the latter and, more importantly, casts it in a counterfactual form: one discovered not just in the absence of any verification through experience or history, but in spite of all the betrayals of experience, and in the face of all historical evidence to the contrary.

What Yeats realized with astonishing clarity is that the kind of collective identity called for in "The Statues" must be counterfactual in this more profound sense. The ability (whether granted to Pearse at the General Post Office or to the Paudeen in the street) to claim Irish "themes" or myths as a national heritage (that could license action on behalf of a nation) depends, not on the discovery that they are one's "suppressed" history (as Said would have it), but on the ability to claim for oneself an identity that has no foundation in the actual past, "suppressed" or otherwise.

II. "I Shall Have Made Him One"

John Hutchinson's *The Dynamic of Cultural Nationalism* provides a concise account of the general aims and methods of the cultural nationalist project, with special reference to the Irish case.

> What is behind this cultural politics is a drive to resurrect the personality in all its dimensions in space and time. . . . National symbols are chosen on pragmatic grounds to objectively affirm a specific vision of historical continuity and to differentiate the group from others. But, if pragmatic, these symbols . . . may have the capacity to elicit powerful historical memories that impel groups towards certain cultural, political and territorial goals.[34]

There are several elements in Hutchinson's formulation that are central to any postcolonialist reading of Yeats. First, of course, is the investment in symbols. Such symbols are not quite as contingent as the term "pragmatic" might imply. As the critics of liberalism never tire of reminding us, there are always factors that constrain and condition the individual's capacity to imagine a relation to a community; the cultural nationalist views these constraints as both the sign and the substance of a natural or divinely ordained nation. Thus, to qualify as a *national* symbol—one capable of affirming a vision of history and a significant distinction between historical communities—a symbol must be thought to be constitutive of the life of a collectivity rather than being merely a product or representation of that life. It must be less like the flag to which the proclamation calls its Irish revolutionaries (a flag derived from the revolutionary tricolour that, in any case, very few of the initially bemused spectators at the Post Office had *ever* recognized as their own), and more like the summoning voice that the proclamation ventriloquizes. A short list of constitutive symbols or symbolic systems that have been useful to cultural nationalist arguments might resemble Edward Said's "common history, religion and language" (*Culture and Imperialism,* 223), to which catalogue a somewhat less doctrinaire historian might append common racial or ethnic characteristics.[35]

Language has been the first resort of cultural nationalism since Herder. Armed with two convictions—that language is the precondition of thought, and that each individual language emerges from nature by design—linguistic nationalists believe language coextensive with the forms of life (beliefs, literatures, practices, institutions) that thought produces. Thus in Ireland, the task of reconnecting the inhabitants of a modern society to its ostensibly natural and national forms of life (spiritual, lyrical, anti-materialist, and agrarian) through the resurrection of the Gaelic tongue was taken up by the Gaelic League under the leadership of Eoin MacNeill and Douglas Hyde. The Gaelic League emphasized the conceptual split between the cultural and political nationalist projects; In Hyde's well-known formulation of the matter in 1892, "The Necessity of de-Anglicizing Ireland" was not felt as a need to reform parliament in order to represent a set of emergent political interests, but rather to cure the Irish consciousness as a prerequisite to *any* authentic political action whatsoever:

> I would earnestly appeal to every one, whether Unionist or Nationalist, who wishes to see the Irish nation produce its best—and surely whatever our politics are we all wish that—to set his face against this constant running to England for books, literature, music, games, fashion, and ideas. I appeal to every one what-ever his politics—for this is no political matter—to do his best to help the Irish race develop in the future along Irish lines, even at the risk of encouraging na-tional aspirations, because upon Irish lines alone can the Irish race once more become what it was of yore—one of the most original artistic, literary, and charming peoples of Europe.[36]

While the League did, despite its anti-political rhetoric, achieve a number of political triumphs—not the least of which was to make the language question one which politicians could ignore only at the risk of losing their nationalist credentials—their small and elite membership was finally unable to revive Gaelic as a living presence outside the economically backward and ever-shrinking *Gaeltacht*. The linguistic "symbol" failed to assert its totalizing claims on the personality of the producers and consumers of Gaelic Revivalism; it was opposed on the former front by a strong tradition of Irish writing in English that sought to measure its national prod-ucts on the scale of European culture, and on the latter front by the Davisite tradi-tion of popular sympathies and sentiments that appealed to a mass audience of middle-class readers who had neither the time nor the interest in the consonantal twists of the Irish tongue nor in the metaphysical terms of a Celtic literature.[37]

Wherever the rhetoric of linguistic nationalism is employed, however, other or-ganicist justifications of community—race and religion—are seldom far behind. And although race and religion did offer Ireland a ground to assert affiliations that bound segments of the population into more than contingent alliances against the encroachments of outsiders, neither racialist nor religious rhetoric could overcome the disunity *within* Ireland—a division that might usefully be exemplified by the split within the leadership of the Gaelic League itself. The Protestant Hyde, though a representative of the Anglo-Irish Ascendancy, was not averse to buttressing his linguistic arguments with claims that were essentially racialist in character. "[T]he Gaelic race," he proclaimed of northeast Ulster, "was expelled and the land planted with aliens, whom our dear mother Erin, assimilative as she is, has hitherto found it difficult to absorb."[38] This is, no doubt, an odd (though not wholly uncommon) conception of racial purity—one that can assimilate those descended from the Anglo-Irish "plantation," but not, apparently, the more recently transplanted.[39]

But the appeal of an assimilative ethnicity is clear when contrasted with the alternative proposed by MacNeill, for whom Gaelic identity was a brotherhood in faith rather than blood. To MacNeill, Gaelic meant Catholic above all else. His copious and meticulous historical scholarship pinpointed the birth of Irish civilization at the precise moment of St. Patrick's arrival in Ireland in the sixth century. St. Patrick, MacNeill argued, healed the divisions between pre-Celt and Celt, as well as the conflicts between the Celts themselves, through *conversion*. And it is only through conversion that "we see the clearly formed idea of one nation, composed of diverse peoples, but made one by their affiliation to the land that bore them—the clearest and most concrete conception of nationality to be found in all antiquity."[40]

This account of national identity, of course, could not but exclude a significant segment of the nation's population—including many of the most enthusiastic supporters of the Gaelic movement. Thus, though MacNeill professed to desire "a brotherhood of adoption as well as of blood,"[41] his conflation of adoption with conversion offered even less hope that the sectarian population might come to *wish* for assimilation. Finally, *neither* racial nor religious affiliations provided much help in coping with a heterogeneous Irish reality that was best described by G. B. Shaw: "There is no Irish race. We are a parcel of mongrels: Spanish, Scottish, Welsh, English and even a Jew or two."[42]

When supposedly "natural" forms of life seem irresolvably multiple and conflictual beyond rational redescription, there is a temptation to resort to a still greater level of generality—to a trait or institution that seems to admit all without exception or exclusion: thus the cultural nationalist assertion that a common *history* offers another possible principle of affiliation. This is also the point at which cultural nationalist arguments tend to converge with the claims of contemporary anti-essentialist theorists of national identity like Said. For the claim that history is itself the possession a community holds in common, and is itself that which justifies the community *as* a community, seems equally effective whether that history is believed to be the manifestation of a divine intention or a mere sequence of contingent but still formative events.

Practically speaking, of course, there are problems with the idea of a common history. A people whose history is a centuries-long history of invasions and defeats, for example, might find it more difficult (or at least disheartening) to claim that history as the essence of an identity. Or else, as was undoubtedly true in the Irish case, such a people might use their unfortunate history to construct an account of national identity that is essentially tragic and self-annihilating, triumphant only in loss. Furthermore, history is not always clear about its own significance. The same events produce radically different relations of identification; thus, while the tensions between England and its representatives in Ireland may have been sufficient to produce in the Anglo-Irish a feeling of solidarity with the Irish lower classes based on a common history of oppression, parallel tensions in Ireland between the governors and the governed worked in precisely the opposite direction, to consolidate the predominantly Catholic lower classes against their "cosmopolitan" or traitorous representatives. But even if history does have as its outcome a relatively well-integrated community with readily definable traits—institutions, personality types, physical or linguistic peculiarities—it is not at all clear why it would be necessary or desirable to appeal to history as the *ground* of identity rather than appealing to the traits that distinguish one community from another. The appeal to history *as* difference rather than as the cause of difference is itself evidence that history has failed to produce sufficient conditions for differentiation, or else that the actual ground on which difference is constituted is perceived as an embarrassment.

Just this embarrassment may be detected in Michael North's reading of Yeats's politics. North argues that the competing descriptions of Ireland's national soul presented a particular problem for Yeats because virtually any claim that could be laid upon the "common stock of memories, customs and stories" that made up the Irishman's "history" as he understood it, tended finally not just to exclude many, but to exclude Yeats himself, and the Anglo-Irish Protestant more generally. To prevent his own persecution (and that of his friends) at the hands of a movement he had, in large measure, created, North argues, Yeats turned in the 'teens in the direction of the universalist liberalism he had early on professed to despise. Through a series of what he terms "figurative extensions," North connects Yeats's increasing recourse to aristocratic themes and images, not with a concern for ancient hereditary rights, but with the rhetoric of *individual* rights. The litany of heroic names with which Yeats represents the Ascendency figures the class as a group of heroic and solitary individuals, or a "class of the classless" (64). That class in turn comes to represent the nation from which it has been excluded; Yeats champions its rights as one might champion the rights of an individual against repressive rule. By abandoning his dream of a truly popular revival and asserting the solitary virtue of the aristocrat, North argues, Yeats was "implicitly admitting that liberalism provides the only model that can settle controversy without oppressing the losers" (35).

North's analysis depends upon the claim that Yeats's supposed turn to liberalism was a consequence of his realization that history had conspired to select one group (the Catholic lower and middle classes) over another (the Protestant governors and intellectuals he valued) as the proper inheritors of a tradition of customs and stories he himself had confected. Having been thus betrayed by the history he had assembled, Yeats had no choice but to abandon "history" altogether for the ahistorical construction of liberal citizenship. Such an argument, however, unaccountably conflates *tradition* with *history,* or "customs and stories"—which could presumably be acquired by anyone with a mind to listen and learn—with "memories," which are the possessions of a particular person or group. Viewed in this way, though, it is difficult to understand why the Catholic majority should not *also* be excluded by a stock of pre-Christian epics they never had the opportunity to forget until the Gaelic scholars made them available in translation in the nineteenth century, folktales they had never heard until the folklore boom of the 1890s, or a language they had never spoken until the early years of the twentieth century and then spoke haltingly at best. If *one* such group can claim to inherit (rather than merely to *learn*) a particular set of memories, beliefs, and practices, then there is no theoretical reason why another group could not claim them as well; all that would be required is a technology of access to those beliefs and practices—a way to claim them as their own.

Yeats's attempt to provide just such a technology returns us to the difficult question of how a "symbol," however pragmatically or strategically chosen, can "elicit" a powerful historical *memory*. When Thomas Davis selected texts for the Library of Ireland project beginning in 1845, books like McNevin's *History of the Irish Volunteers,* Duffy's *The Ballad Poetry of Ireland,* and John Mitchell's *Life of Aodh O'Neill* were chosen for their explicitly pedagogical character, as "examples of public service and warnings against national sins and transgressions."[43] Similarly, any literary symbol is part of an archive of related terms, uses, and contexts which, when recovered through historical, philological, and iconographic research, reveals a genealogy that "objectively affirms" a set of literary, religious, and political values. And while it is easy enough to understand how histories, poems, and models of behavior might be *acquired* along with the values that they purport to represent, it is less obvious how one goes about acquiring histories, poems, models, and values *as memories.* In order to "elicit" history as memory, as an account of personal origins, the archive must, by some means, be transformed into a mirror. Casting one's mind upon "other days" must do more than provide an image of a past or future self; it must give one back one's own perfected image without any feeling of estrangement or discontinuity.

This fact, which strikes North as Yeats's insurmountable problem, Yeats offers as his solution:

> All day I'd looked in the face
> What I had hoped 'twould be
> To write for my own race
> And the reality;
> The living men that I hate,
> The dead man that I loved,

The craven man in his seat,
The insolent unreproved,

. . . .

Maybe a twelvemonth since
Suddenly I began,
In scorn of this audience,
Imagining a man,
And his sun-freckled face,
And grey Connemara cloth,
Climbing up to a place
Where stone is dark under froth,
And the down-turn of his wrist
When the flies drop in the stream;
A man who does not exist,
A man who is but a dream;
And cried, 'Before I am old
I shall have written him one
Poem maybe as cold
And passionate as the dawn.'

("The Fisherman")

Seeking the face of a nation in his immediate surroundings, the prospective national poet of "The Fisherman" discovers a reality that opposes his ideal of unity as
the despised living oppose the beloved dead. Indeed, as we have observed, the
difference between hope and reality is even greater than the difference between
the living and the dead, for the figure whose face and body represent the face and
body of the desired nation *does not exist*—does not constitute part of the reality
that subsumes even death—but rather stands in a counterfactual relation to that
reality at the height of ecstatic ascent and dream. The difference between "The
Fisherman" and poems like "A Deep-sworn Vow" or "The Statues"—which present
a similar anamnetic structure in similar terms—is that "The Fisherman" imagines
and names a *material* mediation between dream and reality that is more stable,
repeatable, and communicable than revolutionary sacrifice, wine-maddened revelation, or death. That principle is *the poem itself,* not just as an archive of information about "Irishness" that might be learned—as the imaginary man is a collection
of "material" qualities that might be imitated (the sun-freckled face of pastoral life,
the rude cloth of an anti-materialistic culture, the graceful habitus of contemplative
labor)—but as a literature of construction or transformation. The true image of the
Irishman is given to the reader as if for the first time ("suddenly"), and at the same
time given to the reader as an account of who he actually is ("always").

Thus the projected vocation of the poet ("Before I am old I shall have written him one / Poem") imagines a striking conflation between writing for a man who does not yet exist and writing that man into existence.[44] The "cold and passionate poem" (which, we should note, the poet promises, but which is not identical with the poem as produced) is imagined as a technology for the production of persons after a type. The name of this type, as Yeats announces early in the poem, is "race." Yeats's increasing fascination with aristocratic heritage, then, is not, as North would have it, an oblique appeal to individual rights; it is, rather, an appeal to a version of "inheritance" that combines the cultural implications of aristocratic lineage with the biological implications of eugenic science—uniting both with the occult power of the symbol that transforms both soul and body. "The Fisherman" announces the transformation of the poem from a vehicle of cultural production and transmission into an agent of racial production and reproduction. The Irishman is Irish by blood—but by blood that can be *made*.[45]

III. The Necessity of "The Necessity of Symbolism"

Even in his earliest theoretical speculation about the nature of poetic language (in the critical edition of Blake edited in collaboration with Edwin Ellis), Yeats understood the symbol to be, not merely useful—a generic resource alongside other resources—but necessary.[46] The necessity of symbolism was not, at the early point in Yeats's career, a *national* necessity—in 1889, when Yeats began his work on Blake, he had not yet aligned his poetic future with his future in Irish politics. It was, rather, an existential necessity. For what seemed to be at stake in discussions of symbolism was not the possibility of an identity for a nation but the possibility of identity *per se.*

Informed by his reading of Blake and Swedenborg, Yeats understood the cosmos to be divided into two orders of reality: a Divine Essence or "energy" which, after the 1901 essay "Magic," Yeats would regularly refer to as "Great Mind" or "Great Memory" (*Essays and Introductions,* 52), and a heterogeneous created world of matter, individual minds, and individual memories. The task of the poet, or mystic, or philosopher, as Yeats perceived it, was to discover a relation between transcendent mind and incarnate mind that would redeem the latter as more than a fatal shadow of the former—as divinely purposive rather than merely accidental— and that would not simply collapse mind into organism, spirit into matter.[47] The difficulty in imagining such a relation stemmed from the fact that, according to Yeats's inherited antinomian cosmology, the human world was separated from its inhuman origin by an apparently unbridgeable gulf at the cataclysm of creation.

Within such a world system, relational terms such as "cause and effect," "producer and produced," and "first and after" are not continuous with one another, but separated by "discrete degrees":

> The materialistic thinker sees "continuous" where he should see "discrete degrees" and thinks of mind as not merely companioning but as actually one with the physical organism . . . for discrete degrees are related to each other by "correspondence" and by that alone, for all other methods imply identity.[48]

Having ruled out both identity and cause as principles of relation, Yeats could only imagine an analogical principle of "correspondence" or "companionship." Thus, while Yeats did provide a hierarchical and even a temporal declension by which an "unmanifest eternal" is succeeded by a "manifest eternal" and then again by the "manifest temporal"—"first a bodiless mood, and then a surging thought, and last a thing"—the only path he could imagine by which the human mind might reverse the movement of creation and come to know itself in terms of its origins was the uncompromising and ambiguous way of "completion"—as in the famous declaration, "The most perfect truth is simply the dramatic expression of the most complete man" (*Works of William Blake*, 286). As Yeats would repeatedly discover, however (first, perhaps, in "The Madness of King Goll" [1887], and then over and over throughout the poems of the 1890s), the attempt to complete the personality, or to embody the universal energy (or "mood") in a mortal being could be accomplished only at the cost of individual personality or identity:

> And now I wander in the woods
> When summer gluts the golden bees,
> Or in autumnal solitudes
> Arise the leopard-coloured trees;
> Or when along the wintry strands
> The cormorants shiver on their rocks;
> I wander on, and wave my hands,
> And sing, and shake my heavy locks.
> The grey wolf knows me; by one ear
> I lead along the woodland deer;
> The hares run by me growing bold.
> *They will not hush, the leaves a-flutter round me, the beech*
>   *leaves old.*
>
> ("The Madness of King Goll")

"The Necessity of Symbolism" produces a virtual gloss on Goll's transformation from one whose "word was law" to a "natural" whose own songs are submerged within the unceasing speech of the multitude: "He who has passed into the impersonal portion of his own mind," Yeats proclaimed, "perceives that it is not a mind but all minds" (244). "Completion," that is, is useless as a principle of personal identity because it means the end of the personal. Similarly, a cosmology that envisions the completion of history is useless as a support for national identity because it requires the transcendence, not only of the conceptual horizons of a nationalist ideology, but of the created world.[49] The *necessity* of symbolism, then, is the need for a mediated relationship between the fact of existence and the ground of existence, or for an object of perception that conveys both the knowledge and the experience of divine origins to the mind in history without destroying either mind or history in the process:

> All sounds, all colours, all forms, either because of their pre-ordained energies or because of long association, evoke indefinable and yet precise emotions, or as I prefer to think, call down among us certain disembodied powers whose footsteps over our hearts are called emotions; and then sound and colour and forms are in a musical relation, a beautiful relation to one another, they become, as it were, one sound, one colour, one form, and evoke an emotion that is made out of their distinct evocations and yet is one emotion. The same relation exists between all portions of every work of art, whether it be an epic or a song, and the more perfect it is, and the more various and numerous the elements that have flowed into its perfection, the more powerful will be the emotion, the power, the god it calls among us. (*Essays and Introductions*, 156–57)

The work of art, as Yeats argues here in the "The Symbolism of Poetry," through its deployment of sound, color, or form, evokes emotions that are in fact synonymous with the "powers" of divinity as expressed in the individual. But by locating "power" or "god," not within the mind, but in the meeting between the artistic symbol and the receptive mind, Yeats imagines a state that he calls "reverie" or "contemplation" in which the created being can know the creative power as its own origin — in which the mind in history can feel the presence of Great Mind. The knowledge of self as other than individual is the *ne plus ultra* of poetic experience: "the moment of contemplation, the moment when we are both asleep and awake . . . in which the mind liberated from the pressure of the will is unfolded in symbols" (159).

Yeats, it should be noted, offers two explanations for the symbol's power to evoke knowledge as emotion. And while his writings on mysticism do provide examples of objects that evoke visions of divinity apparently by virtue of "pre-ordained energies," Yeats's primary poetic interest is in symbols that are symbols by virtue of "long association" — symbols whose powers over the mind are more plausibly a product of their continued material existence across historical and cultural divides than they are a *cause* of that continuity. If a symbol is most frequently knowable as a symbol by being discovered or received (and Yeats received his symbols from a range of traditions more numerous and diverse than any Anglophone poetic predecessor), a symbol must also, at some point, originate.

One speculative account of the creation of a symbol may be found in the "Dust Hath Closed Helen's Eye" chapter of *The Celtic Twilight,* which documents Yeats's first visit to Thoor Ballylee in search of the story of the blind poet Raftery and his love for Mary Hynes (*Mythologies,* 22–30). Yeats's redaction of the folktale collates at least fifteen separate versions, which range from the "first-hand" testimony of an old woman who claims to have known the two (23), to that of "a man by the shore of Kinvara, who is too young to remember Mary Hynes," but knows what "everyone" has said of her (27). The story, as Yeats is careful to point out, is altered as it passes from person to person—"tradition," he notes, "gives the one thing many names" (25). But the outcome of this alteration and multiplication is characterized not as adulteration—a falling away from the singular reality of history—but rather as the perfection of the myth, an alchemical transformation of "mere material" into superior substance by successive retellings. "It may be," Yeats speculates, "that in a few years Fable, who changes mortalities to immortalities in her cauldron, will have changed Mary Hynes and Raftery to perfect symbols of the sorrow of beauty and of the magnificence and penury of dreams" (30).

This emphasis on the constitutive power of tradition marks the crucial difference between the Yeatsian symbol and the Jungian archetype it otherwise resembles. For if the archetype manifest in minds throughout history may be taken as revealed or manifest evidence of a common human heritage, the symbol creates by consolidation the common heritage *as heritage.* Born of the subliming passage of generations, the perfected symbol transmits the knowledge of an origin in eternity; at the same time, it retroactively "rewrites" the history of its own transmission as a line of historical succession or inheritance. This twofold power has consequences for both personal and national identity, as dramatized in the climactic episode of *The Celtic Twilight*:

> Last night I went to a wide place on the Kiltartan road to listen to some Irish songs . . . Somebody sang *Eiblín a Rúin*, that glad song of meeting which has always moved me more than other songs, because the lover who made it sang it to his sweetheart under the shadow of a mountain I looked at every day through my childhood. The voices melted into the twilight, and were mixed into the trees, and when I thought of the words they too melted away, and were mixed with the generations of men. Now it was a phrase, now it was an attitude of mind, an emotional form, that had carried my memory to older verses, or even to forgotten mythologies. I was carried so far that it was as though I came to one of the four rivers, and followed it under the wall of Paradise to the roots of the Trees of Knowledge and of Life. There is no song or story handed down among the cottages that has not words and thoughts to carry one as far, for though one can know but a little of their ascent, one knows that they ascend like medieval genealogies through unbroken dignities to the beginning of the world. (*Mythologies,* 138–39)

In this brief account of the crepuscular moment "when we are both asleep and awake," Yeats is "moved" by song (symbols "in a musical relation") in a sense that is only secondarily affective—for the primary movement he describes is a movement away from the materiality of "a phrase" to an "attitude of mind" to "an emotional form" that carries the listener all the way to Paradise (and here we might note the reversal in thought of Yeats's narrative of origins: "first a bodiless mood, then a surging thought, and last a thing"). The poet is also moved away from the world as "a congeries of beings" to a unified state of Being: many voices, trees, and words become the four rivers (Pishon, Gihon, Tigris, and Euphrates), which become the two trees in Eden, which in turn melt away to reveal the singularity at "the beginning of the world."

The path of the song's transmission—from mythic first maker to anonymous folk on the Kiltartan road to Yeats himself—resembles neither a "medieval genealogy" nor an "unbroken dignity."[50] It does, however, over the course of the passage, begin to resemble a *community*—one mind shared between voyager and cottager, as the particularized "I" is transformed into the generic "one." The sharable experience of song is like the shared experience of the Irish landscape: Yeats shares the emotion of the song's ancient maker much as he shares his unchanged view of Ben Bulben—both are what might be termed "commonplaces" of national life. But unlike Ben Bulben, which is merely material continuously perceived, the "glad song of meeting" (because of its curiously idealized materiality) is subject to a particularly intense account of reception: the poem forges the communal relation between Ireland and Eden, individual listener and Great Mind.

IV. Esoteric Racism

It has often been observed that Yeats's obsession with old age and bodily decrepitude began unseasonably early, his fears of failure emerging well before he had reached the peak of his powers. The poet's anxieties about the failure and dissolution of Irish culture were even more premature—scarcely had he begun the laborious project of bringing such a thing into existence when he started to lament its disappearance. As was so often the case with his hopes, Yeats's fears were emblematized by the fate of the Gregory family and its aristocratic seat at Coole Park:

I thought of this house slowly perpetuating itself and the life within it, in ever increasing intensity of its labour, and then of its probably sinking away through courteous incompetence or rather sheer weakness of will . . . and I said to myself, "Why is life a perpetual preparation for something that never happens? Even as Odysseus only seems a preparation to think of ruin or remembrance.

Is it not always the tragedy of the great and the strong, that they see before the end the small and the weak, in friendship or in enmity, pushing them from their place, and marring what they have built, and doing one or the other in mere lightness of mind . . . (*Explorations,* 121)

It is characteristic of Yeats's thought that the very passage of generations that produces the "oldest of the aristocracies of thought" in the symbolic tradition seems to work against the continuation of the aristocracy of the flesh. It is precisely this anxiety—not over the confection of culture, but over its continuation and maintenance against the human drive toward ruin or mere remembrance, that culminated in what Elizabeth Cullingford has mildly termed "the most questionable" of Yeats's enthusiasms, his advocacy of eugenics as a means to ensure the survival of a culture.[51]

Yeats gleaned what knowledge he had of scientific eugenics primarily from his reading of R. B. Cattel's 1937 *The Fight for Our National Intelligence.*[52] Countering progressive or "reform" eugenicists like Julian Huxley, who argued that the observed physical and intellectual disparities between the social classes were more a result of structural and environmental pressures than genetic ones, and that the goal of the movement therefore ought to be "the equalizing of environment in an upward direction," Cattel's conservative or "mainline" eugenics took an almost exclusively hereditarian and alarmist approach to the problem of social order.[53] Armed with a battery of faulty statistics, Cattel repopularized the myth of the "differential birth rate" which attributed social ills to the fact that "superior stocks" were not reproducing themselves as rapidly as "degenerate stocks," or else were interbreeding with them and diluting their vital forces—an argument that confirmed Yeats's deepest fears about Irish culture. The documentation of falling intelligence scores lent scientific support to the poet's already firmly entrenched belief that Ireland was on the brink of a "breeding" disaster. Yeats thus drew heavily on Cattel's authority in his splenetic 1939 pamphlet *On the Boiler*:

Since about 1900 the better stocks have not been replacing their numbers, while the stupider and less healthy have been more than replacing theirs. Unless there is a change in the public mind, every rank above the lowest must degenerate, and, as inferior men push up into its gaps, degenerate more and more quickly.[54]

There has been much debate about when Yeats's involvement with eugenic thought "proper" began. But as the chronicle of Yeats's early thought makes clear, the poet's romance with eugenics, like his flirtation with fascism, arose less out of an empirical commitment to scientific population management or out of a political commitment to national and racial purity, than out of a lifelong search for new vocabularies to address a persistent philosophical problem, and to grant them the confirmation of the real. The eugenicist's anxiety about *biological* reproduction is a repetition and confirmation of the Neoplatonist's judgment against the incarnate world—for substance is always susceptible to decline as it moves further from its origins in divinity. This connection may be clearest in the explicitly eugenicist play *Purgatory* (published along with *On the Boiler* in 1939), in which father kills son in order to halt the degeneration that began with his own begetting.

But Yeats's concern with versions of this quasi-eugenic thought began as early as 1904. In the play *On Baile's Strand,* for example, when Conchobar taunts the warrior Cuchulain with the fact that he has no heir, Cuchulain responds by pronouncing procreation as a doomed enterprise:

Cuchulain:
> For you thought
> That I should be as biddable as others
> Had I their reason for it; but that's not true,
> For I would need a weightier argument
> Than one that marred me in the copying,
> As I have that clean hawk out of the air
> That, as men say, begot this body of mine
> Upon a mortal woman.[55]

In Cuchulain's weighty argument, even the "purest" imaginable form of conception, the mating of hawk with mortal woman, produces a "marred" copy of the "clean" origin. In the logic of the play, the mating of even the most exemplary mortals can only mar the line further, producing a still more denatured being. Thus, when Cuchulain's son, whose existence is unknown to his father, attempts to demonstrate his nobility by displaying his warrior's arm as proof of his heritage, Cuchulain can only find that arm deficient compared to his own: "That arm had a good father and a good mother," he declares with unconscious irony, "But it is not like this." The very "errors" in transmission that had been so useful in the purification of the symbol have the opposite effect on the purity of a heritage—for not only is the son's arm less strong than the father's, it is, crucially, *unlike* it: an unlikeness that signifies the end of an aristocratic line even before Conchobar succeeds in tricking Cuchulain into killing his only son.

In 1919 Yeats had offered his technical solution to the failure of civilization to renew itself—the eugenic powers of the poem itself:

> [T]he sexual choice of man and woman should be the greater part of all poetry. A single wrong choice may destroy a family, dissipating its tradition or its biological force, and the great sculptors, painters, and poets are there that instinct may find its lamp. When a young man imagines the woman of his hope, shaped

for all the uses of life, mother and mistress and yet fitted to carry a bow in the wilderness, how little of it all is mere instinct, how much has come from the chisel and brush. Educationalists and statesmen, servants of the logical process, do their worst, but they are not the matchmakers who bring together the fathers and mothers of the generations, nor shall the type they plan survive. (*Explorations,* 274–75)

One (unexceptionable) way to construe this passage (and others like it) is as a claim that poetry aids in the sexual choice of man and woman by providing them with culturally sanctioned models for desire.[56] Thus, Paul Scott Stansfield argues that this claim must be understood to qualify Yeats's commitment to a "mainline" eugenic position, since it posits an environmental influence upon reproduction that is, strictly speaking, euthenic rather than eugenic.[57] To understand the function of the cultural artifact even in this limited way is still to grant literary culture a powerful pedagogical function—one that is consistent with Davis's intentions in assembling the Library of Ireland; consistent also with many contemporary critiques of literary culture's complicity with the disciplinary project of cultural institutions.

But the account of the sort offered in Yeats's play *The King's Threshold* (1904) is finally more extreme and more bizarre—and it is more fully Yeats's own. In this play, Seanchean, Ireland's chief poet, must explain why he is prepared to starve himself in protest of his king's violation of "the ancient right of poets" to sit on the royal council. By way of justification, Seanchean has his oldest pupil repeat his oldest lesson:

Oldest Pupil:

      I said the poets hung
      Images of the life that was in Eden
      About the Child-bed of the world, that it
      Looking upon those images, might bear
      Triumphant children. But why must I stand here
      Repeating an old lesson, while you starve?

Seanchean:

      Tell on, for I begin to know the voice.
      What evil thing will come upon the world
      If the Arts perish?

Oldest Pupil:

      If the Arts should perish,
      The world that lacked them would be like a woman
      That, looking upon the cloven lips of a hare
      Brings forth a hare-lipped child. (*Variorum Plays,* 264)

Figure 1.1. Irish coinage, restruck from 1928 proofsets in 1961. Photo @ John Stafford-Langan.

By this point, the logic of this poetic argument will seem familiar. The proper direction of the future is assured, not by imitation, but by encountering an ideal image of prior life, "the life that was in Eden." Such forms are affronted by merely accidental relationships (like a chance encounter with a rabbit). Resuscitating ancient folk tradition on behalf of poetic privilege, Yeats here claims that poetic symbols are *not* pedagogical—there is no sense in which the birthing mother *learns* a tradition of images from Eden—but rather transformative. Images of originary life conflate (as Yeats does in *If I Were Four and Twenty*) "tradition" with "biological force."

This version of the argument emphasizes two important elements—first, the agency of the poet, who has access to *Anima Mundi* and who brings us to significant knowledge of origins by virtue of his images, and second, the recasting of this ancient topos so that knowledge of self results not in despair or blood sacrifice, but in the production of an actual future: "triumphant children." Two episodes from Yeats's involvement with practical politics demonstrate the odd (and occasionally comical) literalism of his attempt to imagine the material consequences of symbols derived from what are, essentially, idealist commitments. The first is Yeats's role as the chairman of the committee to commission a new Irish coinage (see figure 1.1). In his speech to the senate, "What We Did or Tried To Do," Yeats gives a brief account of the committee's search for artists, and the competition held between the various designs. But Yeats's most interesting remarks concern the alterations in the final designs that had to be made on the recommendation of the Irish Ministry of Agriculture:

> As certain of the beasts represent our most important industry, they were submitted to the minister of Agriculture and his experts, and we awaited the results with alarm. . . . The coins have suffered less than we feared. The horse, as first drawn, was more alive than the later version, for when the hind legs were brought more under the body and the head lowered, in obedience to technical opinion, it lost muscular tension; we passed from open country to the show-ground. . . . The first bull had to go, though one of the finest of all the designs, because it might have upset, considered as an ideal, the eugenics of the farmyard, but the new bull is fine, in a different way. I sigh, however, over the pig, though I admit that the state of the market for pig's cheeks made the old design impossible. . . . With the round cheeks of the pig went the lifted head, the look of insolence and wisdom, and the comfortable round bodies of the little pigs. We have instead querulous and harassed animals, better merchandise but less living.[58]

The pragmatist Yeats, in what is surely one of the most bizarre forms of pragmatism on record, recognizes the unfortunate necessity of compromising the artistic integrity of the designs so that the *proper images* would be in general circulation. The "eugenics of the farmyard" are not quite those of Ireland. They are driven by the sort of ideals espoused by the Ministry of Agriculture rather than those of "insolence and wisdom" (for which the pig, apparently, has no need). But they are eugenics nevertheless.

The second example, somewhat less amusing (though no less odd), stemmed from Yeats's involvement in what has come to be known as the Hugh Lane controversy.[59] The broad outlines of this controversy are well known: Hugh Lane, nephew of Lady Gregory and talented collector of art, bequeathed thirty-nine distinguished, mostly French, paintings to the Dublin Corporation with the intention of establishing a respectable modern collection in Dublin. After heated debate, the Dublin Corporation refused to allocate the funds for a gallery to house the work. In response to the public snub, as well as to the aggressive indifference of the middle classes and the open hostility of journalists, Lane bequeathed the paintings instead to the National Gallery in London. This in itself might have been enough to inspire controversy on sheer grounds of cultural prejudice. But the real difficulty began after Lane's death on the *Lusitania*. For it was only then that Lady Gregory discovered among Lane's papers the so-called "codicil of forgiveness"—an unwitnessed codicil to Lane's will that expressed his intentions to return the paintings to Ireland after his death. The National Gallery, of course, refused to honor the codicil (having the letter of the law on its side), setting off a cultural battle that remains to date incompletely resolved.

These events made a considerable impression on Yeats and spurred him into furious activity. By his own account, it was one of the three "controversies" (along with the Parnell controversy and the *Playboy* riots) that shattered his faith in the Irish public and turned him away from popular politics: "These controversies, political, literary, and artistic, have showed that neither religion nor politics can of itself create minds with enough receptivity to become wise, or just and generous enough to make a nation," Yeats proclaimed in the notes to the 1914 edition of *Responsibilities* (*Poems,* 818). In addition to the poems in that volume that dealt explicitly with the controversy ("To a Wealthy Man" and "To a Shade"), Yeats published at least ten articles, interviews, and letters to the press between 1915 and 1926, as well as arguing in the senate (in 1926) a motion requesting the government to pass a resolution to demand the return of the paintings. If neither religion nor politics alone could consolidate minds into a nation, Yeats was determined to insist that images could.

In his prose as well as his poetry, Yeats makes it quite clear that the primary significance of the lost paintings is not the most obvious one: that they would, if recovered, enable Ireland to participate in the cosmopolitan culture of modernism. This pragmatic rationale for the return of the paintings is on display in the copy of Bodkin's *Hugh Lane and His Pictures* presented to the Harvard College Library by Eamon de Valera, President of the Executive Council and Yeats's ideological enemy. The bookplate—a letter on Department of the President stationery pasted on the flyleaf and signed in de Valera's hand—reads: "This Book, which deals with the career of an Irishman who strove nobly to serve the cause of culture in his country, has been prepared as a gift from the Government of Saorstát Eireann to those who love justice and to those who love the arts. As President of the Executive Council, I have the honour of offering this copy to the Library of Harvard University." Where de Valera emphasized the relation between his country's culture and the general ideal of "culture" and "the arts" or the instrumental and institutional relation between the Irish government and the international community of culture and arts lovers, Yeats emphasized the role that the arts play in forming a distinctive culture, and fostering a love for it, insisting that the paintings would serve to "educate" the Irish in their primordial identity: "Dublin is the capital of a nation," he proclaimed, "and an ancient race has nowhere else to look for an education" (*Senate Speeches*, 120).

One must actually see the images in question in order to register the full oddity of Yeats representing these paintings by Corot, Monet, Manet, Courbet, Degas, and others as fit materials for the education of an ancient Irish race. The paintings were, first of all, in a style that Yeats deplored, having long associated this sort of work with his father's commitment to the impressionists. He considered this style of modern painting "mere portraiture" when compared to the significant Pre-Raphaelite symbolism he favored and whose mood he had emulated in his early poems. But even the most cursory glance at the paintings themselves makes Yeats's special pleading seem even more bizarre.

Clearly, what is important about a painting like Renoir's *Les Parapluies* (figure 1.2) or any of the other paintings of windmills in Holland, French army officers, or still lives with spectacles and a book is not the way they evoke Yeats's "images of the life that was in Eden." Indeed, In the April 1917 issue of *Burlington Magazine*, Roger Fry had fixed upon Renoir's painting as the one most likely to reinvigorate the modernity of *British* art: "What might not happen to the future art of England if all young painters could study again and again Renoir's masterpiece 'Les Parapluies.' Here are all the hard-won victories over struggles from which British art has consistently turned aside. After having seen 'Les Parapluies' I find it hard to keep an open mind about Dublin's claims to its possession."[60] But if the paintings do not model a distinctively Irish style as an alternative to the modish and the modern, still less do they present some crucially Irish image-ideal with which a viewer might identify. The painting Lane identified as *The Slave* (figure 1.3) is particularly revelatory or perverse in this regard. While the dignity of the figure is unquestionably intact, no association between Irish citizen and an African slave was likely to lift a contemporary viewer's mind, through Yeats's "unbroken dignities," to the beginning of the world.

What Yeats values in these images—not just over their form and content but *against* form and content—is the fact that they are valid images. As the work of genuine artists—a claim Yeats was willing to take on faith on the judgment of Lane (who was, after all, a Gregory, and thus uniquely positioned to speak on behalf of hereditary mysteries) such works have the appropriate origins in collective mind and might therefore serve as well as any other images the high function of cultural renewal. Yeats makes the argument most forcefully in his poem "To a Shade," in which he projects the outcome for the Irish people if given the opportunity to look in these particular faces:

> A man
> Of your own passionate serving kind who had brought
> In his full hands, what, had they only known,
> Had given their children's children loftier thought,
> Sweeter emotion, working in their veins
> Like gentle blood, has been driven from the place.

If there is a metaphor in this passage, it is not the comparison of thought or emotion to blood—for emotion is *literally* said to work in the veins of the viewers of the pictures, and to pass down, from generation to generation. Yeats's appeal to the direct influence of symbolism may indeed represent a qualification of Cattel's strictly hereditarian stance, but it nonetheless remains close to the literal and biological. The asserted figure or "likeness" here is, rather, the likeness to *gentle* blood. The person

Figure 1.2. Pierre-Auguste Renoir, *The Umbrellas (Les Parapluies)*, c. 1881–86, The National Gallery, London. Image © The National Gallery, London.

Figure 1.3. *A Black Woman*, Sir Hugh Lane Bequest, 1917; on loan to the Hugh Lane Municipal Gallery of Modern Art, Dublin, since 1979. Image © The National Gallery, London.

reconceived upon the model of art is not quite a literal aristocrat; that distinction remains an inheritance that must be inherited. But if the artistic creation of lineage is less dignified than the "unbroken dignities" of Yeats's feudal imagination, it is more enduring. Continuous exposure to the perfection of symbols solves, for Yeats, the problem of the imperfect transmission of blood that keeps even the aristocratic generations of Coole Park falling away from their origins. The ideal resolution of Yeats's thought is the increasing beauty of both persons and poems: "All dreams of the soul / End in a beautiful man or woman's body" ("The Phases of the Moon").

V. Comfort

We may recall at this point that Edward Said locates the value of Yeats's poetry in its ability to contribute a significant narrative upon which an Irish people could found an identity. And while he initially calls that narrative a *history*, he almost immediately revises his terms, attributing Yeats's successes to his "unerring choice of genealogical fables and figures" (*Culture and Imperialism*, 237). For Said, then, positing the *fictionality* of national identities and genealogies (their status as "fables and figures") is the first step on the path to what he understands as "liberation": a state in which persons and populations are not bound by the "limited or coercive" essentialism of the belief "that all persons have only one single identity" (230). On this account, it is precisely insofar as Yeats failed to recognize that nations and identities are not real that he remains a "nativist" poet, suitable to, and perhaps necessary for, a period of "decolonization" (238), but unable to enter the promised land as a poet of ironic "liberation." What makes poetry particularly valuable to nationalism, it would appear, is our absolute certainty that poets, whatever version of a collective vision they might assert, are always necessarily lying. Though we may, for strategic purposes, bind ourselves to their visions and embrace their images, we can take comfort in the fact that they bind us to nothing of real consequence.

But we must note also that Said defines this state of "liberation" as the possession of *many* identities, rather than of *no* identity. The hedging of negation into multiplication, or of a rigorous anti-essentialism into a conception of self in constant flight from its many possible determinations, suggests another, entirely contradictory account of his—and our—interest in poetry. Which is to say that the only reason that Said retains "poetry" at all as a central term in his argument about the reconstruction of collective life is precisely *not* because a poem is an objectified fiction to which we can respond or not, as we are so inclined, but rather because it is the genre traditionally associated with personhood—with *meaningful* life. What the strangeness of Yeats's ontological poetics suggests is that while we may conceive of merely contingent meaning or purely immanent life, we cannot inhabit it; there is no anti-essentialist account of personhood that is both anti-essentialist and an account of personhood. And insofar as we remain committed in theory to refusing accounts of the self as more than merely contingent and strategic, we are committed to an even stranger version of a eugenic poetics than Yeats ever was. For if Yeats was committed to a form of future society he could imagine achieving only by occult means, Said is committed to a future of "liberation" in which he is theory-bound not to believe at all.[61]

Still, it would be a mistake to imagine Yeats's fantastic eugenic poetics as his final word. Yeats's career is one of a persistent vacillation between sober and humane rational concerns for an achievable social form and an irrational vision of violent purification. The same poet who, in a speech on education to the Irish Literary Society, suggested that the educational goals of a new nation ought to include provisions "to cheapen the price of schoolbooks for the poor, or clothe the poorer children, or make the school buildings pleasanter to a child's eyes, or in some other way prepare for an Ireland that will be healthy, vigorous, orderly, and above all, happy" (*Senate Speeches,* 174) was capable of declaring that an Ireland "half-dead at the top" could no longer benefit from "education" of any kind. In *On the Boiler,* Yeats shifts rapidly from a rather commonplace endorsement of class-based oppression to a fantasy of civil war that is spectacular in its brutality:

> If some financial reorganization such as Major Douglas plans, that better organization of agriculture and industry which many economists expect, enable everybody without effort to procure all the necessities of life and so remove the last check upon the multiplication of the uneducable masses, it will become the duty of the educated classes to seize and control one or more of those necessities. The drilled and docile classes may submit, but a prolonged civil war seems more likely, with the victory of the skillful, riding their machines as did the feudal knights their armoured horses. During the Great War Germany had four hundred submarine commanders, and sixty per cent of the damage done was the work of twenty-four men. The danger is that there will be no war, that the skilled will attempt nothing. . . . 'Dear predatory birds, prepare for war, prepare your children and all that you can reach . . . test art, morality, custom, thought, by Thermopylae, make rich and poor act so to one another that they can stand together there. Love war because of its horror, that belief may be changed, civilization renewed.' (19–20)

While Cattel's strict biologism contributed to Yeats's belief in racial purification as the precondition for cultural reproduction, his Platonism contributed the belief that such purification required superhuman agency. In "The Statues" or the much earlier "A Deep-sworn Vow," Yeats had only hinted at the possibility of destructive violence such agency might entail—the ascent toward death or a "proper dark" as a source of renewal. And in "The Fisherman" it appeared that poetry could reconcile the knowledge of origins with the power to act. In "Among School Children" (1927) Yeats acknowledges that the "worship" of images, or what he called "Presences" (in his poem of that name), might impose a pedagogy of ideal beauty upon actual persons only in a way that is ultimately fatal to their actual existence. The famous question that ends that poem—"how can we know the dancer from the dance?"—resolves the problem only by suspending it as a rhetorical question.

But when the *principle* of life is imagined being made actual, the result is a vision of total annihilation that is not required by Yeats's "science" but rather demanded by his commitment to *truth*. It is the recognition of the constitutive difference between a world of multiplicity and distinction and a vision of the potential world of singularity.

> A man that had six mortal wounds, a man
> Violent and famous, strode among the dead;
> Eyes stared out of the branches and were gone.
>
> Then certain Shrouds that muttered head to head
> Came and were gone. He leant upon a tree
> As though to meditate on wounds and blood.
>
> A shroud that seemed to have authority
> Among those bird-like things came, and let fall
> A bundle of linen. Shrouds by two and three
>
> Came creeping up because the man was still.
> And thereupon that linen-carrier said:
> 'Your life can grow much sweeter if you will
>
> 'Obey our ancient rule and make a shroud;
> Mainly because of what we only know
> The rattle of those arms makes us afraid.
>
> 'We thread the needles' eyes, and what we do
> All must together do.' That done, the man
> Took up the nearest and began to sew.
>
> 'Now must we sing and sing the best we can,
> But first you must be told our character:
> Convicted cowards all, by kindred slain
>
> 'Or driven from home and left to die in fear.'
> They sang, but had nor human tunes nor words,
> Though all was done in common as before;
>
> They had changed their throats and had the throats of birds.

"Cuchulain Comforted," dated a mere fifteen days before Yeats's death, imagines a form of communal life that absolutely subverts the possibility of the violent hero- ism that the poet had sponsored in his vision of terror. The subsumption of the mythical hero—whom Pearse was supposed to have summoned as his revolu- tionary ally—by the strangely depersonalized and inhuman "shrouds" would seem to fly in the face of the argument that I have been making all along: that "poetry," as I have described it, names the poet's interest in a common capacity or knowl- edge as a fundamentally humanizing force. In this poem the secret knowledge ("what we only know") *covers* a human life "of wounds and blood" in an impersonal and undifferentiated shroud that Yeats calls "cowardice," and which he describes as a state in which individual fame and experiential history ("kindred") are renounced (or have been renounced), and in which ancient and inhuman rules (rather than human justice) apply.

But though the vision of communal life this poem presents may seem as terrible as any vision of apocalypse, it might look somewhat different if we were to compare it to the following passage from the preparatory notes to Walter Benjamin's "Theses on the Philosophy of History":

> The Messianic World is the world of total and integral actuality. In it alone is there universal history. What goes by the name of universal history today can only be a kind of Esperanto. Nothing can correspond to it as long as the confusion originating in the Tower of Babel is not smoothed out. It presupposes the language into which every text of a living or dead language must be wholly translated. Or, rather, it itself is this language. Not though, as written, but as festively celebrated. This celebration is purified of every ceremony, it knows no celebratory songs. Its language is the idea of prose itself, which is understood by all humans just as the language of birds is understood by those born on Sunday.[62]

Both Yeats's final "actual" poetic vision of comfort and Benjamin's withheld vision of "the Messianic World" propose a "smoothing" out of histories and languages into a single story and a single "prose" (as Benjamin calls it) with no tune or words, that is universally understood—an "undersong" that, though identical to no human tongue, contains the possibility of every actual human language and every possible event, and that both, remarkably, liken to birdsong. This undersong—*not* identical to the poem achieved, but in Yeats's case, imaged within the actual poem as a picture of its knowledge, constitutive principle, or power—represents nothing less than Yeats's final judgment that potentiality can remain humanizing only by being withheld from actuality.

In "Cuchulain Comforted," as Auden reminds us, nothing is made to happen. And in that particular form of nothing—in this form of speaking silence—Yeats rewrites the poetic Messianism of the left and the right, not as a social festival that might be celebrated, but as a radical vision that can be maintained. Withdrawing from the scene of the actual to the ground of the possible, Yeats himself founds the singular poetic history I have been describing. "Poetry," as Yeats leaves it in this poem, is an image, a wish to reserve the ontological commitments implied by Benjamin's "Messianic World" as a regulative vision, while withholding from the world its consequences in practice.

CHAPTER **TWO**

Oppen's Silence, Crusoe's Silence, and the Silence of Other Minds

Truthfulness is far from a social virtue—but
it is poetic
IT IS THE EXTREME LIMIT OF
THE POETIC IMAGINATION

I. Oppen's Silence

THE LAST CHAPTER ended with a poem, perfect in its paradoxical way. The occasion of "Cuchulain Comforted" was the occasion both of the hero's departure from the land of the living and of the poet's own imminent death. Considered as his final act, the hero's death secures his identity; an appropriately memorable end both demands and assures immortalization. Considered as a final word, the poet's poem rounds out the shape of his legacy and assures us that the distinctive voice will endure. There is tension, however, between the powerful impulse to regard either a poem or a life as having a distinctive shape, and the very particular idea of perfection that "Cuchulain Comforted" offers to thought. For all of its singular mastery and powerful voicing, the poem ends in a self-abnegating paradox, presenting an ideal of social being achievable only through the shrouding of heroic individuality and the silencing of the human voice.

This chapter begins with a silence, perfect in its paradoxical way. Like a poem, a silence has both occasion and duration. The duration of this silence is a well-known quantity: after the 1934 publication of his slim volume *Discrete Series*, the poet George Oppen stopped writing poems, decisively abandoned the class of his origin ("upper class of '29," as he liked to say) to join the Communist Party, and, starting in 1950, lived as a "known subversive" in Mexico to escape FBI harassment for his work as a labor organizer in the Workers Alliance. He would not write another poem for almost twenty-five years.[1]

The occasion of Oppen's silence is less well understood. Considered as an episode in the history of American literary communism, Oppen's story appears at first unexceptional. In 1930, Michael Gold in the *New Masses* had condemned the "verbal acrobatics" of modernism as "only another form of bourgeois idleness."[2] The aesthetics of the Objectivist poets with whom Oppen is associated would come under special censure for expressing what Herman Specter would call

> The limited worldview of a "detached bystander": that is, of a person whose flashes of perception for the immediate esthetics of the contemporary scene are not co-ordinated in any way with a dialectical comprehension of the life-process. . . . The fatal defect of the Objectivist theory is that it identifies life with capitalism, and so assumes that the world is merely a wasteland. The logical consequence is a fruitless negativism. . . . Impartiality is a myth which defeatists take with them into oblivion.[3]

Two years after Gold's broadside, Sherwood Anderson (another would-be escapee from the world of "buying and selling" into the class of artists)[4] would suggest that the problem of art was not limited to a particular aesthetic theory or style—one that was falsely "impartial" rather than passionately partisan, or nihilistically "objective" about the world as found rather than actively in league with "objective" laws of history by which world revolution must eventually be made. Rather, it was a more fundamental problem with the nature of artistic labor. On Anderson's view, the privilege of the artist is itself the result of invidious social and economic distinctions, and all songs are songs of exploitation and inequality. A truly committed artist could best demonstrate his alliance with the working classes by joining them and silencing himself entirely: "If it be necessary that in order to bring about the end of a money civilization and set up something new, healthy and strong, we of the so-called artist class have to be submerged, let us be submerged. Down with us."[5] The annals of the '30s are filled with the mute inglorious Miltons of the left, submerged for better or worse—deliberately or against their will—in the interest of a radical politics.[6]

What makes this particular story more remarkable—what marks it as an episode in the history of what I have preferred to call a radical *poetics*—is that Oppen, once submerged, resurfaced. His next book, *The Materials*, published in 1962, commences with an explicit rejection of Yeatsian aesthetic fantasy and political brutality. The book's second epigraph recalls Yeats's lines from "Meditations in a Time of Civil War":

> We had fed the heart on fantasies,
> The heart's grown brutal from the fare;
> More substance in our enmities
> Than in our love; O honey-bees,
> Come build in the empty house of the stare.

Yet Oppen revises the lines, changing them from an admission—an acknowledgment that Yeats's own excesses of idealization might lead to violence—into an accusation against an unspecified "they": "They fed their hearts on fantasies / and their hearts have become savage."[7] For Oppen, self-incrimination is not exculpating; and no aestheticized form of life (the honeybee's artful construction in the starling's abandoned home) could produce a sweetening compensation for violence. The first epigraph of *The Materials,* drawn from Maritain, does, however, promise some new awakening, some new access of consciousness in which "we" might be included: "We awake in the same moment to ourselves and to things." Oppen's reawakening, his spare but uninterrupted second act in poetry would eventually earn him the Pulitzer Prize (for the 1968 volume *Of Being Numerous*).

The long silence at the center of Oppen's career is a mystery sustained by the many attempts to resolve it, which range from Hugh Kenner's semi-serious denial of the need for explanation (Kenner to Oppen: "it took you 25 years to write the next poem")[8], to Rachel Blau DuPlessis's surfeit of explanation: "a critique of modernism which ran counter to contemporary critical, poetic, and academic thinking, a choice of activism in a deeply felt political crisis, a process of self-testing, a war injury, and recovery; later these were joined by a set of taboos and inhibitions around parenthood, and a fear of his own power" (*Selected Letters*, xiv).

The poet's own slim self-accounting for the occasion of his silence is more interesting than a long pause, more specific than a catalogue of everything that happened to Oppen in the intervening years:

> 25 years to write the next poem means. . . . we didn't know enough from the poetry that was being written; from the poetry we had written. And when the crisis occurred we knew we didn't know what the world was and we knew we had to find out so it was a poetic exploration at the same time that it was an act of conscience.[9]

This not-quite-explanation suggests that it might be necessary and possible to come to know something important about "what the world was" by means of poetry in a time of crisis in which Oppen was—perhaps uniquely among his generation of poets—a participant as well as a witness. Oppen fought at the devastating Battle of the Bulge; the infantry division in which he served has been recognized as a "liberator" unit for its participation in the liberation of the Dachau subcamp at Landsberg.[10] The crisis as it "occurred" to Oppen was not just the ideological conflict in America that made him choose temporary exile but the "total war" and the effort at total extermination that preceded and precipitated it.[11]

In his poem "Time of the Missile" (from *The Materials*) Oppen describes his historical moment as one in which the world—reconfigured by the destructive work of "the mind and eye"—has acquired the autonomous capacity to annihilate the life it had formerly sustained. Such a world "can destroy us, / Re-arrange itself, assert / Its own stone chain reaction."[12] In the world unmade by makers, even the most intimate forms of relationship, which have traditionally served as subjects for poetry and redoubts against history, no longer provide comfort or hope for the future:

> My love, my love,
> We are endangered
> Totally at last.

Knowing conditions of total endangerment as Oppen knew them—intimately and firsthand—what could it mean to know "enough"? When the atomic structure of brute material—awakened to violent action by what Auden had called "[t]he high priests of telescopes and cyclotrons"—can assert itself against its artisans and arrangers, what can poetry say about "what the world was" that would be adequate to justify the existence of yet more art?

If we take seriously Oppen's premise that his silence was undertaken in the interest of a poetic solution to the problem of threatened sociability, we might expect to find that his return to poetry carries about it at least the charge of a problem solved. But what most vexes the attempt to grant some substance to that sense—to credit Oppen's retrospectively implied promise that the next poem would be the next *kind* of poetry, capable of bearing new knowledge appropriate to a world in crisis—is not just that the terms of the promise are so vague; it is that one doesn't know just where to look to see if they are fulfilled. Oppen's most attentive and thorough critics—Peter Nicholls and Michael Heller chief among them—have described Oppen's late style as a deliberate rejection or correction of the poetics of *Discrete Series*, describing the emergence of "a radically different poetry, chastened by having followed a failed path, recognizing it as having failed."[13] But despite the profound changes internal to the poet, his next poems, written after a quarter century's accumulation of worldly knowledge, are—to put it perhaps too bluntly—not profoundly different in *kind* than his first ones. The later may well be characterized by a pared-down diction and loosened syntactic connections; but such features are not a true stylistic departure; in poems early and late, we find spare, tense lyric fragments linked in abstract sequences larded with sententious and didactic passages.[14]

Even where formal differences can be heard or seen, they do not seem in and of themselves adequate to support a claim to transformative or redemptive discovery. The older poet may indeed have turned against the dream of revolutionary engagement that attracted him to Marxism, but the first poems are no more or less transparently *engagé* than the last,[15] and while Oppen's notebooks attest to his *will* to differentiate his newer voice from an earlier self, the poems seem more reticent about precisely what the differences signify, and more reluctant to accept a substantive discontinuity between his early and later work. When, in section 37 of his long poem "Of Being Numerous," he revisits the first poem of *Discrete Series*, written thirty-five years earlier, it is with a mind to restate, rather than to reject.

Here is the earlier poem:

> The knowledge not of sorrow, you were
>   saying, but of boredom
> Is—aside from reading speaking
>   smoking—
> Of what, Maud Blessingbourne it was,
>   wished to know when, having risen,
> "approached the window as if to see
>   what really was going on";
> And saw rain falling, in the distance
>   more slowly,
> The road clear from her past the window-
>   glass—
> Of the world, weather-swept, with which
>   one shares the century.

And here is the later, constructed like a rabbinic gloss that deepens mystery rather than dispelling it:

> ' . . . approached the window as if to see . . . '
> The boredom which disclosed
> Everything—
>
> I should have written, not the rain
> Of a nineteenth century day, but the motes
> In the air, the dust
>
> Here still

In *Discrete Series*, Oppen seemed to propose that the objects of knowledge—whether of "sorrow" (the possibility that an unnamed "you" had considered prior to the poem's beginning), of "boredom" (as the poetic speaker's unidentified interlocutor claims correctively), or of "the world" (which our speaker endorses as the true object of such affective states)—are best approached by attending closely to the changeable atmosphere that distinguishes one particular place and time from another: "rain falling, in the distance / more slowly" (5). Such a notion is given formal expression by the poem's ornately atmospheric syntax, which demands and rewards the devoted eye and ear. In "Of Being Numerous," by contrast, knowledge is disclosed by the unchanging particles of dust that hang in the air now just as they did then—much like the particulate and temporally suspended language of the speaker: "here still." From the former, we are told, one might learn about the world that one occupies at the moment, "Of the world, weather-swept, with which one shares the century"; the latter discloses "Everything."

And yet, even as the poet acts out and points out the difference between the poem then and the poem now, telling us that he should have written something other than what he did write, he also writes what he did write. The passage in quotation marks in "Of Being Numerous" ('. . . approached the window as if to see . . .') is a quotation of the poem from *Discrete Series*; indeed, it is a quotation of Oppen's quotation from Henry James's suggestively named "The Story of It." So while the poem seems to say that its views of where knowledge should be sought—and of what knowledge is knowledge of—have changed since 1934 (just as both have no doubt changed since a "nineteenth century day"), the claim that the difference is substantive is interestingly undercut by the act of self-quotation. If what has changed, in other words, is the idea that true knowledge (of "the world") resides in things that change, like the weather, and the new idea is that knowledge (of "Everything") resides in things that do not, like motes, then the words of Oppen's poems would seem to be more like motes than like weather. Words, *les mots,* like the dust, are "here still" in 1968 as they were in 1934—unchanged even since the "nineteenth century day" that James wrote of in 1902.

Of course just as not all the dust in the air in 1968 is the dust in the air in 1934, not all of the words in the later poem are the same as those in the earlier one. By situating old words in a new context—replacing the earlier poem's elaborate Jamesian syntax, for example, with the minimalist syntax of "Of Being Numerous," or altering what follows the quotation in order to give a new object to the verb "to see"—we discover the difference that context can make for meaning. But Oppen's point is not, as one might imagine, that we need to separate out one kind of word from another, the unchanging, knowledge-disclosing motes from the variable weather-words. Words, or motes, according to Oppen, do not just *occupy* different atmospheres, they *are* those atmospheres. As the stanza continues:

> What have we argued about? what have we done?
>
> Thickening the air?
>
> Air so think with myth the words *unlucky*
> And *good luck*
>
> Float in it . . .

Oppen here undoes the distinction between weather and motes, between words and contexts. Words, insofar as they are "thickened" contexts of argument or action, are the stuff of "myth"—shared systems of understanding that are not knowledge- or truth-bearing but as arbitrary and amoral as luck. "A tale of our wickedness," Oppen proclaims at the beginning of the poem, "is not our wickedness." Oppen's invocation of the myth of the fall is oblique, stripped of the red ripeness of the well-known story's thickly rendered detail and its morally burdened specifics of prohibition and redemption. What reticence implies here is not that we must tell a different, truer story of our wickedness, but rather that we must arrive at a thinking of ourselves somehow without story—free of myth, of tale telling, of the naming and placing that leads always—or would seem—to self-recrimination. But if this is so, a problem arises: how can poems, which are, of course, made of words, and are thus consubstantial with the changeable weather of context and all its moral burdens, disclose *anything*, much less "Everything"? The direction of Oppen's thinking here suggests that such knowledge as poems need—if they have it—must reside in a distinction *not* realized in things that can take on formal differences; not realized, in other words, in words.

In what follows, I offer an account of Oppen's poetic knowledge in precisely these terms. On the other side of his silence, Oppen does indeed retain the intention to know "everything"—by which he means something that matters as only everything can matter—along with a conviction that poetry is a way to know it. More specifically, I argue that for Oppen, "poetry" is not a practice of changeable forms but a courting of unchangeable silence a silence that penetrates his poems as well as bracketing them—and that silence is the medium in which love and its total endangerment can be addressed. Such an account has obvious consequences for aesthetics: if silence is not, as Specter would have us believe, a renunciation of poetry but rather a form that poetry can take, then we will need an account of the art rather different than the ones we have. But this change in our account of poetry has even more serious consequences for the idea of a poetic politics. Oppen addresses the total failure of sociability that accompanies "our" lack of knowledge about "what the world was" precisely by reconceptualizing what it means "to know" in a way that cuts it loose from our objects of sense, and that demands a reconsideration of what forms of attention toward others might be adequate. This is a reconceptualization that can and ought to bear on the question of social recognition.

II. Crusoe's Silence

The serial poem "Of Being Numerous" (1968) is representative of the many pleasures of reading Oppen, but also of one of the major difficulties: for a poet who has been labeled an "Objectivist," he can make it extraordinarily difficult for us to feel grounded in a known or even a knowable world. Though he would praise above all others the "small precise . . . overwhelming gentle iron lines and images" of Charles Reznikoff, whose poems emulated their subject matter, "the girder, still itself / among the rubble," Oppen's poetic precision seems more that of intellect than of iron. By the end of the first five sections of the poem, we have swum through such abstract nouns as "things" (specified only as "An unmanageable pantheon"), "images" (specified not at all), and "people" (of whom all that is said is that "We encounter them"). Verbs are equally abstract and technical ("encounter" is a case in point), or else they appear transformed into passive substantives like "Occurrence, a part / Of an infinite series, // The sad marvels" (147). It is only when we reach section 6 of the poem that we wash up at last on the shore of a proper name:

6

We are pressed, pressed on each other,
We will be told at once
Of anything that happens

And the discovery of fact bursts
In a paroxysm of emotion
Now as always. Crusoe

We say was
'Rescued'.
So we have chosen.

7

Obsessed, bewildered

By the shipwreck
Of the singular
We have chosen the meaning
Of being numerous.

Still, any orienting relief we might feel here at stumbling upon a named person must be tempered by the fact that that person is presented to us not under the auspices of perception but rather through the oblique lens of interpretation. Or, to put to it another way (since interpretation is, after all, a given when dealing with a *fictional* person), what is of interest about Oppen's Crusoe is not the fact of his self-authored story, phenomenally vivid and loquacious as the pages in which it appears: face and body illustrated, LIFE and ADVENTURES foregrounded, origin and profession prominently noted, duration and location observed, tragic highlights and strange travails narrated, with "an account" of his rescue delivered as dénouement (figure 2.1)—but rather the fact that "we" have taken even the most minimal account of him.

The quotation marks I have placed around "we" are a way of noting those that Oppen has placed around "rescued"—and those are quotation marks worth noting. Oppen, like many of his contemporaries, is a quoting poet. Many of his quotations represent moments of substantial philosophical engagement; their sources (Plato, Kierkegaard, Maritain, Heidegger) are traceable with some effort (often aided by the poet himself). Others derive from personal engagements (with Mary Oppen, Zukofsky, Reznikoff); these too have important implications that have been ably documented by editors and interpreters. But in this instance—and a few others in which the quotation consists of a single word and no attribution is given ("And he fails! He fails, that meditative man! And indeed they cannot 'bear' it." [153])—the implication is that what is being "cited" is a general attitude rather than a particular one attributable to an individual source.

Thus, though I will propose two quite specific sources for the *possible* judgment that Crusoe's return to civilization constitutes a rescue (The first is in Marx's *Capital*, the second in a set of debates surrounding Wittgenstein's *Philosophical Investigations*), I am not, in fact, seeking to decide the question of which one Oppen alludes to, or indeed of whether the passage is in fact an allusion.[16] My reading is not, in other words, in the mode of intellectual biography so ably and deeply pursued by Peter Nicholls, who has supplied the fullest accounting of Oppen's reading and influence. Instead, I suggest that choosing between these "sources" really entails choosing between two very different philosophical accounts about what it means to have a general attitude—whether those accounts are traceable to particular influences or not. The question is less a matter of which person Oppen means the quotation to refer to, than of what quotation marks tell us that Oppen thinks it means to refer to a person altogether.

For Oppen, the most ready-to-hand context for the figure of Crusoe would certainly have been Marx,[17] specifically the fourth section of the first chapter in volume 1 of *Capital*, "The Fetishism of Commodities and the Secret Thereof."[18] Here, Marx initially appears to use the Crusoe story to distinguish the simplicity and clarity of value born of labor from the "magic and necromancy" that characterizes

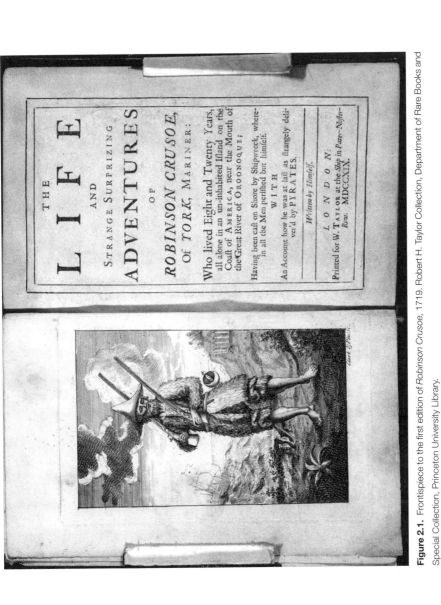

the forms of value specific to a commodity economy (87). Crusoe's needs are immediate, and his labor is unalienated; we know precisely how hard he has had to work to make his unimproved world serve his purposes. But Marx's Crusoe is ultimately not so transparent a figure. For the invocation of Crusoe in *Capital* lies beneath the shadow of his earlier mention in the *Grundrisse*, where Crusoe is revealed, not as an example of man in his natural state, but as a pure creature of ideology. Marx invokes Crusoe in order to contest the way the figure of the shipwrecked merchant had been used in the past by political economists to naturalize and universalize the acquisitive impulse and so give natural warrant to capitalism. For Marx, the judgment that Crusoe needs rescuing could only be true of a Crusoe whose "solitude" was a sham in the first place—"the semblance, the merely aesthetic semblance of the Robinsonades, great and small."[19] The novelistic Crusoe's inexplicably fortunate salvaging of the gold for which he claimed to have no concern, like his diligent bookkeeping and his excessive bower-building, is simply a dramatization of the fact that the Crusoe of the political economist's Robinsonade possesses habits of industry and desires for luxury that are given to him, as it were, from the outside (as products of the historical order of which he is a product) rather than arising from his native inclinations. Such a Crusoe may appear to be alone, but as a good bourgeois he carries his whole class with him wherever he goes.

In his deceptive surfaces and self-deceiving depths, Marx's Crusoe most clearly resembles, not Oppen's, but another poetic Crusoe, that of Elizabeth Bishop in her poem "Crusoe in England."[20] Bishop's Crusoe comes off at first as a good empiricist who spends his time as a castaway diligently numbering his island's volcanoes (fifty-two in all) and cataloguing the variegated colors of his basalt beaches. But despite his diligence, the shipwrecked sailor is nonetheless unable to perceive his island as it is. The pathos of Crusoe's empiricism is that his sense of scale and significance resides elsewhere. Longing for home, he sees turtles as teakettles, snail shells as iris gardens, and waterspouts as "glass chimneys, flexible, attenuated, / sacerdotal beings of glass," conflating in thought the domestic and the spiritual in just that way that we would call bourgeois.[21]

This is nowhere more evident in Bishop's poem than in her Crusoe's attitude toward objects. When Crusoe, having been returned to civilization, contemplates the one tool that he did not make, but that enabled all the rest of his labor, what initially looks like a proper recognition of worth commensurate with its great utility is quickly transformed into that phantasmatic form of valuation that Marx termed fetishization:

> The knife there on the shelf—
> it reeked of meaning, like a crucifix.
> It lived. How many years did I
> Beg it, implore it not to break?

I knew each nick and scratch by heart,
The bluish blade, the broken tip,
The lines of wood-grain on the handle . . .
Now it won't look at me at all.

Of course, nothing in Marx's account of commodities suggests that there is a problem with developing intense emotional investments in objects that have been particularly important to our survival. But the very specific personifying language Crusoe uses here—in which the object is, as it were, hidden behind the figure that is hung upon it—belongs to what Marx calls "the mist enveloped regions of the religious world." By the same token, the knife's apparent capacity to withhold its attention from its heartbroken former bearer bespeaks an order in which "the productions of the human brain appear as independent beings endowed with life, and entering into relation both with one another and the human race" (*Capital*, 83).

Bishop's genteel Crusoe—like the political economist who celebrates Crusoe—has what Marx would take to be a false account of his experience. That is to say, Crusoe misrecognizes his nature (indeed, he misrecognizes it as natural), and therefore he talks about all things in a language that is at once tenderly persuasive and utterly bankrupt. The drama of the poem turns on the way that Crusoe's ability to articulate his exquisitely attuned sensibilities, his feelings of alienation and anomie, breaks down in moments of great feeling, demonstrating the depths of his self-misunderstanding.

Friday was nice.
Friday was nice and we were friends.

Crusoe's impoverished effort to acknowledge the virtues of another person and to describe his relation to him may not quite reach the complete inversion of values Marx imagines when he describes the state of commodity culture as one that imagines "material relations between persons and social relations between things" (*Marx-Engels Reader*, 321). Persons, as well as objects, can legitimately be thought "nice." But the barrenness of Crusoe's recollected sympathy, framed as it is in the language of banal conversation rather than the language of authentic attachments, is the best evidence that this Crusoe suffers determination by a reductive discourse of valuing and a deforming state of social relations.

It is certainly possible to read Oppen's Crusoe in similar terms. Such a reading of "Of Being Numerous" might argue that Oppen intends "our" judgment that Crusoe has been "rescued" to coincide with the political economist's mystifications and with Crusoe's mystified self-assessments. For "us," bound to a misunderstanding of value that we cannot grasp or adjust because it lies external to us, Crusoe's island can only look like a version of our own world. Thus Oppen would seem actually to share Specter's concern that objectivist theory "identifies life with capitalism, and so assumes that the world is merely a waste land," and to set up both Crusoe's plight and "our" aversive reaction to it as a form of inoculating self-criticism. On this account, both the fact of Crusoe's rescue and the judgment that his return is a rescue—that rescue is what "we say"—are not possible outcomes but necessary ones. They are fulfillments of the form of "numerousness" that his apparent solitude conceals from him and that the putative singularity of judgment conceals from us.

Indeed, later in the poem, Oppen does provide some warrant for reading this way, elaborating further on the inability to return to the ground of our activity in order to perceive the actual worth of anything. Contrasting us to man in his primitive state, who can see things as they are, Oppen finds that we are hopelessly blinkered by the good fortune of our civilization:

> Unable to begin
> At the beginning, the fortunate
> Find everything already here. They are shoppers,
> Choosers, judges;. . . And here the brutal
> is without issue, a dead end.

The fact that everything is "already here" for the choosing makes choosing into shopping, a mystified form of voluntarism that conceals the constraints of an economic system that issues only in brutality to others and to the self. It is the same falsely voluntaristic account of "choice," Marx would argue, that underlies the liberal fiction that all social relations are contractual; and it is the same one that leads Bishop's Crusoe to imagine himself responsible for his own alienation:

> "Do I deserve this? I suppose I must.
> I wouldn't be here otherwise. Was there
> a moment when I actually chose this?
> I don't remember, but there could have been."

But at this point, we must confront the difference between Bishop's Crusoe and Oppen's. Bishop's poem is, first and foremost, a complex drama of tone, whose purpose is to evoke by means of voice a gently ironized sympathy, and on that vocal ground, an identification. That is, the point of Bishop's elaborate ventriloquism of Crusoe's self-deceiving words is to see our language in the light of his language and to see Crusoe's behavior in the light of our behavior: to see Crusoe as crucially like ourselves.[22] While Bishop might well have believed that a particular social and economic order gives determinate shape to—or even exacerbates— the misrecognitions that constitute our worldview, her poem is nevertheless consoling on the very ground of its criticism. We may be deceived and thwarted by the fact that what we take to be our languages of expression and valuation are given to us rather than made by us, but such ordinarily tragic and ordinary thwartings are precisely what we share, what makes us us.

Certainly Oppen, too, is capable of pointing out false consciousness of all kinds; he, too, is particularly aware of its consequences for language, which is reduced to "a ferocious mumbling, in public / Of rootless speech." This critique of the way language is abused by being ideologized lies behind a poem like "Song, the Winds of Downhill," which speaks of a longing to jettison those features of language the poet calls "tone" and "pose," aspects which suggest the stresses placed on intention by social obligation—in favor of words like "would with and" that are hard to poison through misuse because it is hard to say they mean anything at all (213).

But we cannot carry this reading of Oppen as a critic of ideology internalized through language too far. Oppen's Crusoe *has* no apparent psychology that might be read as ideology—if only because he makes no appearance at all. We cannot assess the state of his consciousness because we have nothing to go on. He is not loquacious, like the novelist's Crusoe, and therefore he is not acquisitive like Marx's, nor survivalist like the political economist's. He is not even, like Elizabeth Bishop's "Crusoe in England," pathetic or sympathetic, for he has neither tone nor pose: he is *silent*. In fact, the only thing that we know about Oppen's Crusoe is what "we" say about him.

The significance of that fact depends on how we read the syntax of the stanza and construe its causal logic. One could, for example, read the verse as an attenuated argument across the period: "We are pressed on each other. . . . so we have chosen." Read this way, "so" means "as a result": "We are pressed on each other, and as a consequence we have chosen the meaning of being numerous." The implied account of causality here is consistent with the Marxian narrative; it suggests that "our" positive evaluation of Crusoe's return is not really anything we have deliberated or willed. It is, rather, a belief about the nature of persons that is determined by their particular historical condition of "numerousness." "Pressed" on each other, we are transformed by oppressive social relations into reactive objects rather than active subjects.

It is, however, equally permissible to parse the verse so that it reads: "Crusoe we say was 'rescued'. . . so we have chosen." Read this way, "so" would mean something like, "in this manner." This second reading raises the possibility that what is being represented here is not a dramatized foreclosure of choice but an explanation of the manner in which "we" come to decide upon the meaning of any thing. It points us, in other words, toward the other possible source for the image of Crusoe: not in a discourse of class, but in a discourse of mind.

III. The Silence of Other Minds

When Crusoe enters this debate, as he did in a series of explications of Wittgenstein's later thought that followed rapidly on the heels of the

English publication of the *Philosophical Investigations* in 1953, he is obviously not the Crusoe of fiction, nor the "congenital Crusoe" of the political economist. He is, rather, a *structural* Crusoe: a man not left in isolation or reared in isolation but regarded in isolation—prior to and apart from our construal of any of his actions.[23] What has come to be known as Wittgenstein's "private language argument" concerns not just "language" as such; the classic example of a rule-governed activity, used by Saul Kripke in his influential exposition of the paradox in *Wittgenstein on Rules and Private Language*,[24] is the rule of addition. But Kripke selects a mathematical rule for his example only in order to emphasize the generality of the critique—finally, it is meant to apply to *all* rule-governed actions, whether mathematical, linguistic, or merely conceptual.[25]

Briefly stated, the skeptical paradox runs as follows: Imagine that you are confronted by a resolutely skeptical questioner who wants some justification for your belief that your action is consistent with a rule. Or, more precisely, the skeptic wants to know how you know that when following a rule you are acting in accordance with that rule as you have intended it in the past. The problem is that you have in your life set out to follow any given rule only a finite number of times, in a finite number of cases or contexts. (In Kripke's mathematical example, the rule is the rule of addition, and the highest number you have ever added is 56.) What the skeptic is suggesting is that while you may have thought you followed that rule in the past because you performed according to its dictates in every case you have confronted so far, you cannot be certain that the rule you in fact intended was not some *other* rule—one that stipulated that you behave as you have in all the cases you have encountered thus far, but stipulated something else in some as-yet-unencountered and future case. Kripke's example: When you followed the rule for "plus" in the past, the function you intended might indeed have been to add two numbers together—for in the case of every number with which you have thus far been confronted, that is what you did. But on what basis, he asks, can you assert that the rule you actually intended was not the rule more properly known as "quus"? According to the quus function, one proceeds to add all numbers lower than 57 as one would if performing addition; but in *quaddition*, the answer to any problem containing a number higher than 56 is the number 5. You have never added a number over 56 before; you have therefore never formulated any intentions regarding such numbers. You therefore cannot challenge the skeptic's claim that you had meant *quus* all along by appealing to or reporting on your prior mental state.

One possible reply to the skeptic might be to observe that the number of times I have applied the rule of addition cannot possibly matter, since a rule of this kind is not limited in its application to a finite number of cases. Addition is, rather, a general rule (an algorithm) about what to do when confronted by two groups of objects—i.e., you combine them and then count the larger pile. But, the skeptic might retort, this objection also depends on a rule which, in your experience, has only been applied over a finite number of cases—the rule in the exemplary case being the rule of counting. Perhaps in every previous instance, the skeptic suggests, "by 'count' [you] formerly meant quount, where to 'quount' a heap is to count it in the ordinary sense, unless the heap was formed of two heaps, one of which had 57 or more items, in which case one must automatically give the answer '5'" (*Wittgenstein on Rules and Private Language*, 16). Your objection that counting, too, specifies a rule that is independent of the number of objects counted does not help matters; for a version of this critique can be made about any reduced rule, going, as it were, all the way down—until you come to rest upon a rule that you must admit is irreducible to any other—and that rule too will be susceptible to the same skeptical critique.

The conclusion of this argument is intended to be fatal to your conviction that you are behaving now as you once did, since you can no longer be certain what you once did—whether in fact you meant plus or quus. The problem Kripke's paradox poses is not just an epistemological problem that makes it impossible to be certain that the rule you intend now is the same rule you intended before. It is also an ontological problem, potentially devastating to the idea of meaning altogether. For, Kripke argues, "if there was no such thing as my meaning plus rather than quus in the past, neither can there be any such thing in the present" (21). The logical outcome of the paradox is the deeply anti-Cartesian conclusion that there is, *even now,* no fact about you or your mental state that distinguishes meaning plus from meaning quus. And if there is nothing about you that constitutes your intending one rule rather than another, then on one account of meaning, "there can be no such thing as meaning anything by any word" (55).

On Kripke's account, Wittgenstein's solution to the "private language argument" is offered, not as a redemptive account of individual psychology, but in terms of a community of language users, or what he calls a "form of life" (Wittgenstein, *Philosophical Investigations*, 8e). A form of life, as Kripke defines it, is "[t]he set of responses in which we agree, and the way they interweave with our activities" (*Wittgenstein on Rules and Private Language*, 96). According to Wittgenstein, then, I ascribe rule-following to you when your behavior is consistent with my "form of life," by which I mean that (a) you give the same responses I am inclined to give in a situation like yours, (b) you interact "properly" with my community, and (c) the ascription of rule-following to you has some utility in that community. While there are no truth conditions, then, for determining whether a person follows a rule, there are assertibility conditions for our judgment that he does so.

In Wittgenstein's paradox, Robinson Crusoe presents us with two problems, both of which are relevant to Oppen's Crusoe in "Of Being Numerous."[26] The first is an "internal" problem about determining the nature—or, in fact, the existence—of one's own intentions. Considered in this context, Oppen's previously odd-seeming locution about Crusoe suddenly makes a great deal of sense as an argument about intentionality. By saying "so we have chosen," Oppen means not so much that "we" have decided (through internal deliberation or ideological formation) that it is better for Crusoe that he has been brought home; he means that "we" have decided something by talking about him in a particular way. There may not be truth conditions for determining the meaning or value of Crusoe's actions, (since they have no determinate internal or intentional mental realization), but there are assertibility conditions for our calling his return a rescue. And indeed, as the verse goes on to imply, it is *only* by talking about things in a particular way—by sharing a particular form of life—that "we" exist as a communal entity at all.

But it is at this point that the silence of Oppen's Crusoe becomes particularly important—and particularly troublesome for my hypothetical Wittgensteinian Oppen. For what can "we" make of Oppen's decision not to describe Crusoe's activity *at all*? Given a structural Crusoe, it is only when we interpret a person's responses as being in some way consistent with our own that we, in Kripke's exceedingly evocative and resonant phrase, "take him into the community." But what if Crusoe's responses did not resemble any we knew? What if his life was so different from any we might imagine as to be incomprehensible, imperceptible, *silent*? This is the second "external" problem that Crusoe poses. If there was nothing about Crusoe's mental state, nothing beyond our interpretive acts, that constituted his meaning anything in particular, from whence derives our inclination to take that person—man considered in isolation—into our form of life in the first place?

Kripke's phrasing, in other words, presents the question as a question not just of epistemology but of "rights": "If Wittgenstein would have any problem with Crusoe, perhaps the problem would be whether we have any 'right' to take him into our community, and attribute our rules to him" (110). But his tentativeness about the literalness or propriety of the term gets at an interesting ambivalence about the status of the normative in this line of argument. For the problem with annexing Crusoe's actions to our own purposes or purposiveness is less an ethical one than a logical one. Or, perhaps better, it is a logical one *before* it is an ethical one. Kripke acknowledges that "if we think of Crusoe as following rules, we are taking him into our community and applying our criteria of rule following to him" (110). *But he does not explain why we should think of him as following a rule.* How we might come to recognize rule-following as such, what the tests of rule-following-in-general might be if they do not already entail the judgment that someone obeys our rules, is not at all clear.

Oppen here addresses himself to an aspect of the hard problem of other minds that Kripke does not raise: that in some important respect all persons are silent, all responses sufficiently unlike our own to cast radical doubt that we are faced with a fellow rule-follower—which is to say, a potentially recognizable fellow person. If, as Oppen's Crusoe's silence suggests, silent singularity is in some crucial sense the norm, then reason decrees (and history as Oppen experienced it confirms) that it will be all too easy to make mistakes about persons: not just to fail to treat them justly, but to fail to perceive their presence or credit their existence altogether. Such normative silence threatens at every moment to lead to the failure of acknowledgment and care Oppen calls "the shipwreck of the singular."

If we were operating within some other field of inquiry—of cognitive psychology, for example—we might find ready to hand a set of arguments proposing to elaborate a set of procedures for the empirical detection of rule-following altogether. But for Oppen the poet, the solution is posed, not as a formal method or a form of reason, but as a form of patience, as a general attitude—as a silent extension of credit. And the poetic form silent patience takes is, typically, the break, the pause, the caesura. Thus the significance of this section break between 6 and 7, which separates the act of "choosing" from the mental states ("oppressed, bewildered") that determine choice and separates it, too, from the actual choices that are made (the "meaning of being numerous").

Section 6, then, "considered in isolation," suggests yet another possible way of seeing "so": "Crusoe we say was / 'Rescued' / So [you can see] we have chosen." And what you can see we have "chosen" is sociability itself, conceived, not as a particular vocabulary, but rather as the obligation to say *something* about Crusoe, whether we recognize him as being part of our "form of life" or not—because we regard him as having *a* form of life, as being a person like ourselves, though not necessarily as our kind of person. After this choice is made, the particular choice of the meanings we come to assign him ("the meaning of being numerous") may be determined by our form of life, or it may be determined by the relations of production that structure and give form to our lives (pressed, oppressed, bewildered). But the fact that we choose a meaning is dependent only on our acknowledgment of the existence of the other person. We do not "rescue" Crusoe by interpreting his behavior as being consistent with our own; we have already rescued him by granting that his activities need interpretation.

This is the minimalist attitude toward persons that Oppen, citing yet another quoted (though this time, attributed) term, called "curiosity." The final section of "Of Being Numerous" consists in its entirety of a fragment of a letter written by Walt Whitman:

Whitman: 'April 19, 1864

The capitol grows upon one in time, especially as they have got the great figure on top of it now, and you can see it very well. It is a great bronze figure, the Genius of Liberty I suppose. It looks wonderful toward sundown. I love to go and look at it. The sun when it is nearly down shines on the headpiece and it dazzles and glistens like a big star: it looks quite

Curious . . . '

Figure 2.2. The Statue of Freedom, seen "very well." Photo by Jack E. Boucher, 1993. Library of Congress, Prints & Photographs Division, HABS DC-38-C-10.

Figure 2.3. Sunset on the Capitol dome. Library of Congress, Prints & Photographs Division, HABS DC, Wash 1-16.

It is quite striking that the poem's conclusion on Whitman's letter courts, but quite deliberately avoids, a description of how the statue "looks." Despite Whitman's assurances, the viewer—whether close up and at a steeply raked angle, or near level but from a great distance—cannot see the statue atop the capitol dome "very well" at all. Instead, Whitman's insistence on his perception of the obduracy of the great bronze becomes the occasion to describe a whole variety of subjective, imaginative, and affective responses: personification, the registration of preferences (for the way something looks at particular times of day); indeed, perception in this poem becomes something like a vision of subjectivity itself as it emphasizes just those particular qualities of sundazzle on bronze that are the result of one's particular position relative to a thing, and the changes in attitude, atmosphere, or weather that constitute subjectivity across time ("it grows upon one in time").

Nor does Oppen resolve on an account of what it looks *like* (figures 3.2 and 3.3)—for the poetic insistence upon likeness is also what makes possible the misperceptions or projections we call ideological.[27] Whitman's ability to see the feathered headdress that the *Statue of Freedom* atop the Capitol dome wears as itself a star (rather than merely including stars) is finally not all that different from the reason why the statue atop the Capitol dome wears a feathered headdress in the first place, rather than a phrygian cap as was originally intended. Both the constructed figure (Crawford's) and the figured figure (Whitman's) are attempts to secure the legitimacy of a new government by recasting it as having highest possible sanction. For Whitman, union begins in the heavens; in 1863 America, it began by avoiding the divisive implications of topping the statue of freedom with the symbol of freed slaves.

"Of Being Numerous" resolves instead upon an *attitude toward looking*. "Curious" is itself a curious term; it should be contraposed to "beautiful," or even to "meaningful." Isolated in white space, set silently apart from the fluent discourse of the letter, curiosity represents the jettisoning of a concept of "art" in favor of an artless stance toward the object. If "it" looks curious, it is because I look curiously; curiosity toward the other redounds upon the self. What Oppen chooses to emphasize is not a description of this object, nor is it a criterion by which we value it; it is, rather, the name of the disposition to perceive and to value.[28] It is typical of Oppen's poetry that we find consensus-type judgments (of beauty, of meaning) separated from the foundational premise of "curiosity" or care that of necessity precedes them in fact, though it may follow them in verse. Note, for example, the reversed blazon in section 15:

> Chorus (androgynous): "Find me
> So that I will exist, find my navel
> So that it will exist, find my nipples
> So that they will exist, find every hair
> Of my belly, I am good (or I am bad),
> Find me."

Here, the "androgynous" chorus seems at first to imply that persons can only exist insofar as they are acknowledged. And while it is true that they are individuated by being literally incorporated by communal criteria, this peculiar *chora* seems already mysteriously to possess the power of speech, a prior speech that voices what we might call the human (collective) capacity to be found.

The same dynamic structures what is perhaps Oppen's best known short lyric, "Psalm," where the difference between what is judged "beautiful" and the ground on which judgments of beauty are made possible is once again indicated by a silence or caesura, here marked diacritically not by a space but by the dash:

> In the small beauty of the forest
> The wild deer bedding down—
> That they are there!

The poem's epigraph—"Veritas sequitur . . . "—invokes and alters Aquinas's doctrinal *Veritas sequitur esse rerum* ("Truth is a consequence of the existence of things"), a doctrine originally formulated to counter and divinize the Aristotelian (and, we might say, proto-Wittgensteinian) idea that truth is a consequence of cognition about things. But Oppen conspicuously and typically omits Aquinas's *esse*, which contained in it the assumption of the divine origin of "thing" (which, in other words, inscribes the "truth" that follows from objects as a particular theologically sanctioned form of value) and replaces it with a paraphrase posed less as a metaphysical dogma and more as an astonished exclamatory premise.

The difference between doctrine and premise is made even clearer in the *Daybook*, where Oppen meditates on the same passage:

> Truth ~~follows~~ must follow
> after things

> *Nevertheless, Truth follows*
> *The existence of <u>something</u>* 29

In the first formulation, Oppen strikes out the dogmatic proposition of (theological) certainty and replaces it with a statement of logical necessity. In the second, squared-off formulation, it is not "things," but simply the premise that an abstract "something" exists, that makes subsequent "truth" possible. This something—less certain, more abstract, but also more humane—is what Oppen means by "knowledge." This intention toward persons, the attitude "That they are there," is unconditioned by particular historical forms of belief, unspecified as to the particular qualities of objects, but it is forcefully stated. From this "judgment" for the existence of a necessary truth, all other sorts of judgments (like sympathy, like small beauties) may follow.

IV. A Vision

> I am talking of a being
> I am not ~~talking of~~ displaying a dialectic. I am talking of
> a vision.

> Only I am talking of any vision. of all vision
>
> . . . .
>
> NOT A DIALECTIC
> BUT VISION.—Not a dialectic
> but vision . . . [30]

It is hard not to feel sympathy for Oppen, whose long poetic silence was sub-tended by boldfaced repetitions of "visionary" intent that have gone unheard. It is as if the poet himself was speaking a private language. The earliest criticisms of Oppen's work denied the poet's vision focusing on the way that the particulate materiality of his poems rendered them incomprehensible, and characterizing their maker as a sort of idiot-boy stutterer:

> Mr. Oppen's offering exhibits that extreme parsimony of words that is taken today to imply infinite profundity. I don't believe it implies anything of the kind. His writing is like listening to a man with an impediment in his speech.[31]

More recently, however, precisely this critique has been revived as praise: "I am not sure I completely understand this poem," admits Peter Nicholls when con-fronted with the late poem "Occurrences" (1972), "but nor am I sure that I am meant to. The syntax seems broken, precarious, though to describe it as frag-mented would misleadingly assume a reconstitutable logic of propositions."[32]

One of the central features by which Oppen's "alternative" poetic is distin-guished as alternative is by its supposed emphasis on a textual materiality that eschews claims of "vision"—or even of propositionality altogether. Thus, in Mi-chael Davidson's reading, as in Nicholls's, "Oppen's paratactic logic, truncated syntax and ambiguous use of antecedents" do not signify an impediment of speech but a resistance to it. Such fragments "embody the shifting attentions of a mind dissatisfied with all claims to closure."[33] For Davidson, the workings of that shifting and resistant mind are most emphatically on display, not in the finished and published texts of Oppen's poems, but in what he calls the "palimptexts" of the daybooks—the drafts of poems in which line revisions are typed on cut scraps and pasted on drafts in impasto twelve leaves deep; the "book" formed by ham-mering a set of sheets into a piece of plywood with a nail; the "fascicles" fastened by metal screws, brads, and pipe cleaners. But though his description is filled with the romance of labor, his point is avowedly anti-romantic. Davidson means to argue that for Oppen, writing was not the act of creating unified and rarified "works," but rather a sort of homely work:

> My purpose in describing the material component of Oppen's work is to suggest the degree to which writing was first and foremost something ready-to-hand—as immediate as a coat hanger or a piece of wire. The pipe cleaners, metal clasps

and glue are visible representations of those "little words" that Oppen liked so well, the basic materials of a daily intercourse. (77)

Or again:

What we see in the typescript page but not in the published poem is the dialogue between individual sections, each responding to and qualifying the previous. . . . Language is both the vehicle and the object of Oppen's speculations as he oscillates between competing propositions. Such dialectical progress can be seen in the published version to be sure, but the page—with its spelling mistakes, holograph emendations, and variable lineation—provides a "graphic" indication of how immediate and personal that progress is. (75)

One might point out that the "little words" used to write poems on paper are themselves visible representations of the little words Oppen liked so well. But the point of Davidson's parallel between pipe cleaner and word is less that one part of a work should be seen to be in "dialogue" with another or that the meaning of any part of a work is "qualified" by acknowledging the contingent materiality of the language in which it is rendered; it is rather that meaning—as something that does not change—is effectively *vitiated* by that materiality. The word, viewed as a commonplace object, makes writing a form of jerry-rigged, practical, daily labor that issues not in meanings at all, but in objects. "Dialectic," on Davidson's account—and on many accounts like it—is not a movement from contradictory assertions toward a higher synthesis. Rather, by taking the materiality *of* language to qualify or compete with the intention to mean anything in particular *with* language, the proponents of this version of dialectic make conceptual synthesis unnecessary by canceling out anything so brutally final as an assertion, and imagine that political consequences follow from the rejection of a conceptual finality seen as inseparable from violence.[34] Or, as Jerome McGann's argues,

. . . when the physical aspects of writing—its signifying mechanisms—are made a conscious part of the imagination's activities, writing opens up the subject (and even to a limited extent the possibility) of unalienated work.[35]

It should go without saying that Oppen is not afflicted with other-speech—a verbal disability that threatens to exclude the speaker from a speech-community altogether. But, as may be evident from his insistence that his work is "NOT A DIALECTIC," neither does he intend that his poems embody difficulty in order to suggest some other to speech—a material text that would be "unreconstitutable" in terms of some "form of life" or another. Rather, if Oppen's poems seem "broken" or "parsimonious" it is because he does not really want to be making "poems" at all. "The poem replaces the thing, the poem destroys its meaning— —I would like the poem to be nothing, to be transparent, to be inaudible, not to be."[36]

On this note of self-abnegation, we might once again recall the singular harshness of Oppen's single mention of Elizabeth Bishop's poetry. Oppen never does tell us which line in "The Fish" he regards as "the silliest line ever written," but on the basis of the argument thus far I am willing to hazard a guess. The speaker of Bishop's poem recounts the story of the capture and release of a "tremendous fish" with all the attention to detail and imaginative sympathy that we expect from this most precise of poets. But more than that, she presents the release precisely as a triumph of the power of sympathetic sight to make available the story of an alien other. The first appearance of the fish as it is hauled halfway from the water and into the poem finds it barely recognizable as a living thing or a thing of value—as "stained" and "homely" as faded wallpaper. If the stain is a faded trace rather than a dynamic sign of life, it is also the objective trace of a past action or series of actions, as vivid a phenomenal realization of the fish's history as the collection of hooks and lines embedded in its lip, "a five-haired beard of wisdom / trailing from his aching jaw." The relation between the wear upon the creature's body and the wisdom it has achieved is decisive for the poem, and for the poet. For the more attention the speaker pays, the more the dulled and "battered" exterior of the animal yields to her attention images not just of history (and its pain) but of an imagined interior at once delicate, vivid, and charged with passion:

> While his gills were breathing in
> the terrible oxygen
> —the frightening gills,
> fresh and crisp with blood,
> that can cut so badly—
> I thought of the coarse white flesh
> packed in like feathers,
> the big bones and the little bones,
> the dramatic reds and blacks
> of his shiny entrails,
> and the pink swim-bladder
> like a big peony.

Of course, Bishop's speaker is aware of the awful costs of such observation. What makes such close examination possible is the fact of capture, the alienating "rescue" of the fish from its proper form of life into our own terrible air. In the contact zone between our life and its life, breath itself is a zero-sum game. The gills through which the blood courses might also draw our blood; its "freshness" is our wounding. In coming to see the fish's flesh as bird flesh or flower, Bishop briefly imagines the creature as though it could thrive in an atmosphere that is in fact fatal to it. But her mode of figuration registers the approximateness or falsity of this thought.

Thus in "The Fish," the narrative of the poem is the story of empirical sight producing the vision that compels its own renunciation.

> I stared and stared
> and victory filled up
> the little rented boat,
> from the pool of bilge
> where oil had spread a rainbow
> around the rusted engine
> to the bailer rusted orange,
> the sun-cracked thwarts,
> the oarlocks on their strings,
> the gunnels—until everything
> was rainbow, rainbow, rainbow!
> And I let the fish go.

"Rainbow rainbow rainbow!" would have offended Oppen not—or not only—for its sentimental performance of its speaker's faux-naïve astonishment, and not just for the capacity to detect beauty in bilge and rust. These are mere matters of decorum and sensibility, and even Oppen's sparest poems are not immune to moments of sentimentalized description. What offends Oppen's epistemology ("sensibility" seems here a singularly question-begging word) is the fact that the poem's "victory"—the speaker's decision to let the fish go—is made to depend upon the occurrence of a form of wonder based entirely in perception—a sort of phenomenal luck which is no less a trick of the light than the glinting of the sun off the Capitol dome.[37] And what offends Oppen's ethics is the idea that one's conviction that a meaningful life is present should arise as a projection of a desire originating wholly within the self.

The dependence of care upon the chances of sense is a central trope in Bishop's oeuvre—that monument to perception in which, as she puts it, "the crudest scrollwork says 'commemorate'" just as clearly as the finest filigree of art. Initially recoiling from the vision of her "Filling Station" ("Oh! But it is dirty!"), the speaker of that poem gradually discovers a series of well-placed (if homely and faded) objects that transform what she perceives as an alienated and alienating place of labor.

> Somebody embroidered the doily.
> Somebody waters the plant,
> or oils it, maybe. Somebody
> arranges the rows of cans
> so that they softly say:
> ESSO—SO—SO—SO

to high-strung automobiles.
Somebody loves us all.

The relation between the signs of maternal care in the filling station—the stitching of the doily, the maintenance of the plant—and the signs of artisanal care that has been taken with the poem (the way the "oil-permeated station" is materialized by the embedding of "oil" in doily, for example)—is brought to its fullest conjunction in the sibilant stuttering of the artfully arranged cans. In this poem, as in "Of Being Numerous," so much depends on the word "SO." But for Oppen, "so" is purely a logical operator. Just as "the meaning of being numerous" was not learned by observing any particular way of talking about another person, so too, the meaning "so" (in "so we have chosen") is precisely indifferent to the particulars of what has been seen. In contrast, Bishop turns the word "so" itself into a thing to be seen, and makes seeing the thing make all the difference. Conflating the object that the word is with the causality that the word denotes, the poet of "Filling Station" insists that the act of perception itself can serve as *evidence* that we too are seen, and known. It is Bishop, in other words, rather than Oppen, who treats language as material; Bishop, rather than Oppen, who makes "the physical aspects of writing" a conscious part of the speaker's imagination. And in so doing, it is Bishop who makes the relationship between the arrangements in a work of art and their consequence into a consoling one. To see "so"—not once, but many times, metered, arranged and arrayed, is to feel the force of the word as an argument. The materialization of the word, its transformation into soothing whisper or deliberate pattern, offers concrete evidence for the conclusion of universal love.

V. The One Thing

I would like the poem to be transparent, inaudible

. . . .

"Because I am not silent the poems are bad"

Over and over again (here in *Conjunctions*, 3) we find Oppen trying to indicate one great "vision"—though quite unlike Bishop's vivid pictures, it turns out to be an extraordinarily difficult one for his readers to see. In his own terms, Oppen aspires "to construct with language something other than language"; such a construction properly entails not a craftsmanlike attention to the origin and consequence of words but rather an indifference to words: "the poem begins without the words or with one word or with any word." The something other than language that is intended by this sort of poem is not a meaning; or, as Oppen puts it, "It is not what a poem says, but what it is talking about" ("Philosophy of the Astonished," 220).

What a poem is talking about with any, one, or no words is "poetry," which Oppen understands not as a collection or series of objects, not as a set of rules about their proper construction, but as what he calls "the power to originate": "the power to originate lies not in aesthetic man (the exercise of taste) but in ontologic man; man as he confronts the world" (225).

Such statements, collected from the strange and scattered fragments of Oppen's notebooks, are not, regardless of any editorial fiat, poems. Rather, they address a problem that Oppen sees as endemic to poems: no matter how spare they become, they are still too fluent. Poems always seem to be saying something; or, in what amounts to the same thing, they are always making themselves available for particularizing judgment. This is what Oppen means when he says that all poems are "bad" insofar as they fail to be silent. Silence, on the other hand, is not fluent enough; not *properly* "inaudible," it appears merely to be saying nothing at all. The daybooks form a continuous running undersong whose genre is uncertain—as is, therefore, the relationship to readers that is projected by this form of writing. If neither poems nor silence alone succeed in "talking about" the right thing, then the daybooks, imagined as a speaking silence, aim to be at once fluent *and* inaudible. They aim not to say anything but to "disclose everything."

Oppen writes, in section 10 of "Of Being Numerous":

But I will listen to a man, I will listen to a man, and when I speak I will speak, tho he will fail and I will fail. But I will listen to him speak.[38]

As with the "man" the speaker describes, Oppen's critics have listened and failed. What Oppen means to point to (again, gesturing at his point with the resonant silence that separates the articulated sense that poetic utterance "will fail" from its compensatory solution) is the determination to listen: "But I will listen to him speak." Oppen addresses the problem of other minds not by submitting them to the chances of style but by at every moment supposing that there is something there to understand, someone who means something: the person, who needs us not in order to exist, but just in order to be found.

> One must not come to feel that he has a thousand threads
> in his hands,
> He must somehow see the one thing;
> This is the level of art
> There are other levels
> But there is no other level of art

Despite his injunction against empiricism in section 27 of the poem, Oppen is not a moral intuitionist. He does not exactly believe that moral principles or value judgments are self-evident, nor that we have a special faculty that detects and sorts values.[39] Neither, however, is he a full-blown skeptic. If the injunction to "somehow" see the "one thing" is to mean anything at all, then Oppen's account of "art" cannot be reduced to the argument that communication is always doomed to failure. Like the skeptic, the poet casts doubt upon the idea that listening or looking, feeling, or thinking might bring us to value what most needs valuing. Like the intuitionist, however, Oppen insists upon a kind of attentiveness that encourages and dramatizes the greatest possible opening of the self to the possibility that a morally salient thing could be present. It is only by failing to attend to the silent peculiarity of *this* art that we could conclude that what was most important to bring to light about persons or poems was their individual "sound" or "feel," their thousandfold particularities and social distinctions, rather than their basis in the truth of one common "thing."

An attention to truthfulness, as the epigraph to this chapter suggests, is "far from a social virtue," because Oppen's understanding of the truth of poetry is precisely at odds with any account of virtue that depends on the social determinations of a "form of life." Oppen's lesson to twentieth-century poetry is that a poetry sufficiently abstract to provide social hope will appear to be not just "anti-aesthetic" but altogether anti-phenomenal—opposed not just to the idea of literary quality but to the idea of quality itself. Communication may indeed fail: but the curious fact ("that they are there" prior to recognition, prior to obligation) is the sort of success made possible by being willing to fail aesthetically, by being silent in the right way.

The Justice of My Feelings
for Frank O'Hara

the final opinion does not glow in the dark

I. For the Times

Yesterday I accepted an invitation to a party. But I had no
    sooner arrived and let my coat tumble, exhausted, onto a
    bed, when a perfect stranger whom I immediately and
    unwittingly admired asked me if I were a poet.
Many guests crowded around the two of us, as at a wedding.
    "I suppose I am," I said, "for I do write poems."
"Well write one now, will you?" he said, smiling fiercely. Faces
    aureoled at his shoulders and elbows. A few tendrils of hair
    escaped the opening of his shirt, fled upward to his neck,
    and they were not the color of his eyebrows!
"I'm sorry, but I don't feel like one just now, if you don't mind,"
    I said, thinking of many things, chiefly, perhaps of child-
    hood, when I would make myself vomit so I wouldn't have
    to go to parties.
"Well what makes you feel like writing one?" he said, and
    kicked me in the balls.
Ugh!

As I hobbled to a chair, however, I managed to somewhat re-
gain my composure. "You needn't be afraid of me," I said,
turning. "I don't love you."[1]

This odd poem, entitled "Prose for the Times" (1952), exemplifies in condensed
form many of the problems that a reader inclined to take poems seriously encoun-
ters when approaching the poetry of Frank O'Hara. Unlike Oppen's self-inflicted
silence, so burdened with moral gravity, virtually everything about O'Hara's voluble
poem seems designed as if to affront the dignity of the poetic vocation, no matter
the terms in which that vocation is imagined. Note, for example, the resolutely
trivial nature of the poem's "occasion"; an inconsequence that is registered both
narratively—as the strange goings-on recorded by the poem take place at a party
that is apparently last-minute and louche—and generically: for while the poem
alludes to an "occasional" genre—the party is said to resemble a wedding—it
refuses to commit much to the resemblance, or to ornament that short time into
"endlesse moniment." This "prose" brings its news (whatever that might be) for
"the times," rather than for all time.

Or perhaps (O'Hara himself never published it and so there is no authoritative
typographic or bibliographic indication to prevent the reading and there is some
anecdotal information to recommend it),[2] O'Hara means to suggest that this is
prose for *The Times,* which would identify the poem with ephemeral middlebrow
journalism rather than the high-demotic and subversive ephemera of the "mimeo
revolution" to which this poet would be such an enthusiastic contributor.[3] "Prose
for the Times" presents itself less as the "deep gossip" of which Allen Ginsberg
would proclaim O'Hara the master[4] than as the sort of gossip item one might find
in the society pages; it is neither Pound's "news that stays news" nor (certainly)
Yeats's immortal song.

The self-negating self-identification of the title, too, renounces the honorific
generic title of "poem" without compensating that loss with the semantic com-
pressions and symbolic energies of the prose-poem. Here (in contrast to his self-
mocking stance toward his own prose poetry in "Why I Am Not a Painter"—"It is
even in / prose, I am a real poet"), O'Hara flouts not just the tradition of the well-
made lyric, but the "alternative" tradition of flouting that tradition; he betrays not
just the sons of Eliot (a poet who, O'Hara declared in the same year he wrote this
poem, had "a deadening and obscuring and precious effect"[5] on epigones like
Lowell and Wilbur) but also his chosen family, the "Fathers of Dada!" he celebrated
in "Memorial Day 1950."[6] The *correspondences* of Baudelaire and the "*déregle-
ment de tous les sens*" of Rimbaud were avant-garde gestures with which O'Hara
was more than passingly familiar; he had read and indeed imitated each of these
poets at various times in his early work[7]—but this prose resembles the work of
neither of these masters, nor does it recall the "prose" of Reverdy, allegedly so

close to O'Hara's heart that he once poetically confused the two ("My heart is in my pocket / it is Poems by Pierre Reverdy" [*Collected Poems,* 258]).

These devaluations and renunciations of the entire range of poetic contexts barely get us to the first line. Reading further, one is perhaps not surprised to discover that the ambiguous generic status of the poem predicts its subject matter, which explicitly takes up the status of O'Hara's vocational identity. Here, I am struck at once by O'Hara's rhetoric of supposition (rather than conviction) when aggressively confronted with the question of whether or not he is in fact a poet; struck too by the circular logic with which that supposition is supported. The only proof on offer that he *is* a poet is that "I do write poems"—surely an underwhelming claim in the light of our doubts about whether it is a poem in which the claim is being made. The oddly compelling, artificial, and inexplicably admirable stranger who confronts O'Hara in the whirl of social life that is his natural habitat—the world in and out of which he composed—stands in for us and asks the question we are most inclined to ask.

What *are* we asserting when we assert that O'Hara is a poet? Certainly O'Hara does make poems—many poems, hundreds upon hundreds of poems. But one may legitimately question whether any of them are "written" in the sense in which we ordinarily mean the term. O'Hara's poems are tossed off on lunch hours, scribbled on napkins in the midst of parties, banged out (perhaps the story is apocryphal) on floor models in typewriter shops; they are inserted into letters and mailed, never to be seen again; they are stuffed into underwear drawers to be retrieved by more pragmatically minded editors—each one, like this one, providing evidence that could be taken either to confirm or deny O'Hara's supposition that he is a poet.

The way the stranger deals with O'Hara's attempt to deflect the confrontation only deepens the question. Perhaps recognizing the futility of an argument that bases the definition of a poet on the poet's own inclination to declare the objects of his activity poems (O'Hara wrote more than fifty poems entitled simply "Poem," and at least eleven poems he called "Odes," though they obey no particular generic constraints), the stranger's next question—"what makes you feel like writing one?"—presses on, turning the question about poetic identity away from a demand for objective evidence and toward a more subjective inquiry about the origin of what we would, under more ordinary circumstances, be inclined to call O'Hara's inspiration. What is it that O'Hara's "feeling like it" stands for that gives him claim to the title? Is he a poet (even in the absence of poems) because he is moved by "natural feelings" whose "spontaneous overflow" can be neither compelled nor curtailed? Is he a poet because he consciously and deliberately turns from "sincere emotion" in order to express "impersonal" but "*significant* emotion"?[8] For "Prose for the Times," neither the Romantic valuation of "genius" (granted only to a few by spiritual election) nor the modernist valuation of mastery (achieved by learned diligence and devotion to tradition) will do.

But neither will the postmodern appeal to the value of "liberation." For the one moment in this poem that even merits quasi-poetic consideration is O'Hara's reactive "Ugh!" I call this ejaculation "quasi-poetic" for reasons internal to the narrative itself (it is, after all, what O'Hara makes in response to the "social demand" for poetry); but also for formal reasons: for its insistent (if unmusical) vocality, for the way it flirts with traditional figures like onomatopoeia or apostrophe. In this case too, there is a recursive quality to the story, in which internal events anticipate our external queries. For the utterance that stands, as it were, "in the place" of the poem is—whatever else it might be—a noise *forced* from the poet by a vicious external assault. Kicking makes O'Hara do something whether he feels like it or not. The fact that the exclamation is conspicuously *not* in quotation marks like the rest of the dialogue identifies it not (or not just) as a part of the story being told but with the act of the telling itself, the implication being that the whole of "Prose for the Times" might be understood, not as a declaration of freedom from constraining models, but as a reflexive response to a timely shock ("the times," "The age demanded"). The question of inspiration (and its implications for any assessment of the poem's value) would thus be answered by suggesting that this "poetry" is not evidence of any autonomous capacity, but is, rather, a mere emanation of a mechanism, making the poet a sort of object himself rather than a subject—or at best the sort of subject who is formed by a constitutive wounding and subordination, as might be the case if the same story were told (a version of it essentially is) by Jacques Lacan.

Approaching this poem in these terms, with their implied demands for general principles, may feel like training outsized weapons on a very slight target. But the questions that thinking about O'Hara raises—in part because of the characteristically offhanded way the same questions come up about and within his work—are serious questions, and bring to bear a much greater awareness of literary historical problems than might initially be apparent. Whatever else it is, "Prose for the Times" is a thinly veiled parody of one of the founding stories of the poetic tradition in English—the story of Caedmon's vocation. As that story is narrated—in *Latin* prose—by the Venerable Bede, Caedmon, the first named poet we know of to make a religious poem in English (more precisely, Anglo-Saxon), was also confronted by a mysterious *quidem,* a someone, who demanded that he make a poem—though in Bede's account, Caedmon had initially succeeded in avoiding such a confrontation at the party he had been attending, fleeing it before it was his turn to sing (he knew no songs). And while Caedmon's argument takes place after a party, in an actual dream rather than a surreal semblance of one, the terms of the stranger's demand are virtually identical: "Well, write one now, will you?" Or, as the dream-visitation commanded the illiterate lay brother Caedmon: "Caedmon, sing me something!"

The story of Caedmon, along with the poem that Caedmon sang, originally appeared in the Venerable Bede's *History of the English Church and People*. This situation of poetic history as a subset of ecclesiastical history is paradigmatic. Caedmon, one among the *illiterati* and *idiotae,* sings his poem again for Hilda, abbess at the monastery at Whitby. It is she who validates the poem as authentically the work of God—in effect deciding the up-to-that-point ambiguous doctrinal question of what poetry stands for and where it comes from, and founding a tradition of religious verse that would be normative practice until the late nineteenth century.

But Caedmon's hymn is *also* to be found at the beginning of any of the standard histories of English poetry available up through the middle of the twentieth century, including the one that O'Hara encountered at Harvard College at the beginning of James B. Munn's course, English 1b, "History and Development of English Literature from the Beginning to 1700," which O'Hara took as a sophomore.[9] This situating act is also paradigmatic. If Caedmon's song was appropriated by the Catholic Church and *made to be* consistent with canonical doctrine, the resulting poem has been subsequently incorporated as part of the *literary* canon, an institutionalized body of texts that aspires to make poems project an image of cultural totality for the twentieth century in much the same way that the canon of scriptural texts did in the seventh.

O'Hara's version of the Caedmon hymn, we should note, has led a very different institutional life than the original. "Prose for the Times" does not appear in any anthology that purports to understand its selection as a representation of the literary canon; it does not even appear in what passes for the "O'Hara canon": the massive Knopf-published volume of O'Hara's *Collected Poems.* I have retrieved it instead from *Poems Retrieved,* a volume that gathered previously unknown poems, the majority of which were never published or even prepared for publication. To my knowledge, this poem has never been featured in *any* anthology whatsoever, mainstream or experimental, nor discussed in any work of criticism. Insofar as I have been able to determine, I am the *only* writer on O'Hara ever to reproduce it at all.

The very different history of these two vocational "hymns"—one objectified, reproduced, fetishized, canonized, appropriated by institutions and recruited into a disciplinary project; the other barely a poem at all, self-canceling, retrieved only out of my own odd affection as a way of trying to demonstrate that O'Hara can be thought about rather than that he is valued in any previously sanctioned terms—produce what are, in effect, two very different ways of thinking about what the history of poetry is, and about what kind of work goes into the valuing of poems.

The argument of this book thus far has been that an adequate account of poetic thinking of a certain kind requires that we emulate the stranger in O'Hara's poem, redirecting our categorizing interest away from the question of what sort of object the poet produces and toward the question of the conception of the person indicated by its production. A second major argument is that this reorientation ought to produce a history of twentieth-century poetry less afflicted by false divisions based on the surface differences between objects. But the reading of "poetry" I have offered in the preceding chapters raises an odd problem: for the first of these claims seems to interfere with the second, making it difficult to understand how "poetry in the general sense" could have a history at all.

O'Hara, I will suggest, provides us with an opportunity to think through both these problems. For he is a poet whom other poets want, for whatever reason, to claim as part of *their* history, and also a poet deeply interested in finding a history for himself; he thus provides an opportunity for others to struggle with the way that the fetishization of poetic styles produces a sense of determinism even as he suffers that sense of determinism in his own work. O'Hara's poetry in general also provides us with the opportunity to think through the complex relation between questions about form and questions about vocation. The first is what we might call an ontological problem: What are the features that we point to in identifying a poem as a poem? The second is a social problem: What values are sponsored by our acts of valuing?

These problems have roots in the oldest discourses of value and branches in analytic aesthetics. But O'Hara is a poet virtually without a philosophical vocabulary or political inclination; his education was conducted almost entirely in art. Because we begin thinking about poetry firmly entrenched in the world of poems, I take seriously O'Hara's admonitory recollection in "Memorial Day 1950": "those of us who thought poetry was crap were throttled by Auden or Rimbaud." What I hope this argument will begin to demonstrate and theorize is one way that an interest in what I have called "poetry" as principle can be consistent with a hermeneutic impulse, and so foster a "non-crap" relation to poems even as I insist upon their secondariness.

Or, to put the argument in its properly inductive form, I would like to show how an encounter with one's throttling love for poems can end up pointing away from them; how an insider's preoccupation with the details and distinctions and personages of the art world, with its constrained occasions and modes of valuing, can be made to disclose the widest possible view of the human world. O'Hara's imaginary solution to the problem of having a style was to imagine poems that had no style, and were therefore not actual poems. But O'Hara lacked Oppen's philosophical inclination to imagine his poems to be ontologically different—or ontologically anything, for that matter. He remained an inveterate if conflicted maker of poems, and of himself as an artifact: "against my will / against my love / become art" (*Collected Poems,* 257).

O'Hara's real contribution to the poetics I am describing is rather a reconceptualization of poetic history, less as a sequence of valuable objects, and more as a *medium* in which we can privilege our disposition to value altogether. It is O'Hara's determination, not to evade literary judgment, but rather to totalize it, that allows us to imagine the possibility of a kind of poetic (as opposed to aesthetic) valuing that is bound neither to particularizing histories nor to particular kinds of institutionally sanctioned objects. The criterion of poetic value is not any criterion of *taste*, but rather a criterion not subject to historical determination or institutional oversight—what O'Hara (in "Prose for the Times") calls "love."

II. Secondariness, "Second Avenue"

As my discussion of "Prose for the Times" might suggest, O'Hara occupies an odd place in the literary canon. No one seriously challenges his right to it, and yet at the same time no one can say precisely on what basis he belongs in it. Early reviews of his work were quite mixed, finding him too slight, too trivial, too coterie bound; and at the same time (once the shocking size of the *Collected Poems* was revealed), too much, too monumental. Pearl K. Bell's review of *The Collected Poems* in the *New Leader* is fairly typical:

> For the occasional arresting passage . . . one must endure huge trash-heaps of what he calls his "I do this I do that" poems, full of campy gossip, silly jokes, travel notes, subway rides, newspaper headlines, sentimental shadows of anxiety. Mainly he drew on his vast collection of celebrated friends, in an extended family album of Larry Rivers, John Cage, Edwin Denby, Virgil Thomson, Jackson Pollock, and a lesser cast of thousands. The names may glitter, but O'Hara's poems to and about them do not. For the reader, the cumulative effect of this colossally self-absorbed journal of happenings is numbness, not pleasure.[10]

If the initial implication here is that O'Hara's poetry is parasitic—stealing its pale fire from the glittering stars of his celebrated friends—Bell's subsequent insistence on the poet as journalist of "self-absorption," as well as her classing his poetry alongside various genres of ephemera (gossip, notes, inside jokes), suggests that the real problem lies elsewhere: not in the poet's drawing off star quality, but in his insistence on drawing in men and women *without qualities* who round out the scene of O'Hara's art without filling it with significance or making it shine—a "lesser cast of thousands" that this reviewer does not stoop to name, but whom O'Hara could not stop naming.

Poets determined to commemorate subjects of uncertain or just unpublished distinction rely upon various strategies of generalization. Milton rewrites the ordinary "Edward King" as "Lycidas," a name that brings with it the complex resources of praise and fame made available by pastoral elegy. Yeats, by judicious selection and generous augmentation of aristocratic virtues, made Major Robert Gregory into "soldier, scholar, horseman" and so into "all life's epitome." Robert Lowell writes the names in own extended family album into transhistorical significance as a reenactment of Freudian family romance. O'Hara exercises none of these options. It is not that V. R. Lang, Patsy Southgate, Mike Goldberg, John Button, and Joan Mitchell have no virtues that could be indicated or elaborated, or that O'Hara knew no paradigmatic stories in which they could be made to take up their characteristics as character. O'Hara's maximal lists of minimal names—Bunny and Patsy and Mike, Robin and Don and Joe and Jane and Kenneth, Ashes for Ashbery—suggest a deliberate effort to make poetry out of *particularity* rather than *specificity*.

I want to pause here to emphasize the difference between two terms that might appear to be synonyms. Specificity is a category of qualitative experience, existing on a continuum with generality. Someone could have a quality (or collection of qualities) so specific as to be unique without those qualities ceasing to be general— sharable on principle, even if not shared in practice. Particularity, on the other hand, is a *logical* category—it admits of no degrees and it is not a feature of my experience, though I can become aware that it applies to my experience when I become aware of something as *my* experience.[11]

To restate Bell's objection, then, a "lesser name" is lesser not because it is of lesser quality, but because it is not presented in qualitative terms at all. (This is the importance of the "thousands," which, however large the number, indexes the numerical particularity, and thus the inaccessible idiosyncrasy, of the unnamed.) However well known the name, O'Hara's names name his particular attachments rather than their attributes, value, or other logically general qualities. The same may be said of what O'Hara himself called his "I do this I do that" poems, which provide itineraries of his peripatetic wandering through New York but which, unlike Aristotle in Athens, frame no lesson and posit no telos. We may trace O'Hara's footsteps, but he gives us no way to walk un his shoes. (That is why, for Bell, his "pleasure" can only be our "numbness".)

This repeated poetic attachment to particulars is, we should note, unproblematic—or at least intuitive—with respect to actual persons. Our ideology of love is such that attachments to persons are intuitively understood to be nonfungible— nontransferable to others even if they possess to the greatest degree of specificity imaginable the same qualities that we profess to love in the beloved. We aspire to love others, as Yeats suggests, as perhaps only God can—for themselves alone, and not for their yellow hair. But to profess attachment to *poems* in this way—as logical particulars defying qualitative analysis or quantitative measure—would seem at the very best like a failure of critical competence; at worst it seems like a failure of rationality. Though expressed negatively, this objection hits precisely on what has always seemed most odd about O'Hara's positive reception, or about the fact that he is in the canon at all. O'Hara's poems seem to be valued all the more highly to the degree that people find themselves able to attribute their valuation *of* them to no qualities *in* them; or else to attribute to them only the most attenuated and self-negating of qualities.

Thus John Ashbery, in what is still among the most influential essays on O'Hara, describes the dilemma faced by those who aspire to think about O'Hara as a part of their poetic history.[12] Contrasting O'Hara to artists who "feel compelled to band together in marauding packs," Ashbery finds him to be a poet without a tribe: "O'Hara's poetry has no program and therefore cannot be joined." Ashbery offers a few negative examples of what it might mean to have a program (thinking most obviously of Allen Ginsberg, but his remarks would apply equally well to Robert Lowell): "It does not speak out against the war in Viet Nam or in favor of civil rights; it does not paint gothic vignettes of the post-Atomic age." But if Ashbery finds it difficult to attribute an affiliation to O'Hara on the basis of what he speaks *about,* it is even more difficult for us to imagine an affiliation on the basis Ashbery's account of *how he speaks*. As Ashbery describes O'Hara's poems, they are

> big, airy structures unlike anything previous in American poetry and indeed un-like poetry, more like the inspired ramblings of a mind open to the point of dis-traction. The result has been a truly viable freedom of expression which, together with other attempts at technical (Charles Olson) and psychological (Allen Gins-berg) liberation, has opened up poetry for today's generation of young poets. In fact, without the contribution of poets like these, and O'Hara in particular, there probably wouldn't be a young generation of poets committed to poetry as something living rather than an academic parlor game. (ix)

O'Hara exemplifies a freedom that is not specifically "technical" like Olson's, nor "psychological" like Ginsberg's, nor ideological, nor semantic—but that despite apparently being devoid of qualities altogether nevertheless has a fructifying effect on future poetry, making it possible to commit to poetry as "living" rather than as "playing."

This is, of course, something like a formal wish, rather than a formal reality. For in some ways O'Hara has proved to be one of our most imitable of poets, provid-ing a set of moves, gestures, and features that are, perhaps too easily, reproduced and transported. The poets most committed to understand themselves as the direct inheritors of O'Hara's "living" poetic were those of the second generation of the "New York School"—a loose confederation of poets, some of them friends of O'Hara's and some of them merely *soi-disant*—who appear in *An Anthology of New York Poets*.[13]

The editors of this volume—Ron Padgett and David Shapiro—use their preface to disavow the very notion of the existence of anything like a "New York School" ("most poets of any interest these days are so enlightened that they automatically reject, in their lives and work, the unhealthy idea of being part of a literary move-ment" [xxix]). Explaining why statements on poetics (of the sort appended to

Don Allen's anthology) were unnecessary, however, they give two interestingly incompatible reasons: first, though all the poets included could be said to share "tastes and affections," none of them would want to enshrine their principles in anything so "eternal" as a manifesto; but second, because all of the poets included have found their principles enshrined in a manifesto already—O'Hara's famous "Personism: A Manifesto," which, they say, "in many ways speaks for us all" (xxxi).

I will return shortly to the matter of "Personism" and to the notion that it may speak for "us all," but first I would like to take up the claim that the New York Poets do not share anything in their poems beyond affection and a commitment to emphasize their own particularity. As an example of the interesting way these two qualities can stands at odds with each other, I would point to Ron Padgett's "Strawberries in Mexico":

> At 14th Street and First Avenue
> Is a bank and in the bank the sexiest teller of all time
> Next to her the greatest thing about today
> Is today itself
> Through which I go up
> To buy books
> . . . .
> I like these old pricks
> If you have an extra hair in the breeze
> Their eyes pop out
> And then recede way back
> As if to say, "That person is on . . . dope!"
> They're very correct
> But they're not in my shoes
>
> In front of a Dubuffet a circus that shines through
> A window in a bright all-yellow building
> The window is my eye
> And Frank O'Hara is the building
> I'm thinking about him like mad today
> > (As anyone familiar with his poetry will tell)[14]

Padgett's elegy to O'Hara is indeed quite emphatically particular. It describes *his* day, *his* bodily location at a particular intersection, his own desires (taking care to indicate that they, unlike O'Hara's, are heterosexual). Perhaps the most important indication that the "old pricks" who pass judgment on the speaker are correct in finding him "different" is *not* (as one might expect) that he has taken drugs—for while drugs may alter the mind, they are perfectly consistent with a lifestyle. It is, rather, Padgett's positioning himself before a painting by Dubuffet. This in and of itself might seem to be odd grounds for self-differentiation. In purely formal terms, spectatorship is utterly undifferening; anyone—hip or square—can stand in front of a painting.[15] In practical terms, few things mark you out as a particular *kind* of person more clearly than visiting the Museum of Modern Art to look at the work of a contemporary French painter in the middle of the afternoon on a workday. But for Padgett, as for Whitman before the Statue of Freedom, being in front of a work of art is the ultimate demonstration of the fact that "they're not in my shoes." The idiosyncratic experience and subjective judgment solicited by an art object represents the *ne plus ultra* of what it means to be the particular person you are.

But what is most striking about the poem is that however unlike Frank O'Hara Padgett may be in his particulars, he is virtually indistinguishable from him in his *particularity*. It is not so surprising that the evasion of style should turn out to be just another style; it is more surprising that particularity should be so firmly and fascinatingly associated with one particular individual. This attachment is thematized in the poem itself, which conflates thinking about Frank O'Hara and thinking like Frank O'Hara in a way that seems on the face of it quite mad. We initially thought (as indeed he had thought) that Padgett was thinking about himself; but the fact that in thinking about himself he is thinking about O'Hara is evident long before he tells us. The poem suggests that "liking" O'Hara (in the sense of finding him to your *taste)* is hard to differentiate from being *like* O'Hara: "The window is my eye, and"—or, one would want to say, *but*—"Frank O'Hara is the building."

Padgett's elegiac embrace of a sort of stylistic apprenticeship under the auspices of particularity brings to mind the poem in which O'Hara attempts to rid himself of his own stylistic apprenticeship. "Second Avenue" (1953) is widely regarded as O'Hara's breakthrough poem, in which he comes most decisively into his own style:

> Quips and players, seeming to vend astringency off-hours,
> celebrate diced excessives and sardonics, mixing pleasures,
> as if proximity were staring at the margin of a plea . . .

The most distinctive feature of the opening is its reproduction of the whole range of styles available to an apprentice poet of the period. Here are obvious echoes of Crane ("excessives and sardonics"), Eliot ("mixing pleasures"), and probably Stevens as well, in the intensely musical sound-over-sense mode of *Harmonium*. In O'Hara's early Hopwood manuscript poems (so clearly influenced by Coleridge, Wyatt, Apollinaire, and others), imitation was the mark of an earnest craftsman trying on styles and techniques to see what they have to offer. But the rapid-fire centriloquism of "Second Avenue" has both a surer and a more polemical purpose. This is O'Hara's attempt to *pass judgment* on the stylistic resources of modernism:

> This thoroughness whose traditions have become so
>   reflective,
> your distinction is merely a quill at the bottom of the sea
> tracing forever the fabulous alarms of the mute
> so that in the limpid tosses of your violet dinginess
> a pus appeared and lingered like a groan from the collar
> of a reproachful tree whose needles are tired of howling.

Though this passage hardly needs explanation (it oscillates between clarity and deliberate surreal impenetrability), O'Hara glosses it anyway in the "Notes on Second Avenue" (provided at the request of *Time/Life* editor Rosalind Constable): "To put it very gently, the philosophical reduction of reality to a dealable-with system so distorts life that one's 'reward' for this endeavor (a minor one, at that) is illness both from inside and outside" (*Collected Poems*, 495). It is not difficult to connect O'Hara's disparaging remarks about "philosophical reduction" to the inheritance of a high modernist poetics. If such systems and styles were once vital, the modernism of these great stylistic predecessors refracted through the poetry of Robert Lowell or Richard Wilbur now seemed submerged in an ocean of "reflective" tradition.

Having already proclaimed the exhaustion of modernist "thoroughness"—the ambition to reconstruct the world on the order of style—one might legitimately expect a gesture toward a new style. But the odd thing about "Second Avenue" is that after beginning with this emphatic critique, the poem does not change. It continues as a torrent of recycled idiom, a canyon of reflective echoes. What the poem provides is repetition and wild parody; a travesty of "The Waste Land" gone mad because it has nothing else to offer in its place:

> Candidly. The past, the sensations of the past. Now!
> in cuneiform, of umbrella satrap square-carts with hotdogs
> and onions of red syrup blended, of sand bejeweling the
>   prepuce
> in tank suits, of Majestic Camera Stores and Schuster's,
> of Kenneth in an abandoned storeway on Sunday cutting ever
>   more
> insinuating lobotomies of a yet-to-be-more-yielding world
> of ears, of a soprano rallying at night in a cadenza, Bill, of
> "Fornications, la! garumph! tereu! lala la! Vertigo! Weevy! Hah!"

"Second Avenue," in other words, looks less like a practical rejection of a particular literary genealogy (an anxiety of influence) than like a wishful rejection (per impossible) of genealogy as such. For the poem, like Padgett's poem, appears to suggest that having a style at all makes one subject to endless opportunities for determination.

O'Hara did try in various ways to avoid the pitfalls of having a style. One of these ways was his peculiar mode of (non)-publication. When Allen wrote the introduction to *Poems Retrieved,* he noted that "O'Hara was never very sanguine about publishing his poems" (xv). In fact, this considerably understates the fact of the matter as it emerges from Allen's own testimony:

> When I set out to edit the *Collected Poems* in the late sixties, I felt that I had little or no indication of what O'Hara himself might have included in such a volume had he lived—apart, that is, from the poems he had already published in books and magazines. True, I had studied a manuscript of some 100 early, short poems in 1961 when he wanted my advice on what to include in *Lunch Poems.* And he had shown me at various times the poems that were later published as *Love Poems,* as well as some longer poems for possible publication in *Evergreen Review, The New American Poetry* and other projected collections. . . . But there remained many poems of which I had never heard, or doubted that he would have published without revising, ones that seemed too similar to other poems of the same period or were too fragmentary. In the course of restudying the manuscripts and collecting his correspondence, however, I came to realize that O'Hara at one time or another would most likely have published all of his poems, and that the present volume was the logical and necessary completion of the publication of all his poems. (It is of course entirely possible that more unknown poems may yet come to light.) (xvi)

It is worth pausing over this remarkable statement. Despite his early experience helping O'Hara to select poems for one of his published volumes—*Love Poems (Tentative Title)*—Allen professes to have *no idea* what O'Hara's criteria for publication were. Editing a volume of love poems had provided no notion of thematic coherence, none of order, none of kind—and, perhaps most strikingly, none even of quality. The conclusion that Allen draws is, remarkably, that O'Hara would have wished, not for none of his unpublished poetry to be published, but rather for all of it to be published. If Allen is correct about the "logic" of O'Hara's production, this would make O'Hara a poet vastly different from Whitman (the poet he understood himself to be emulating)—for Whitman had consistently understood himself to revising a single great work. It would make O'Hara into a poet who "chose" everything, and as a result made no stylistic choices at all.

Another account of what it might look like not to have a style is "pictured" in "Second Avenue." The poem was originally conceived as a sort of challenge to Kenneth Koch to write a poem in which you "go on as long as you can." Just what that might mean is explained by another "gloss" in the "Notes on Second Avenue."

For, as O'Hara explains, the poem contains "a true description of not being able to continue the poem and meeting Kenneth Koch for a sandwich while waiting for the poem to start again" (496): "Kenneth in an abandoned storeway on Sunday cutting ever more / insinuating lobotomies of a yet-to-be-more-yielding world / of ears . . . " Given the complexity of the passage, O'Hara's "explanation" is suspicious in its simplicity: "('He was continuing to write his long poem as he waited')." While the referent for "He" is presumably "Kenneth," we might also recall that we have also just been told that it is *O'Hara* who is "waiting for the poem to start again." The resulting pun turns out to be a surprisingly apt description of "Second Avenue"—a poem that "goes on" even when its writer is supposedly not able to continue "writing" it, just as the poet may still be a poet even when not "writing" poems.

Of course, going on "as long as you can" imagines some limit to capacity, though it does not specify what the limit is. O'Hara frequently ends poems by invoking just such a limit, a summation that can only be expressed in some as yet uninvented language. "Second Avenue" itself ends with the announcement that "You have reached the enormous summit of passion / which is immobility forging an entrail from the pure obstruction of the air" (15), while "Ode to Michael Goldberg('s Birth and Other Births)" ends by imagining a miraculous being who might one day achieve that originary style of which O'Hara can only dream: "and one alone will speak of being / born in pain / and he will be the wings of an extraordinary liberty" (298).

O'Hara does imagine at least one poet who embodies the extraordinary liberty he speaks of here, in one of the poems he titled "Poem":

> To be idiomatic in a vacuum,
> it is a shining thing! I
>
> see it, it's like being inside
> a bird. Where do you live,
>
> are you sick?
> I am breathing in the pure sphere
>
> of loneliness and it is sating.
> Do you know the young René Rilke?
>
> He is a rose, he is together, all
> together, like a wind tunnel,
>
> and the rest of us are testing
> our wings, our straining struts.

Here, O'Hara imagines the young Rilke, the Rilke of *Neue Gedichte,* on the model presented by one of Rilke's own poems. According to O'Hara, Rilke's bowl of roses exists in a space wholly outside the world of striving where "two boys / ball themselves into something that was hatred and writhed on the ground," away from the theatrical display of "actors, towering exaggerators." Rilke, like his roses, has power precisely because of his indifference to being perceived. Though he, like the roses, has the potential to be made to be anything, he achieves that infinite potential by remaining only himself. Imagining a poet in these terms is to imagine the poet as freedom and flight, or rather to identify him with the medium of freedom and flight—not so much with the bird as the wind tunnel that alternately buoys and buffets.

In relation to this sort of poet, all subsequent acts of creation are not just acts of apprenticeship or fledgling efforts but "straining struts"—a phrase that beautifully captures the sense of the preening effort that accompanies self-display in a world in which expression has become reflective and mechanical.

The problem for O'Hara, then, was not how to create a different kind of poem— for by his own lights there is no such thing as a different kind of "poem." The problem was rather how it might be possible to think about poetry in such a way as to allow poems to be "idiomatic in a vacuum"—to reconceive the poetic world itself to allow for the valuation of particulars without imposing the oppressive atmosphere of a norm.

III. Personal Poem

Now when I walk around at lunchtime
I have only two charms in my pocket
an old Roman coin Mike Kanemitsu gave me
and a bolt-head that broke off a packing case
when I was in Madrid the others never
brought me too much luck though they did
help keep me in New York against coercion
but now I'm happy for a time and interested

I walk through the luminous humidity
passing the House of Seagram with its wet
and its loungers and the construction to
the left that closed the sidewalk if
I ever get to be a construction worker
I'd like to have a silver hat please
and get to Moriarty's where I wait for
LeRoi and hear who wants to be a mover and
shaker the last five years my batting average

is .016 that's that, and LeRoi comes in
and tells me Miles Davis was clubbed 12
times last night outside BIRDLAND by a cop
a lady asks us for a nickel for a terrible
disease but we don't give her one we
don't like terrible diseases, then
we go eat some fish and some ale it's
cool but crowded we don't like Lionel Trilling
we decide, we like Don Allen we don't like
Henry James so much we like Herman Melville
we don't want to be in the poets' walk in
San Francisco even we just want to be rich
and walk on girders in our silver hats
I wonder if one person out of the 8,000,000 is
thinking of me as I shake hands with LeRoi
and buy a strap for my wristwatch and go
back to work happy at the thought possibly so

The most common critical response to a poem like this one in O'Hara's "mature style" (should we be inclined to admit the existence of such a thing) is the effort to recuperate its seeming triviality of choices by finding evidence of O'Hara's ability to inflect a catalogue with consequence, and by demonstrating that O'Hara's mode of poetic juxtaposition allows for the registration of a wider (and more "engaged") awareness of social conditions than he is usually given credit for. For Marjorie Perloff, this awareness is registered in the "thinly veiled anxiety" of the poem's tone; it is also evident in O'Hara's reference to the beating of Miles Davis by a "cop" outside "BIRDLAND" in a poem otherwise filled with what would appear to be biographical charms and aesthetic quirks. Such news, Perloff announces, is "terrifying . . . for the gay speaker as well as for his black friend, given the raids on gay bars frequent in those years."[16] But this reading of a transparently representational "politics" (perhaps surprising coming from a critic who is ordinarily determined to privilege form as the site of significant poetic engagement) reads like the result of a critical will to impute significance where none is forthcoming. Perloff's ability to find "terror" in this poem, in other words, seems to be a way of compensating for the leveling effect that form has on tone—for the poet's manifest indifference to the suffering of the "lady" who appears in the very next line, and who is denied even a nickel on the perverse grounds that "we don't like terrible diseases." When the poem is viewed in its actual discursive mode (rather than through a projection of what a "gay speaker" must feel in "those years") it seems difficult to think about Miles Davis's suffering as anything other than another element in a catalogue of things to which O'Hara registers dislike.

I use the word *dislike* (rather than Perloff's preferred terms, "terror" or "anxiety") in order to emphasize how much of this poem seems to revolve around the statement of preferences or value judgments in just these mildly affective terms. There is simply nothing about the poem (though there may be much about the sensibility of the critic) to suggest that the problem of racial violence ought to be granted significance according to some other set of criteria than those that apply to the matter of "who wants to be a mover and a shaker." Ultimately it makes no more sense to praise O'Hara for his alertness to the concerns of identity politics than it would to condemn him for his blindness to those of class politics—both seem equally beside the point.

Perhaps it is in response to the poem's refusal to offer anything other than preference as its "point" that other readers have undertaken laborious efforts to give O'Hara's judgments a provenance, in the hopes that telling the story of how they came about might reveal them to be more than merely arbitrary. Reva Wolf, for example, has argued that the expression of artistic preferences ought to be considered under the rubric of what she calls "gossip," which she understands as the fundamental discourse of artistic relationships: "being blind to the force of gossip in history, we often fail to see the fullness of relations between people that makes art a vital, human thing."[17] Claiming to be "reading between the lines," then, she attributes O'Hara's "liking" Don Allen to the fact that "Allen was a supporter of [his and Jones's] work (which he included in his highly successful 1960 anthology *The New American Poetry*)" (17). David Lehman—whose own past experience as Lionel Trilling's research assistant at Columbia University leads him to believe that logrolling of the sort Wolf describes is insufficient explanation to justify what to him can only appear as the perverse inversion of values expressed by O'Hara's preference for "the little-known Grove Press editor" over "the Columbia eminence at the height of his influence"—does much more legwork to solve what he regards as a "literary mystery." After entertaining and rejecting a number of possible grounds for disliking Trilling (e.g., "the Robert Frost brouhaha of 1959"), Lehman suggests that O'Hara's judgment is actually a response to something written by *Diana* Trilling—the memoir of her marriage in which she announced Lionel's preference for "seriousness" over "happiness". In this mediated way, then, "Lionel Trilling" represents, not a publication in which O'Hara could not appear (*The Partisan Review*— in which, after all, he did appear), but rather a "value system" of which O'Hara disapproves.[18] (By virtue of what mediations Don Allen represents the opposing pole of that value system—"happiness"—is left up to the reader's powers of detection.)

If we are interested in solving the "literary mystery" in this way, there are probably better solutions than the ones that we have been offered. As long as we are interested in literary "gossip," for example, why not consider O'Hara's "liking" Melville as a coded "gossipy" way of hinting at a relationship of identification that existed between O'Hara and the critic F. O. Matthiessen at Harvard?[19] And as long as we are supposing that judgments of taste encode personal "value systems," we would probably do better to note the complex network of poetic and identitarian affiliations specified by O'Hara's choice of Melville over James: for the choice is consistent not just with Phillip Rahv's well-known aesthetic and quasi-anthropological division of writing in the period between the "Redskin" and the "Paleface," but also with a choice for a set of specifically homosocial poetic affiliations that would include Hart Crane ("At Melville's Tomb"), Charles Olson (*Call Me Ishmael*), and even D. H. Lawrence (in *Studies in Classic American Literature*).[20] The link to Matthiessen seems a much more complex and subtle way of "reading between the lines" than the rather transparent sort of information that Wolf presents; it is also more plausible as gossip goes, given the fact that *The New American Poetry 1945–1960* would not be published until a year after "Personal Poem" was written. The relation to Rahv or to Crane offers a more expansive, historically informed, and literary vision of the values that literary preferences can stand for than Lehman's anecdote-hunting will allow.

But finally, such sleuthing misses altogether the force of the problem that "Personal Poem" presents, a problem that has less to do with the question of what *kind* of research we ought to be doing in order to decode the meaning of the poet's preferences than with the question of why we need to do any research at all. Why, one might fairly ask, does a poem that announces itself to be "personal" make us work so hard to *personalize* it? What such dogged researchers fail to theorize, in other words, is that biographical detective work is made necessary in this instance by the fact that the criteria for the judgments made in the poem are withheld by the poem. They also fail to acknowledge (a necessary prelude to such theorization) the rather obvious and important fact that the preferences in the "Personal Poem" are not actually presented as *personal* preferences at all, but rather as *collective* preferences—not as statements of what "I like" but of what "we like"—which makes biographical explanation seem potentially misguided (or at least oversimplified) from the outset.[21]

One possible way to account for both the fact that the criteria of judgment are apparently shared *and* the fact that their meaning is not made explicit in some other terms is by considering such judgments under the rubric of Pierre Bourdieu's concept of the "literary field":

> The social microcosm I call the *literary field* is a space of *objective* relations between positions—between that of the celebrated artist and that of the avant-garde artist, for example. One cannot understand what is going on without reconstructing the laws specific to this particular universe, which, with its lines of force tied to a distribution of specific kinds of capital (economic, symbolic, cultural, and so on), provides the principle for the strategies adopted by different

producers, the alliances they make, the schools they found, and the art they defend.[22]

For Bourdieu, then, the field constitutes what he calls a "space of possibles"—aesthetic positions (formalism, realism, "engaged art," or "art-for art's sake") that correlate with social locations (the academy, the fireside, or "bohemia") and, through various complex mediations, with economic interests. "Above and beyond individual agents," Bourdieu notes, "this space functions as a sort of common reference system that situates contemporaries . . . by virtue of their common situation within the same intellectual system" (541).

According to the logic of positions available in the literary field, the judgments artists make (like the artifacts they produce) are not explained so much as they are correlated. In the "space of possibles" made available in the fifties in America, then, to like Don Allen over Lionel Trilling just *is* to prefer Melville to James; O'Hara and Jones, occupying virtually identical positions within the literary field (Jones having not yet seceded from the Lower East Side bohemia to take up a more militant Black Nationalist "position" as Amiri Baraka), do not state their criteria because from their perspective, the criteria go without saying. The fact that Trilling is not liked at all, whereas James is not liked "so much," might be a response to some negative personal associations with Trilling (Lionel *or* Diana), or some (milder) negative formative experiences with the work of Henry James; but more importantly, such judgments of taste are a way of registering something "objective" about the "rules" of the literary field as such that from the position of the bohemian avant-garde artist, any artist (even an artist of the wrong kind) is always (for *some* reason) going to be found preferable to a critic (academic critics in particular being those who attempt to reinscribe the avant-garde artist in terms palatable to bourgeois readers); while it also goes without saying that an artist of the right sort would be liked above all.

Once we begin thinking about O'Hara in the context of a "rigorous science of cultural works" (Bourdieu, "Flaubert's Point of View," 539), what initially appeared to O'Hara's early readers as a problem about O'Hara's work—its tendency to reduce the entire world to a mere record of an artist's actions ("I do this I do that"), a roster of his friendships, or a catalogue of his aesthetic likes and dislikes—becomes something like a scientific virtue. The more "personal" O'Hara becomes—the more enthusiastically he makes manifest his judgments—the more *typical* he appears to be: for in his singular determination to act without reflecting upon anything, his actions are revealed as refractions of the field that determines him.

This way of reading justifies the trope most commonly applied to this poet—that of typicality or "inseparability." Thus when Helen Vendler writes that "Frank O'Hara's charms are inseparable from his overproduction," or Mutlu Konuk Blasing argues that "his aesthetic values are inseparable from his culture's vices,"[23] they are using different (and actually not all that different) vocabularies to note the same thing: that precisely what makes O'Hara appealing is the degree to which we are able to appeal to him to clarify the logic of a cultural condition that we are in fact presumed to share.

On this account, what becomes important about a poem like "The Day Lady Died" is the way it decodes the avant-garde poet's pretentions by recording his *purchases*:

> I walk up the muggy street beginning to sun
> and have a hamburger and a malted and buy
> an ugly NEW WORLD WRITING to see what the poets
> in Ghana are doing these days
>   I go on to the bank
> and Miss Stillwagon (first name Linda I once heard)
> doesn't even look up my balance for once in her life
> and in the GOLDEN GRIFFIN I get a little Verlaine
> for Patsy with drawings by Bonnard although I do
> think of Hesiod, trans. Richmond Lattimore or
> Brendan Behan's new play or *Le Balcon* or *Les Nègres*
> of Genet, but I don't, I stick with Verlaine
> after practically going to sleep with quandariness

Of course, the interest of Bourdieu's argument derives from his premise that the various "fields" that constitute the social world (like the artistic, the scientific, and the economic), while they are complexly related to each other, remain "relatively independent" (541), and appear *entirely* independent to those who participate most fully in them. Thus, while from the perspective of the analyst the expression of literary choice through shopping may reveal that "O'Hara's aesthetic belongs in the larger historical context of the commodification of the avant-garde" (Blasing, *Politics and Form,* 32), from the perspective of the artist, choices made within the field appear to be significant (to induce "quandariness") entirely in virtue of their own values. This, for Bourdieu, is what it means to be a "player" in any particular social "game":

> Every social field, whether the scientific field, the artistic field, bureaucratic field, or the political field, tends to require those entering it to have the relationship to the field that I call *illusio*. They may want to overturn the relations of force within the field, but for that very reason, they grant recognition to the stakes, they are not indifferent. Wanting to undertake a revolution in a field is to accord the essential of what the field tacitly demands, namely that it is important, that the game played is sufficiently important for one to want to undertake a revolution in it.[24]

Bourdieu's concept of *illusio*—or what he also calls *"investment"* ("in the double sense of psychoanalysis and of the economy" [*Practical Reason,* 78])—improves on the crude Marxist reduction of aesthetic (or religious, or scientific, or political) values into economic ones. As Bourdieu would have it, "external factors—economic crises, technological change, political revolutions, or simply the demand of a given group—exercise an effect only through transformations in the structure of the field where these factors obtain"; or, to put it more pithily, "the field *refracts*" ("Flaubert's Point of View," 544). This way of thinking about the socio-logic of literary judgment has the considerable virtue of acknowledging the fact that literary judgment is exercised in a literary way—as a passionate choice of texts, styles, affiliations, heroes and *isms*—and *not* as the expression of a *Weltanschauung* or (still less) an elaborate form of publication credit.

Finally, though, I want to suggest that this way of thinking about O'Hara crucially misses the point about the kind of work that the totalization of "preference" or "judgment" does in his poetry. By totalization, I mean two things. First, preference appears *everywhere* in O'Hara. When, for example, no less august a personage than *the sun* deigns to speak to O'Hara (in "A True Account of Talking to the Sun at Fire Island"), it is precisely and only in order to say:

> Frankly, I wanted to tell you
> I like your poetry. I see a lot
> on my rounds and you're okay.

But I also mean to note that preference applies to *everything*. This is, I take it, the real point of the otherwise irredeemably cruel joke of O'Hara's "misunderstanding" (in "Personal Poem") of what it means to be asked to give money "for terrible diseases." Of course, it is entirely possible to imagine a sociological account of "liking and disliking" extending even to describe this sort of "judgment" as an effect of a shared position in the field; it is another of the great (and sometimes frustrating) strengths of Bourdieu's method that *nothing* escapes the engine of sociological correlation. Thus, we could point to the Pre-Raphaelite Brotherhood (a literary coterie in which O'Hara had a strong interest)[25] as a historical example of a literary school formed precisely on the correlation of aesthetic dispositions with *charitable* dispositions. Similarly, Oscar Wilde's particular instantiation of the "position" of art-for-art's-sake aestheticism is entirely consistent with the *uncharitable* judgments O'Hara makes here—for, as Wilde put it in his preface to *The Picture of Dorian Gray,* "No artist has ethical sympathies. An ethical sympathy in an artist is an unpardonable mannerism of style."[26]

But to identify O'Hara as the simple (or perfect!) embodiment of the logic of his position in the literary field (the postmodern version of the Wildean "aesthete" or the "professional man of taste"), is, we might say, to *miss the joke;* and to miss the joke is to miss precisely why it is serious business. For what O'Hara displays in his totalizations of liking and disliking and in his conflation of different categories of liked and disliked things is his refusal to allow the field to "refract," or even to remain a field. The modality of O'Hara's choosing is not that of disinterest—which Bourdieu in any case reads as a form of "passion," as just another position in the space of possibles (*Practical Reason,* 84). It is, rather, the one affect Bourdieu claims you cannot have within a field or social game and still count as a player in the game: the affect of indifference.[27] By indifference, I do not mean indifference toward suffering; I mean an indifference to confining "literary" judgments to literary objects, combined with a refusal to properly value literary preferences as such with the appropriate degree of "investment":

> But how can you really care if anybody gets it, or gets what it means, or if it improves them. Improves them for what? For death? Why hurry them along? Too many poets act like a middle-aged mother trying to get her kids to eat too much cooked meat, and potatoes with drippings (tears). I don't give a damn whether they eat or not. Forced feeding leads to excessive thinness (effete). Nobody should experience anything they don't need to, if they don't need poetry bully for them.[28]

The central action of "Personal Poem" is not the correlation of literary preferences, which is premised on making distinctions in a literary way, but rather the act of *having* preferences of whatever kind. It is one thing not to see the difference between a charitable transaction and a bacteriological infection because of the way in which one's position in the field expresses itself as a *habitus*—a set of embodied dispositions to see certain things and not others, to do this but not that. It is quite another thing to perform acts of judgment "indifferently" in order to dramatize or hypothesize the possibility of using a single scale to determine whether one values something, regardless of what sort of thing it is. What matters on this account is *not* that one likes Melville *more* than one likes James, or that one likes Don Allen a great deal and Lionel Trilling not at all, but rather that the various things that one values—whether they are literary critics, authors of literary works, literary works themselves, or even terrible diseases—are valued in the same way.

There is a deep logic behind O'Hara's rewriting the entire world in literary terms while simultaneously professing that nobody needs literature as such. The function of restriction to a single vocabulary—that of "liking and disliking," for example—is not to elevate judgments of taste (which, as every critic of Kant has argued, is a category that may appear to be free, but is actually complexly restricted to some classes and denied to others). It is, rather, to elevate valuing as such in order to demonstrate that *that* is an activity that is not bound by particular histories or restricted to particular communities.

Both of these tendencies (the restriction to one vocabulary or scene of value and the totalization of the activity of valuing) are on display in a poem like "Manifesto," a mock statement of purpose for what may or may not have been an actual little magazine, *The Benjamin Franklin Review*:

> Literature will now open its big face
> in the pages of this publication
> and slily, in the spirit of FRANKLIN
> and with the amusement of his policy which
> is foreign, sit on it. The word "savoir" will now
> be translated as "to die." No longer will things
> be said to be "beautiful," "amusing," "passionate,"
> "moving"; the sanction of the gang who appear here,
> the Downtown trapezists, will be indicated by
> the phrase "killingly funny," and greatness,
> whether it be of Michelangelo or of Bebe Daniels,
> will not be surprised by the appellation.
> A blush, as at a secret enthusiasm, will spread
> over the world, the Red World and the White World.

What is "foreign" about the policy of *Franklin* is *not* that it refuses to adopt conventional terms of literary evaluation—that is, after all, what the countercultural little magazine exists to do. Nor is it evidence of a "foreign" sensibility to refuse to distinguish between the artist of the cathedral and the diva of the music hall—even a virtuoso of the literary field like T. S. Eliot had proclaimed that the poet ought to aspire to the condition of the music hall comedian.[29] Rather, what makes the policy of *Franklin* "foreign" is the way in which "killingly funny" is imagined less as an aesthetic criterion particular to a social group, than as a "phrase" that will enable anyone to recognize and embrace greatness. For while the term may initially represent the sanction of a coterie (the bohemian and elevated "Downtown Trapezists"), it ends up being transformed into an affect—a "secret enthusiasm" that is not *so* secret that it fails to be available to the "whole world." The division of the "whole world" into a set of warring worlds—"Red" and "White"—gestures not only at the possibility of division, but at the multiplicity of possible *kinds* of division—ethnic (black and white, native and colonizer); literary (perhaps a reference to Rahv's "redskins" and "palefaces"); ideological (Red vs. American)—without quite referring properly to any of them. For finally, the function of translating the various criteriological demands of a plurality of worlds (or fields) into a single "literary" world is to imagine the replacement of socially divisive distinctions by a universally sharable affect or enthusiasm—a libidinal blush that reconciles the difference between any local colors.

O'Hara's poetry persistently proposes subjective-seeming categories of "aesthetic" evaluation as though they were the be-all and end-all of evaluation. In the poem "Having a Coke with You," for example, the titular action

> Is even more fun than going to San Sebastian, Irún, Hendaye
> Biarritz, Bayonne
> Or being sick to my stomach on the Traversa de Gracia in
> Barcelona
> Partly because in your orange shirt you looked like a better
> happier St. Sebastian
> Partly because of my love for you, partly because of your love
> for yoghurt
> Partly because of the fluorescent orange tulips around the
> birches
> Partly because of the secrecy our smiles take on before
> people and statuary

In this poem, the judgment that something is "fun" does the same work that the judgment that something was "funny" did in "Manifesto." O'Hara's desire to bring together under one named criterion things that might ordinarily be considered fun (going to San Sebastian, for example, is great fun), and things that are not at all obviously fun (being sick to your stomach, even in Barcelona, seems like no fun at all) is made even more significant by his capacity to imagine any number of utterly heterogeneous qualities contributing to the judgment that something is fun. Thus, resemblance to religious icons, gustatory pleasures, natural beauties, and even personal affections can all be valued in the same way at the same time—though not necessarily to the same degree.

IV. Love

There is no O'Hara concordance. But if there were, it would no doubt reveal that the paradigmatic affective mode of evaluation in O'Hara's poetry is not liking and disliking, or "fun" or "funny"—but rather "love."

By invoking love at this point, I do not mean to induce a solemn hush of assent. Quite the opposite, I mean to point to a set of philosophical problems that arise in thinking about the relationship between emotion and evaluation—problems that "love" raises in particularly striking ways. The effort to understand love as a possible mode of evaluation gives rise to what Ronald de Sousa has called "Alcmene's Problem,"[30] a conundrum named in honor of the faithful wife of Amphitryon (and eventual mother of Hercules), whom Zeus was able to seduce only by taking on the form of her husband. "Alcmene's problem" is a potential *problem* for judgment because it poses the question of *what* we love when we love: is it a "bundle of qualities" that could be possessed by various persons or things in varying degrees? Or is it, rather, a nonexchangeable ("nonfungible" [98]) individual? If the former, there seems to be no *logical* reason for our commonsense judgment that Alcmene has done something wrong in sleeping with Zeus in the guise of her husband—for (we presume for the sake of argument) Zeus, as a god, has it within his power to assume every single one of the qualities that Alcmene loves about Amphitryon, and to possess them in the same way and to the same degree that Amphitryon possesses them.

If, on the other hand, the latter case is true—if Alcmene's love is directed at an individual (Amphitryon) *independent of any qualities that he possesses*—then our commonsense intuitions about love might be confirmed, but only at the cost of making love appear to be a deeply irrational and indeed arbitrary fixation upon an individual—an attachment for which Alcmene could, if asked, supply no reason at all.

De Sousa purports to solve Alcmene's problem by giving a "natural metaphysics" of emotion, describing love's intentional structure in such a way that it can in fact be understood as an attachment to qualities, but only as qualities are instantiated in particular individuals. De Sousa posits a developmental narrative of the moral subject that turns an initial state of undifferentiated receptivity into nonfungible attachments to individual embodiments of qualities. Thus, according to the natural metaphysics of emotion,

> our attachments are to particulars, and if there are no particulars, or if we have the wrong one, then something has gone wrong with the ontological correlate of our emotion. The psychological answer, in brief, is that we are so wired as to acquire attachments in the course of our causal interaction with such individuals as are posited in our metaphysics. (134)

According to this reasoning, the accounts of the rationality of O'Hara's preferences given by Wolf or Lehman, while perhaps not precisely the right accounts, are nonetheless accounts of the right kind. For insofar as we are involved in the attempt to track down the "causal interactions" that lead O'Hara to form the particular attachments that he has, we are in the business of giving reason to his preferences by giving them biographies.

Bourdieu makes a similar argument with respect to his account of libido; but in place of a biographical narrative, he demands a sociological one:

> One of the tasks of sociology is to determine how the social world constitutes the biological libido, an undifferentiated impulse, as a specific social libido.

There are in effect as many kinds of libido as there are fields: the work of social-ization of the libido is precisely what transforms impulses into specific interests. (*Practical Reason*, 79)

The account of "love" that opposes this one is Plato's. As put forward in Diotima's speech in the *Symposium,* Plato's argument is that love can be made a tool of an objective ethical science (rather than a narrative account of subjective reasoning), because it can (with some effort on the part of the philosophical pedagogue) be made to serve as an assessment of the degree to which all things possess a sin-gle kind of value—that which goes by the name of the *kalon* (a complex term that unites the notions of beauty and value in one package).[31] In Plato's account the developmental narrative runs in precisely the opposite direction than the one that De Sousa describes. Diotima admits that the lover (her paradigm, too, of the person engaged in judgment by emotion) begins by valuing the *kalon* of a single body, but

Then he must see that the *kalon* in any one body is related to the *kalon* in an-other body; and that if he must pursue the *kalon* of form, it is great mindless-ness not to consider the *kalon* of all bodies to be one and the same.

As Martha Nussbaum argues, the logic of this commitment to a single value term is inexorable, and drives its holder to the extreme limit of commensuration: "we must see the beauty or value of bodies, souls, laws, institutions, and sci-ences as *all* qualitatively homogeneous and intersubstitutable, differing only in quantity" (115).

O'Hara's poetry is torn between these two conceptions of love—love as funda-mentally bound to individuals on the basis of his own experiences, and love as the universalization of a single valued quality that holds its value independent of any experience. In his "Ode: Salute to the French Negro Poets," for example, O'Hara laments living in "the terrible western world" where "one's specific love's traduced by shame for what you love more generally" (305), while in a poem like "Medita-tions in an Emergency," he associates a love that makes distinctions (as between the shaven and the unshaven) with the invidious and death-dealing form of libidi-nal limitation he calls "heterosexuality":

Now there is only one man I love to kiss when he is unshaven. Heterosexuality! you are inexorably approaching. (How dis-courage her?)

What O'Hara means to accomplish by totalizing the "literary world"—by rewriting love as "literary"—is to discover a form of commensuration that can universalize the work of valuing without universalizing the demand to value a particular quality. Note, for example, the multiple terms in which O'Hara celebrates love ("the pecu-liar decision to get married") In "Poem Read at Joan Mitchell's":

It's so
Original, hydrogenic, anthropomorphic, fiscal, post-
    anti-aesthetic, bland, unpicturesque and
    WilliamCarlosWilliamsian!
it's definitely not 19th Century, it's not even
    Partisan Review, it's new, it must be vanguard!

The genre being parodied here is the epithalamium, and it is chosen for a particular purpose. In epithalamium, as in Spenser's great example of the genre, the
poem serves to summon representatives of all of the valuing institutions that structure the social world (divine angels, royal handmaidens, merchants' daughters,
etc.), so that they can bear witness and give sanction to the love being celebrated.
In O'Hara's version of epithalamium, all these value terms are also drawn from a
single "institution"—an aesthetic institution. But the difference between the art
world as defined by O'Hara and the cosmos as defined by Spenser is a difference
of boundary or limit. Some of O'Hara's terms are drawn from the actual literary or
artistic discourse of the moment ("original," "post-anti-aesthetic," "WilliamCarlos-
Williamsian"), but some of them merely parody that discourse while at the same
time breaking it open to admit heterogeneous or even inimical terms ("hydrogenic," "fiscal"). O'Hara's point is twofold: first, that judgments of "taste" are not
necessarily, or even primarily, aesthetic judgments; but second, that judgments of
"love," though they posit our common participation in a single world in which valuing is absolutely essential, do not restrict us to positing a single *value* (like the
aesthetic, or like *kalon)* that can actually be instantiated in all things. For O'Hara, a
community is not a place where everyone who is the same values the same things,
but where everyone is the same insofar as they have made the commitment to
find value.

I can't believe there's not
another world where we will sit
and read new poems to each other
high on a mountain in the wind.
You can be Tu Fu, I'll be Po Chü-I
and the Monkey Lady'll be in the moon,
smiling at our ill-fitting heads
as we watch snow settle on a twig.
Or shall we really be gone? This
is not the grass I saw in my youth!
and if the moon, when it rises
tonight, is empty—a bad sign,
meaning "You go, like the blossoms."

O'Hara's absolute refusal to believe that an afterlife could look any different than the life he actually leads—a life that consists of poetic exchange with friends—is not, as Helen Vendler declares, a "prescinding from the metaphysical" (*To Be True to a City,* 235); it is the form the poet's metaphysics takes. The complex and many-layered imagination of sociability in "To John Ashbery" is dependent on the collapse of all scenes of valuing—past and present, real and imagined, national and international—into a single reimagined world. What initially appears in the poem as a sort of historical mistake (Tu Fu and Po Chü-I provide poor models for mutual valuing in that they never exchanged poems with each other, the former having died two years before the latter was born), or else as evidence of a sort of pedagogical determinism (the only "mountain" on which these poets can exist side by side is "The Jade Mountain"—the anthology in which O'Hara most likely encountered them in the first place[32]), is revealed instead as O'Hara's effort to depict a world in which value is universal; not a world in which there is no difference between loving persons and loving poems, but in which the world recast as "literary history" universalizes the opportunity to exercise the capacity to value.

In his recent book on O'Hara as a coterie writer, Lytle Shaw describes *coterie* as "a figure, an idea, a mode of thinking, rather than a binding imperative governing our relation to a real historical context."[33] On his account, coterie has to do with "an idea about how the engines of literary history might be confused into inclusions through the guerilla use of proper names," and so reflects a "meta-communal concern" in which literary history is used to promote alternative models of kinship (10, 11). While I agree that O'Hara's emphasis on what might be called coterie—what I more expansively have termed "the literary world"—is a "meta-communal" discourse, I suggest that the target of that discourse is precisely not the literary dynamic of canonization. Rather, O'Hara's adoption of a literary vocabulary is the means by which he accomplishes his refusal to accept "merely" literary forms of distinction and valuing. This is why, in "Personal Poem," "we don't even want to be in the poets' Walk in San Francisco." It is a sign of participation in O'Hara's peculiar understanding of the literary world that one refuses such canonizing forms of literary distinction (the poets' walk) in favor of commensurable measure. But not a *single* commensurable measure. The reason why "we just want to be rich" is not because money is being made the measure of all things, but rather (and for once) money merely symbolizes the possibility of a like measure of all things. But in this poem, so does wearing a silver construction worker's hat. Both are emblematic of what O'Hara called "the shining thing": the perceptibility (or susceptibility to value and to be valued) that both being "rich" and being "silver" confer.

O'Hara's form of love—love of the medium in which the act of valuing takes place—is his effort to respect both particularity *and* abstraction that inhere in emotional judgments. Thus O'Hara's poetry forcefully acknowledges the need to make distinctions in a "crisis": "In times of crisis, we must all decide again and again whom we love." But time and time again, what O'Hara "chooses" to love is precisely something that by its very nature defeats the logic of singular choice.

This explains too his identification of poetry with another "medium"—that of film. In his poem "To the Film Industry in Crisis," O'Hara's ecstatic catalogue of the qualities of the cinematic medium—"glorious Silver Screen, tragic Technicolor, amorous Cinemascope / stretching Vistavision and startling Stereophonic Sound," whose capacity to encompass the whole palette of experience reaches "heavenly dimensions and reverberations"—lists precisely the expansive properties that seem capable of defeating *merely* literary distinctions. Indeed, the poem begins by rejecting such distinctions as unacceptably allied with the scarcity of value:

> Not you, lean quarterlies and swarthy periodicals
> with your studious incursions toward the pomposity of ants,
> nor you, experimental theater in which Emotive Fruition
> is wedding Poetic Insight perpetually, nor you
> promenading Grand Opera, obvious as an ear (though you
> are close to my heart), but you, Motion Picture Industry,
> it's you I love!

Film (and a poetry reconceived on its example) enables a seemingly endless procession of actors and actresses to appear, and who, because they *can* appear, are all equally worthy of notice. Thus, not only can O'Hara both state the need to acknowledge the multiplicity of "the Tarzans, each and every one of you"; he can at the same time fail to translate that noting of distinction into a difference in valuation ("I cannot bring myself to prefer Johnny Weissmuller to Lex Barker, I cannot!"). The medium of film, which is not "lean" like that of the periodical, but "stretching" and accommodating like Vistavision, is not susceptible to the impoverished forms of criteriological measure applied to so-called high art like "emotive fruition" or "insight." And while O'Hara recognizes that "the heavens operate on a star system," he also argues that it is the nature of such a divine medium that the capacity to appear is sufficient to confer value, if not always to the same degree. Credit is rendered in the one standard he recognizes—love—which is equally granted (though not, again, granted equally) to the brightest stars *and* the most ephemeral:

> Elizabeth Taylor blossoming, yes to you
>
> and to all you others, the great, the near-great, the featured,
>   the extras
> Who pass quickly and return in dreams saying your one or
>   two lines,
> my love!

V. Personism

At last we are in a position to say why the "Personism" manifesto is in a position, as the "New York School of Poets" asserted, to speak for everyone without necessarily requiring everyone to commit to some set of stylistic or ideological entailments.

"Personism: A Manifesto" is most often read as though it advocated treating poetry as a form of interpersonal conversation, a reading that is buttressed by O'Hara's own decision to locate the origin of the movement in and as an anecdote:

> It was founded by me after lunch with LeRoi Jones on August 27, 1959, a day in which I was in love with someone (not Roi, by the way, a blond). I went back to work and wrote a poem for this person. While I was writing it, I was realizing that if I wanted to I could use the telephone instead of writing the poem and so Personism was born. It's a very exciting movement which will undoubtedly have lots of adherents. It puts the poem squarely between the poet and the person, Lucky Pierre style, and the poem is correspondingly gratified. The poem is at last between two persons instead of two pages. (499)

But even the slightest doubt about this orthodox interpretation ought to call our attention to the oddity of the fact that the realization that the poet could simply call his beloved on the telephone does not lead him *in fact* to call his beloved on the telephone. Not to notice that "the poem" as defined by "Personism" is in fact a rejection of communication (rather than the literary emulation of it) is also to miss the fact that O'Hara's announced topic in "Personism" is not in fact particularity but rather abstraction. It is worth quoting at some length what comes before these lines:

> Abstraction in poetry, which Allen [Ginsberg] recently commented on in *It Is,* is intriguing. I think it appears mostly in the minute particulars where decision is necessary. Abstraction (in poetry not in painting) involves personal removal by the poet. For instance, the decision involved in the choice between "the nostalgia *of* the infinite" and "the nostalgia *for* the infinite" defines an attitude towards degree of abstraction. The nostalgia *of* the infinite representing the greater degree of abstraction, removal, and negative capability (as in Keats and Mallarmé). Personism, a movement which I recently founded and which nobody knows about, interests me a great deal, being so totally opposed to this kind of abstract removal that it is verging on a true abstraction for the first time, really, in the history of poetry. . . . Personism has nothing to do with philosophy, it's all art. It does not have to do with personality or intimacy, far from it! (449)

Returned to the context of what O'Hara actually wrote, it seems clearer that the "anecdotal moment" at which it occurs to O'Hara that he might call the man he loves on the telephone and does not do so—that is, he continues to write the poem—is the moment at which we must ourselves reject the account of O'Hara's poetry as fundamentally "personal" in the sense of being a communicative act directed at a single loved person, and re-open the question of what it means to locate a poem *between* persons, or what it means to evoke what O'Hara calls "overtones of love without destroying love's life-giving vulgarity . . . sustaining the poet's feelings toward the poem while preventing love from distracting him into feeling about the person" (499).

When we reach the final lines of "Personal Poem" (which is, after all, the poem that "Personism" was composed to explain),

> and buy a strap for my wristwatch and go
> back to work happy at the thought possibly so

it is with the sense that O'Hara's happiness and conviction that even one person in "the 8,000,000" might be thinking of him cannot be adduced from the actions he has just performed (bidding farewell to a fellow poet, purchasing a band for his wristwatch). These are actions that *place* him, distinguish him, mark him as a player in the various social games that specify their own forms of distinct valuation. What O'Hara is interested in is the fact that his capacity for making choices and for choosing actions are evidence that he is also susceptible to being perceived and chosen.

The poem's "happy" conclusion snaps shut on a couplet—it is the only rhyme in the poem. But this "possibly so" is a non-closural closure. Even as it secures the formal actuality of the work, it announces as happiness the formal dependence of the actual upon the possible. In this instance what closure announces is not the completion of a thought, but the thought that O'Hara is *thinkable*. O'Hara is in a poem because he *can* appear—as a particular, prior to the attribution of qualities— and thus he is susceptible to valuing, whether or not such valuing, such love, such a poem, should actually come to pass. "Possibly so." And such possibility is the happiness that O'Hara's poetry names.

CHAPTER FOUR

Language Poetry and Collective Life

Oh for just one more decisive conference
concerning the abolishment of all conferences!

BOB PERELMAN'S 1996 *The Marginalization of Poetry*[1] ends its scholarly and autobiographical account of the recent American poetic avant-garde with an allegorical fantasy. Before Perelman's dreaming eyes, Frank O'Hara—discerning lover of the world, aficionado of the mess of experience—and Roland Barthes—passionate reader of the world, systematizer of the codes of experience—meet for the first time in death as they did not in life. Appearing in an ersatz heaven crowned with haloes and wreathed in fog-machine smoke, the two trade barbs and witticisms, quote poems and texts back and forth. As they speak, it gradually becomes apparent that they are not just fictions but symbols. Perelman's O'Hara is a knowing naïf who strove (ultimately in vain) to write of a pleasure in life that defeats reflection: "I was happy and I wrote. I stopped, you know" (164). His Barthes is a passionate intellectual, denied happiness in life by the rigor and comprehensiveness of his own thinking: "Imagine reading where you know the sense *perfectly*, yet you couldn't touch the world" (165). Regarding his own inventions with a critical eye, the poet-intellectual rebukes them both for the "impasses" that they reached as writers mistakenly devoted to but one of the Yeatsian antinomies of life or work. "Contemporary cultural information has to be *challenged*," Perelman declares, "just reading it or celebrating one's navigation among its shoals won't do" (164).

Increasingly aware of their present existence as mere props in a project of literary-historical explanation and artistic self-justification, the poet and critic assume the poet-critic's mandate of challenge, turning upon their maker and wryly ironizing their own function even as they act it out. "He wants to conjure up the birth of language writing from personism and the heroic decodings of taste," O'Hara declares, "God knows why" (165).

In this chapter, I assay an answer to this question, and an account of the logic behind Perelman's dream—his wish to produce a poetry that *will* "do" out of an uneasy marriage of O'Hara's worldliness and nervy freedom from forms and Barthes's semiotic and taxonomic rigor. My broader goal is to provide an analytic, rather than descriptive or autobiographical, reading of the movement Perelman represents: the phenomenon more commonly known as "Language poetry."[2]

By calling my argument "analytic," I mean first of all to distinguish it from *critique*.[3] Language poetry was conceived as a response to two roughly contemporaneous if incommensurable developments—the American government's involvement in the Vietnam War and the American university's enthusiastic reception of continental literary theory—but its practitioners remain active and visible well after the end of the former and the institutional domestication of the latter. Having survived the historical situation it originally addressed and transcended the most explicit reference to the intellectual framework that underwrites its practice, Language writing promises to outlive as well the institutional ethos (that of the "voice centered" poetry writing workshop) whose dominance initially justified the movement's sense of itself as embattled from the very moment of inception. There may be newer claimants to the mantle of the poetic avant-garde; but the stylistic practices bequeathed by Language poetry remain central to ambitious American poetry in the present, whether that inheritance is regarded with reverence or ambivalence. In such a changed literary scene, critique seems not only too late (Language poetry having already triumphed over its detractors) but also beside the point. The ever-widening reach of a Language-informed poetics, and the energy with which it has charged the scene of contemporary poetry, suggests that the mere critique of Language poetry as historically belated or theoretically benighted must be missing something important about the work.

Nor, however, should analysis be thought synonymous with *defense*. For while the account I will give of Language poetry does provide what I take to be a compelling rationale for its modes, forms, and attitudes, it nonetheless should not count as an explication or endorsement of the Language poets' own sense of their enterprise. Because I believe that Language poets have tended to resist or even to misdescribe some of the most serious and interesting implications of their own practice, I am under no illusion that the account I am about to offer will be appealing to them (or even that they will agree that it is their practice that I describe).

Language poets have made dramatic claims for the "challenge" that Language poetry presents to contemporary culture, arguing for the contribution "oppositional" poetry makes to the reader's freedom and to social justice. At the same time, Language poetry has understood itself to be *itself* something like a culture—a "provisional institution" that grounds "an alternative system of valuation."[4] In reality, of course, the actual social arrangements that make up the ensemble of practices called Language poetry are more normative than alternative. It is not only that Language poetry survives most fully in the academy; it is that avant-garde poetic movements are in practice hardly distinguishable, in their affections, affiliations, infighting, gossip, and institutional dynamics, from past literary movements—or social life altogether. I will suggest that this disparity between theory and practice—between imagined and actual forms of collectivity—arises from precisely the pair of contradictory commitments that Perelman's story allegorizes: a commitment to a radical concept of freedom on the one hand and to a repressive hypothesis of cultural determinism on the other. The theoretical assumptions that ground Language poets' totalizing analyses of subject formation and of institutional power make their desire for freedom incoherent, leaving Language poetry at a familiar theoretical impasse which it has noted, but to which it has not adequately responded.[5]

The affirmative analysis I offer is, I should say up front, only implicit in the present form of the practice of Language poetry. But it is deeply implicit: so much so that I will immodestly argue that it may be said to constitute the group's *functional* motive. What it lacks in the assent of the poets concerned, it makes up for by dealing with their poems in the forms in which they really exist, rather than in forms that might be wished for. A responsible description of Language poetry, however respectful of experimentation and formal inventiveness, can ignore only at the price of its persuasiveness to all but the converted what I take to be an objective and, indeed, deliberated feature of the work: the overall thinness or insubstantiality of the poems Language poets have made. One might call this quality their an-aesthetic:

Not this.
What then?
I started over & over. Not this.
Last week I wrote "the muscles in my palm so sore from halving the rump roast I cld barely grip the pen." What then?
This morning my lip is blisterd.
Of about to within which. Again & again I began. The gray light of day fills the yellow room in a way wch is somber.
Not this. Hot grease has spilld on the stove top.
Nor that either. Last week I wrote "the muscle at thumbs root so taut from carving that beef I thought it wld cramp." Not

so. What then? Wld I begin? This morning my lip is tender, disfigurd. I sat in an old chair out behind the anise. I cld have gone about this some other way.[6]

The an-aesthetic of a poem like Ron Silliman's *Tjanting* may not be immediately apparent to someone coming to it for the first time. Certainly it will not be apparent if the reader is engaged or enthralled. But it may be equally inapparent to the reader who is shocked or put off by the poem's lack of emphasis on design appreciation: what Dante Gabriel Rossetti terms "proportion" or what Clement Greenberg calls "rightness of form."[7] What I mean by an-aesthesis is not the same as *ostranenie,* the renovating estrangement Silliman claims as justification for his repetitions and opacities. While seeking to subvert easy pleasures, defamiliarization is nothing if not an aesthetic effect, its goal, as Shklovsky declares, "to increase the difficulty and length of perception because the process of perception is an aesthetic end in itself and must be prolonged." And as is the case with all such prolongations and operations upon perception—with the sunlight striking stars off the bronze head of Liberty, for example—what may dazzle or undeceive the eye is highly dependent upon context and sensibility, subject to chance and change. The jarring startle of the poem's opening negation may be overcome in any number of ways: by education or habituation, by sheer good luck, or by the reader's enthusiasm for engaging with the kinds of questions it raises—questions about the simultaneity of representation and misrepresentation raised by a poem that begins by pointing away from itself: "Not this." Likewise, the disillusion that comes from being denied a sense of what (if any) details are essential to a story ("Nor that either") may be re-illusioned if we come to be absorbed, for whatever reason, in the "story" that unfolds in these nondiscursive rhythms. Estrangement is its own form of enchantment; difficulty can always be reconstituted as a subject matter of potential interest—and of pleasure—if that difficulty is to your taste.

But imagine for a moment that *Tjanting* goes on for more than one hundred pages in the same deliberately hobbled mode (because it does). Imagine, too, that the poem is only a single part of its author's projected life work: one that includes *The Alphabet* and projects a *Universe*; one that explicitly subordinates the unit of the poem to the abstract and unfolding category of "poetry" (because it is).[8] And now imagine that there are thousands upon thousands of other poems by other poets that bear more than a passing resemblance to this poem—not in their precise technique of ongoing, idiosyncratic diction or autobiographical detail, but in paratactic structure, low affect, quizzical tone, and theoretical orientation (because there are). Consider them together as a whole, as "Language poetry": a vast, overwhelming corpus whose internal logic (like that of *Tjanting* itself, structured after the Fibonacci sequence) is the open-ended algorithm of addition. Soon, the rising tally of similarities and texts places impossible demands on our capacity and will to attend to the manifest differences between one poem and another, to articulate the fine distinctions of tone or affect; until the effort to immerse oneself in Language poetry produces the sensation that language as Language poetry imagines and manifests it has neither affect nor tone, and that poetry as Language poetry imagines and manifests it demands neither articulation nor, precisely, attention. Imagine language, in effect, without a speaker. I will suggest that under these conditions, indifference and inattention to the specifics of what is being said is not only a plausible response; it is the strong response that such writing demands. Our indifference to "actually existing" Language poems, in other words, is not a form of contempt, but a recognition that these poems do not mean to be well understood, do not ask to be revisited with devoted care, do not even seek to be finely perceived. In the most general terms, they do not seek to become available for judgments of taste. And I will suggest it is in this indifference as well that we register a significant sense in which Language poetry is experimental, and a compelling sense in which Language poetry might be said to be social.

Language poets are *experimental*, that is, because they treat their poems neither as semantic tokens nor as aesthetic objects but as experiments or examples. And it is the curious nature of both experiment and example that while there must be enough of them to warrant an inference, in none of them is it self-evident just what is being demonstrated or exemplified. Language poems are *social* in that what they take poems to be examples of is the unique capacity to produce language altogether, and thus to announce—as nothing else at the present moment seems to be able to do with the same persuasiveness—the existence of something fundamentally human on which the very possibility of social life can be predicated. Language poetry considered under this description is not, strictly speaking, a literary practice, for it does not produce objects that belong to *any* category of language use, let alone a literary one. Nor is it, properly speaking, an aesthetic practice, for it is not oriented toward *aesthesis,* or perception, at all—never mind the refined or shattering perceptions traditionally associated with an aesthetic sensibility. It is, rather, an ontological and ethical practice. Language poets produce poetry that is precisely equivalent to language, where language is considered as a kind of creatural knowledge or potential; therefore Language poets tend to treat the objects of their art—poems—as epiphenomenal evidence of a constitutively human capacity for free and creative agency that is the real object of their interest.

In this very particular sense—and despite its avowed interest in what Charles Bernstein (perhaps the movement's best known theorist and practitioner) calls "the local, the particular, the partisan, the committed, the tiny, the peripheral, the unpopular, the eccentric, the difficult, the complex, the homely" ("Provisional Institutions," 143)—Language poetry does in fact succeed in being universal, general, uncommitted, vast, central, and, at the very least, quite moving in its intention, if not precisely beautiful in its actualization. The question Language poetry poses to American poetry is not a classifying question—What do you call a group of poets?—but a philosophical question: How do you recognize a group of persons?

I. Leningrad

In August of 1989, four American Language poets traveled to the then-Soviet city of Leningrad at the invitation of Poetic Function, a circle of experimental Russian poets. This gathering took place at a particularly dramatic historical moment, as Silliman, one of those American visitors, notes retrospectively, falling "during that brief window in world history between the Tiananmen Square massacre in Beijing and the fall of the Berlin Wall and the Eastern bloc."[9] The "window" Silliman imagines here is a window of opportunity that history would soon close to the imagination. For while the long-term significance of the revolutions of 1989 for "world history" certainly has yet to be determined, these events have been widely received as history's judgment on the legitimate forms human social life could take.

The most notorious theorization of this judgment is Francis Fukayama's essay for *The National Interest,* "The End of History?" which argues that the breakup of the Soviet Union must be read as a revelation that "the end point of mankind's ideological evolution" had been reached, and that liberal democracy characterized by free market capitalism constitute the triumphal *telos* of all social striving.[10] While many of Fukayama's liberal critics have distanced themselves from some of his more conservative political and economic conclusions, the events of 1989 did solidify an evolving consensus in liberal moral psychology: the disappearance of historical communism seemed to affirm that no political system that failed to place primary value on the individual's self-esteem could be legitimate and that no political system could properly value self-esteem that was founded on the strong idea of a community. To affirm a community is to affirm an ideology in the invidious or totalizing sense; or, as John Rawls renders the verdict in *Political Liberalism:* "the hope of a political community must be abandoned, if by such a community we mean a political society united in affirming the same comprehensive doctrine."[11]

The end of history has posed a challenge to the political left—it has been addressed in various well-documented ways by communitarians and post-Marxists. But the "brief window" between the loss of a particular socialist future and the end of history altogether posed a challenge of a different kind to the imagination of the American *poetic* left, a challenge received by the visiting writers as a commission. At this precise moment—call it the beginning of the end of history—Russian and American avant-garde poets met for the First International Summer School, as if to pass judgment on the representational structure of the present and to propose a new dispensation for the future. The proposed themes of the conference—"Language—Consciousness—Society"—suggest, by their particular enumeration and ordering of the important "problems of contemporary culture" (*Leningrad,* 1), that the reconstitution of "society" was a task not for politics but for poetics, for representers from cultural capitals like Berkeley or Leningrad rather than for representatives who might convene in Washington or Moscow. When, four months later, Timothy Garton Ash and Václav Havel met in the Prague theater called The Magic Lantern, the product of that meeting would be a democratic government;[12] the product of the meetings in the basement of the Leningrad Composers Union was the American visitors' collaborative poem called *Leningrad* (1991).

The presence of *American Writers in the Soviet Union* (as *Leningrad* is subtitled) represents the fulfillment of a long-standing fantasy in the self-understanding of Language poetry. Though literary critics have often responded to Language poetry as if it were a theoretical argument about language only incidentally *illustrated* by poems, Language poetry has, since its inception in 1971, devoted a significant portion of its energies to the construction of an "alternative" literary culture, founding little magazines such as *This, Hills, o-blek, Temblor, L=A=N=G=U=A=G=E, Poetics Journal,* and *Aerial,* small presses such as Roof, Potes and Poets, O Books, The Figures, Tuumba, and Sun and Moon, and an endless number of mimeos, broadsheets, newsletters, reading series, collaborations, and, of course, conferences. The authors of *Leningrad*—Michael Davidson, Lyn Hejinian, Ron Silliman, and Barrett Watten—represent this collaborative imperative in microcosm: Watten is a cofounder with Robert Grenier of *This* magazine, arguably the first journal of the Language poetry movement, and was the coeditor, with Lyn Hejinian, of *Poetics Journal,* which encouraged the movement's expansion on an international scale; Watten, Davidson, and Silliman are cultural historians of the movement as well as theorists within it; and between the four of them they have published nearly sixty books of poems.

These general remarks about the variety and industry of Language poets' activities cannot hope to stand in for a substantive analysis of the contemporary world of (very) little magazines and small press publishing.[13] The point of this too brief overview is less to provide a thoroughgoing literary anthropology of Language poetry than to suggest that Language poets imagine their literary culture as the kind of thing that anthropologists would be interested in. That is, Language poets regularly represent Language poetry as more than just the sum of its practitioners, poems, institutions, and theories. As Watten suggests, "a community of writers" shares "a collective state of mind" that unites those disparate embodiments.[14] "Imagine that all the nationally circulated magazines and all the trade presses and all the university presses in the United States stopped publishing or reviewing poetry," Charles Bernstein proposes. "New poetry in the United States would hardly feel the blow. But not because contemporary poetry is marginal to the culture. Quite the contrary, it is these publishing institutions that have made themselves marginal to our cultural life in poetry" ("Provisional Institutions," 133). Bernstein is proposing a critique of what he calls "official verse culture"[15]—which he depicts as a sort of conspiracy between the *New Yorker*, the Iowa Writers Workshop, and the literary academy—in the name of a set of "unofficial" publications and institutions. But while the rhetoric of his analysis initially divides "official" from "unofficial," it does so in the interest of conceptually conflating "verse" and "culture." It is just such an anthropological motive that underwrites Language poetry's peculiar forms of self-presentation and preservation—its tendency to publish not just its poems, but its conversations about poems, and not just those conversations, but jokes amidst the conversations, laughter at the jokes, stumbles, interruptions, and silences—as though on behalf of some future civilization studying its own past. Most recently, this retrospective documentary impulse has given rise to *The Grand Piano*: a ten-volume "Collective Autobiography" filled with reminiscence, meditation, theorization, and sociology written collaboratively by ten writers associated with the Language poetry scene in San Francisco in the 1970s.

This motive toward self-documentation runs deep in the formal mode of authorial self-presentation in *Leningrad;* it explains, for example, the inclusion of photographs in the text of the earlier poem. What is being illustrated by this text is not a theory but a state of mind. Note, for example, the way The First International Summer School is depicted as at once stereotypically cultural and stereotypically countercultural. If the long, well-laid table in the first photograph (figure 4.1) mimics the solemn ceremonies of acknowledgment typical of the official sanctioning institutions that actually made the conference possible (the University of California, the Fund for U.S. Artists at International Festivals and Exhibitions, and the Leningrad branch of the Soviet Cultural Fund), what Davidson primarily wishes to emphasize in his contribution to the introduction to *Leningrad* is "the stuffy, smoke-filled basement of the Composers Union, outside the official conference" (*Leningrad,* 21; figure 4.2). It is this literal and figurative "outside" and beneath that gives the idea of a "Composers Union" its imagined countercultural force: "It is here, in the unofficial convention sponsored by the unofficial writers, that our collaboration truly begins" (*Leningrad*, 21). *This* collaboration is depicted as spontaneous, intense, intimate, and unregulated; untrammeled by the weight of ceremony and the material trappings of authority, possessed only of the energy of cultural renewal.

The attempt to represent "verse culture" as culture itself places a great burden of symbolic significance on the poem. In verse culture, verse is the vehicle for the transmission and reproduction of culture, but verse is also the valued culture that is transmitted. This double burden accounts for the curiously recursive structure of *Leningrad*. As a "narrative" poem, the text *documents* the meeting of Soviet and American poets. It records their conversations and exchanges, their troubled efforts to bridge the gap that separates East and West. But at the formal level, the

Figure 4.1. American writers in the Soviet Union, the "official vision." Michael Davidson et al., *Leningrad*, p. 142. Photo by Viktor Nemkinov.

poem is also highly self-conscious occasion for a meeting of the American poets themselves. *Leningrad* was written using a complex procedure for exchanging and circulating manuscripts in progress, allowing the poets to respond to one another and revise in the light of each other's contributions. If the narrative is a meditation on the difficulty of community, then the form proposes to have overcome that difficulty; the great epiphany in writing *Leningrad* is the poets' realization that there is *no difference* between collaborating on a poem and being a community: "As the poem evolved over several months," Silliman recalls, "we began to realize

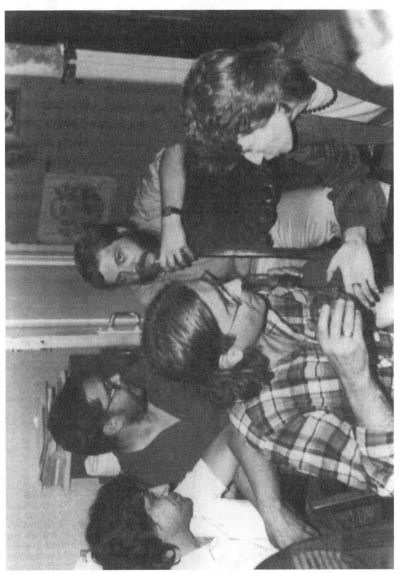

Figure 4.2. American writers in the Soviet Union, the "unofficial vision." Michael Davidson et al., *Leningrad*, p. 112. Photo by Barrett Watten.

Figure 4.3. A. The *Leningrad* icon, "The Five-Year Plan in Four Years." The accompanying text reads in part: "The authors of *Leningrad* have sought to ground the literary movement known as 'language poetry' in a sense of community and to connect it to progressive politics and new social theory. This concern is reflected in the text, in which their four alternating voices run together, collectively forming these essays. B. The authors may be distinguished only by the icons used as a visual key to identify them: a formal element of the text as poem" (Davidson et al., *Leningrad*, p. i). All images from *Leningrad* appear by permission of the authors.

how we had unconsciously replicated the constant passing around of manuscripts which for decades had been the necessary mode of distribution for all but a few Soviet poets."[16] The passing resemblance of these ad hoc generative procedures to the practice of *samizdat* publication is represented as an identity. What initially appears to be a mode of distribution made necessary by the state's censorship of particular ideas and interests is revealed instead to be a *form of life,* a social form reproduced "unconsciously" by poets in California, the spontaneous expression of a verse culture that identifies equally the poets of any nation.

This identification is sealed by a strange sign (figure 4.3). *Leningrad* is constructed in cycles of prose paragraphs, four to a section—one by each of the

Figure 4.3. (*Continued*)

poets. Each poet's contribution is marked, not by a name, but by one quarter of a glyph inspired by a 1930s Soviet textile pattern—a marker that the authors of *Leningrad* term "A formal element of the text as poem" (*Leningrad,* i; see figure 4.4).

Indeed, this image—and its fragmentary iteration—might be said to be the *only* formal element of the text as poem, if only in the sense that it is the only element of the poem that purports to perform the traditional poetic function of formal integration. This integration is symbolic in the most orthodox sense—nature harmoniously reconciled with industry as part of a single design, just as earthly human striving is, in the words of T. S. Eliot, "reconciled amongst the stars." In one fell imagistic swoop, the glyph identifies what would otherwise appear to be scattered fragments as one single poem; it unifies four individual poets into one collective authorial entity; and finally, its very motif signifies the unification of two nations into one verse culture endowed with an almost magical capacity for productivity: the image, after all, is entitled "The five-year plan in four years" (*Leningrad,* i).

When I saw, on the wall of their bathroom, two toilet-paper holders, each full, my first thought was "These people are flaunting it"—later, realizing that this was a communal flat, I understood that each family had its own roll, and wondered if they cheated and stole from one another. My identity is ascertained by a photograph in a small blue book. Brigada S used to be Brigada SS. The gold in your smile shines. Who I am is this pain in my chest, ungratified desire to weep. "No more surprises!" The cab driver (not a cab driver) suddenly lurches his vehicle forward down the unpaved, rubble-strewn street— he wants to buy our dollars, sell us cameras, film, do anything. Arkadii says of another, "He's a Soviet yuppie." Just ten weeks later, the ruble has been devalued by 90 percent. Here, take my insect repellent, please. A trio of giant cockroaches construct an anthology. "I was at Woodstock—they treat me as a goddess."

101

ЛЕНИНГРАД

I too am split—between a temporal sequence (involving events received retrospectively and witnessed as if by a tourist looking at a diorama through glass) and a spatial field in which events seem to repeat themselves like so many columns in one of Rastrelli's colon-

Opposite page: Aleksei Adashevsky and, just behind him, Dmitrii Spivak, Leningrad linguist specializing in the linguistics of altered states.

Figure 4.4. A page of *Leningrad*, exemplifying the way in which symbols designate a particular poet's section. In this case the poets are Silliman (factory) and Davidson (stars).

Given the burden of reconciliation and unification that is placed upon the poem by what ought to be considered an *image* of a poem, it is not altogether surprising that in the text of the poem, "actual" poems of the textual kind seem to appear only with great difficulty. One episode from the poem will suffice to demonstrate this. Standing in a street outside the "Composers Union," one of the Moscow poets, Dmitrii Prigov, hands one of the Americans, Michael Davidson, two "signs"— what Davidson calls "signs of community, in many cases, among total strangers." The first is a business card reading "Dmitrii Prigov, Poet, Artist." The second, offered as if in the hope of confirming the first, is a poem; or to be more precise, a poem that has been shredded into confetti and stapled into small packages the poet calls "Coffins" (*Leningrad*, 45–46).

Hejinian later interprets Prigov's gesture: "The question is who tore the poems, and that is a question of context. If the state tore up the poems, the cultural context is one in which poetry represents a challenge and a conflicting picture of power. If the people tore the poems, the cultural context has turned poetry into litter" (*Leningrad*, 46). Hejinian's interpretation reads like a history of Language poetry: not only of the forms it takes—Language poetry's notorious penchant for fragmented and otherwise destroyed texts—but also its contradictory analysis of its social situation. By making the interpretive question (what the torn poems mean) depend on context (rather than, for example, asking the poet what he intended by the gesture), Hejinian leaves the existence of the poem unexplained—an omission that makes writing into a pathos-laden mystery, a form of agency that comes prior to official judgment or mass refusal. This agency is all the more pure because its consequences are never quite made manifest. This notion of a poetic agency whose significance is intensified by its foreclosure reappears in relation to *Leningrad* itself. When, several years after its publication, Ron Silliman duly revisits the poem in an essay entitled "The Task of the Collaborator" (1995), he performs a remarkable experiment. Using a pair of computer style-checking programs, one called *RightWriter,* the other called *Corporate Voice,* Silliman measures the sentences of the poem against the built-in stylistic norms of the program in order to address the question of, as he puts it (quoting Mayakovsky), "how verses are made," and of what sort of mental action collaboration is.

There are two things to notice about this experiment. The first is that despite its high-tech methods, its mode of inquiry is deeply traditional; in its effort to determine the relation of the poet to culture by measuring the distance between poetic language and "the language of men," it resembles nothing so much as Wordsworth's "experiment" in *Lyrical Ballads.*[17] But where Wordsworth, in his 1800 preface, hoped to secure in advance his audience's goodwill so that they might not rebel at his failure to "gratify certain known habits of association" (155), Language poetry means to *expose* the insidious operation of linguistic habits already in place.

In most ways, of course, Corporate Voice is a less well-equipped reader than Wordsworth. The program (now obsolete) is not really capable of grammatical parsing; it "comprehends" language only in terms of measurable variables like sentence length and syllable count. It has no understanding of word meaning, only an elementary set of rules (verb forms and so on). It has no notion of genre or context, and it has no inkling of pleasure.

For all its obvious shortcomings, there is canny wit to Silliman's method. Corporate Voice may be a less capable reader than Wordsworth, but it is more determined to make distinctions.[18] Originally designed as a tool for assembling and evaluating basal and remedial reading texts, the program uses a mathematical algorithm called the Flesch-Kincaid formula (the same formula used by Microsoft Word's grammar-checking program) to assign any selected text a "readability index" (a numerical value from 10 to 50) that is in turn indexed to grade levels within the public school system (10 is readable by a first-grader, 50 unreadable entirely). But if the primary intention of the style checker is pedagogical, its primary use has been administrative. The Federal Insurance Commission, the IRS, and, perhaps most significantly to Silliman, the Department of Defense all use versions of the same scale to normalize their operations manuals, ensuring ease of comprehension at all levels of the institutional hierarchy, ensuring, for example, that no Department of Defense document will exceed the reading capacities of a fifth-grader. The felicitously named Corporate Voice lends a certain plausibility to the Language poets' association of syntactic innovation with political opposition—an association which usually appears in more epigrammatic form as in Charles Bernstein's slogan "Language control = Thought control = Reality control." The old linguist's joke that "a language is a dialect with an army and a navy" needs to be updated; it also has an educational system, powers of taxation, and a corporate ethos.[19]

Thus, although Silliman had initially claimed that the function of the style checker was merely to generate raw data for stylistic analysis, it appears that not just the form but also the *themes* of that analysis are determined in advance by the tool he uses. Silliman is quite pleased by the (not altogether surprising) fact that Corporate Voice does not know what to make of *Leningrad,* finding it by turns too simple, too difficult, too heterogeneous to target any audience the style checker is programmed to foresee. The program singles out for particular censure the longest sentence in the poem, written by Hejinian:

> The person would reappear, languid—he was said to be an esteemed and assertive mathematician but the problem of being a person seemed to have exhausted him, seated some distance away, whispering with Rosa, but somehow simultaneously he was already outside on the quiet street where a small group of intellectuals hung around gossiping, stooped because of his height, accepting a cigarette—as a theme, troubled—I had been told some months earlier that many people in a Russian audience will not understand the Western notion of subjectivity—which he agreed to translate. (*Leningrad*, 34)

At ninety-three words and several em dashes long, this sentence scores a 40.65 out of 50 on the Flesch-Kincaid scale: "virtual unreadability." For Silliman, however, the sentence is not difficult at all; rather, "Hejinian's sentence is . . . both concise and direct, but to a different standard of perception than the world of reductive surfaces implicit in Strunk and White" ("The Task of the Collaborator," 150). Although Silliman's analysis does not suggest what the sentence means so concisely and directly, his remarks nonetheless do suggest one way to understand how ambitious the consequences of understanding are. Identifying another "standard of perception" with another "world" is a move perhaps most recognizable in literary studies; Stanley Fish, in an oddly parallel "experiment" conducted on his own students and documented in the essay "How to Recognize a Poem When You See One," discovered that different "interpretive communities" have different standards of perception, and that those standards of perception are bound to the institutions that sponsor them.[20] Considered as an internal memo for the Department of Defense, Hejinian's sentence is less than clear; considered as a poem, it calls forth all the interpretive capacities and constraints appropriate for that activity. But the difference is that for Silliman, reading poetry is all capacity and no constraint. This highlights what has always been an ironic fact about poets calling themselves Language poets: they are seriously and programmatically opposed to providing a general account of what a *language* is. In his book *Total Syntax,* for example, Barrett Watten defines syntax as "how . . . the statement of the work is made, both in time and in space. . . . There are no fixed rules for this syntax; 'acceptability of statement' or 'competence in art-language' are time-bound, culturally specific, and a part of the total human situation."[21] What makes "total syntax" total is that it is not essentially linguistic, and it is not essentially linguistic because nothing is *essentially* linguistic.

Thus, if Fish has always been vague about what precisely is required in order to constitute an "interpretive community," the idea of a "total human situation" determining meaning is even less precise. But that lack of precision is salutary. Because all interpretive abilities, aims, and goals by definition belong to what Watten calls "situations," the fact that the Hejinian sentence is readable must count as evidence for the existence and success of another human situation—that of poetic culture as opposed to corporate culture. And it is *only* by leaving the idea of a "situation" unspecified that the failure of Corporate Voice looks like a triumph for the Language poets. Because Corporate Voice cannot read poetry, verse culture can be defined by default as a model for a common world that embodies everything that corporate culture ostensibly opposes: organic community, anarchic creativity, autonomy—what Juliana Spahr has termed "wild reading."[22] The argument is structured like a rhetorical question: Where do you want to direct your efforts— toward the work of cultural reproduction and administration that normative grammar enables you to accomplish? Or *what?* Language poetry offers no alternative, and as a result the idea of the alternative is all that is offered.

If we do follow up on Silliman's claim that the sentence is readable, however, it is difficult to feel that we are sufficiently rewarded for our efforts. For what Hejinian's sentence *says* is that our ability to read it is not any sort of solution at all; rather, it *is* "the problem of being a person." What has "exhausted" the mathematician is not, perhaps surprisingly, the problem of being restricted by a particularly draconian set of cultural conventions supported by institutions (those of life in the Soviet state, for example) but rather the problem of being restricted to social conventions altogether. For if the mathematician seems unusual for being able ("somehow") to occupy more than one place at one time—he is at once "inside" and "outside," at once conversing intimately and gossiping professionally—this is only a literalization of the fact that contexts are all there are to being a person. This is finally the sense of conjoining "assertive" to "esteemed"—for self-assertion is understood only as a function of public evaluation. At this point, it looks as though the ability to pit one context against another (domestic against professional), one kind of communication against another (the urgent and intimate communication of the whisper against professional gossip), or one kind of reading against another (corporate voice against poetic voice) identifies the mathematician as another version of Prigov's "Poet, Artist," written on a business card; his every assertion of poetic identity announces the death of autonomy. Or, as Arkadii Dragomoschenko, another of the Soviet poets, plaintively puts it, "Our independent separate singularity can hardly be spoken of . . . but many people wish it" (*Leningrad,* 34).

Where Silliman initially pits one culture against another—the corporate against the poetic—it now appears that to have a choice between cultures is only to choose a form of subjection. Thus, the fantasy that motivates Language poetry is not the liberal idea of a better situation—a situation with relatively greater autonomy, more freedoms, expanded access to resources for self-definition—but rather a fantasy of no situation. This is why the Hejinian sentence, incapable of eliminating content altogether—there is always some set of conventions that could make sense of a poem, no matter how obscure—makes content seem always to be punitive, as if to demonstrate that your literacy always testifies to your subjugation.

Once again, Bernstein can be relied upon to present the most extreme formulation of this problem. On his account, Language poetry's institutional mandate demands "the formation and reformation, dissolution and questioning, of imaginary or virtual or partial or unavowable communities and/or uncommunities" ("Provisional Institutions," 143).[23] As Benedict Anderson has suggested, "imagined communities" are eminently capable of inculcating real values;[24] the same has perhaps been proved true of "virtual" communities.

Bernstein's resolution on a negation—an "uncommunity"—is the result not of a rich anthropology, but of a theoretical dead end. If there is one thing about which the Language poets seem certain, it is that a meeting of poets, whether at the pastoral First International Summer School or the subterranean Composers Union, must entail the formation of groups organized on some *other* principle, but what that principle is, they cannot say. The poetic effort to construct a nonparodic version of collectivity in the wake of the fall of historical communism—one that would allow full autonomy not only for the poem but for the poet, not only for the poet but for the person—that effort is relegated to fantasy by an inability to imagine that poetry could offer anything other than another set of conventions that come to look oppressive as soon as they are understood to be conventions. Thus, despite their great pains to manifest themselves as a group enterprise, despite the manifest similarity of their texts, Language poets are theory-bound to represent themselves as a group that is not just pluralist but internally differentiated almost to the point of non-existence. Almost, that is, but not quite. For there is at present no claim more characteristic of the uncommunity of Language writing than the claim that Language writing cannot be characterized.[25]

II. Language as Poetry

But if the category of "the person" in Language poetry is, as Hejinian's sentence attests, "as a theme, troubled"—that is, a theme of being troubled, but also troubled because it is only available *as* a theme, as a category structured by conventions—it may be, as a form, redeemed. In the remainder of this chapter, I will argue that Silliman's invocation of the category of "readability" in conjunction with Hejinian's sentence suggests another theory of Language poetry. And as it is also an account that lends a certain limited plausibility to the Language poets' identification of poetry with sociality, and of person with autonomy, I will offer it as something like the deep motive for Language poetry.

Let us, for a moment, take Silliman seriously in his claim that the grammar checker is meant to provide data for a *linguistic* analysis—which involves taking Corporate Voice seriously for a moment, not simply as a sign of the language conspiracy in operation, but as a tool designed to approximate the way readers at various stages of development process sentences. If we do so, the first thing we might note is that the grammar checker's failure is overdetermined. Hejinian's poetic sentence has virtually every one of the superficial aspects that have been empirically shown to make sentences difficult to "use," not just in the context of a Department of Defense manual, but in *any* context. That is, the particular ways in which it is convoluted—repeatedly nesting phrases one inside another, nesting long and complex elements, presenting elements that are not just "embedded" but "self-embedded" (one adversative phrase inside another)—all contribute to the "unacceptability" of the sentence in something like an *absolute* sense.[26] There are, of course, limits to patience, resourcefulness, education, and talent, all of which are contingent on the various situations in which persons find themselves, just as there are limits that context imposes on the acceptability of even quite ordinary language. But there are also limits to the human capacity to process sentences—and these limits are features of *our* mechanism. The foremost theorist of such limits is Noam Chomsky, who has long argued for the crucial distinction between the knowledge of language in the sense of the know-how that allows an individual to speak a *particular* language—national, professional, or private—and the knowledge of language that provides the *a priori* capacity to acquire any language at all. If "language" in the former sense looks something like a habit structure—a complex outgrowth of experience acting on and forming the mind—then "language" in the latter sense is what Chomsky has called *competence:* a system of rules and principles *innate* to the mind that make it possible to acquire linguistic habits in the first place, while at the same time constraining the possible forms languages can take. For Chomsky, only the hypothesis of what he calls a *universal grammar* could explain the remarkable fact that human children are capable of uttering sentences that they have never heard before, as well as the fact that poets can make sentences that have never been said before: "The language provides finite means but infinite possibilities of expression constrained only by rules of concept formation and sentence formation, these being in part particular and idiosyncratic but in part universal, a common human endowment."[27]

In the light of this distinction, Silliman's insistence that Hejinian's sentence, seemingly designed to be "virtually unreadable," *is* readable—that is, *can* be read whether or not it is ever in a situation in which it will be read—looks less like an argument for the existence of a poetic community, and more like an attempt to illustrate the fact that "acceptable" sentences are not the same thing as "grammatical" ones. This seems like an odd point on which to found a poetics, having nothing to do with meaning whatsoever, but only with whether or not the sentence conforms to the abstract rules of an innate mental grammar. Adding to the oddness is the fact that my attribution of this poetic to Silliman—or indeed to any Language poet—is counterintuitive. A rejection of Chomskyan linguistics is something like an obligatory opening gambit in any work of Language poetry theory. Silliman's essay "The New Sentence," for example, begins by citing Chomsky as an example of the way in which the discipline of linguistics has failed to produce an adequate definition of the sentence.[28] Likewise, Watten's "total syntax" is announced to be the opposite of generative grammar—consisting precisely of all the messy instances that Chomsky supposedly sacrifices for the sake of theoretical coherence.[29]

The Chomskyan account is, nonetheless, the *only* account that could make sense of the other claims that Silliman makes about the collaboration. As it turns out, Corporate Voice can do more than read texts against its pernicious built-in norms; it can compare poetic texts to one another. When Silliman, using the style checker, measures each poet's contributions to *Leningrad* against each other poet's, and then each poet's contributions to *Leningrad* against other texts written by the same poet, he discovers that for all their differences in background, experience, and gender, for all their own idiosyncrasies of theme and style, the poets of *Leningrad* write like one another. Indeed, Silliman declares, "a fuller statistical analysis of this work (and probably other collaborations as well) would almost certainly show that poets are more like one another during a collaboration than any one poet is like him- or herself" ("The Task of the Collaborator," 153).[30] Silliman does not specify in what sense poets are "alike" during collaboration; and looking at a passage from Silliman's own part of *Leningrad*, it is difficult to see in what sense they *could* be alike:

Even in the Gardens of Gogol Park the dominant theme was the weeds. One didn't stroll down the Nevsky Prospekt, one jostled. Our plane touched down in Moscow to pick up Ozzy Osbourne and Mötley Crüe. The bathwater filled the tub, as dark as tea. Once she had been a dancer with the Kirov. Instinctively, you squint as you suck on the end of your cigarette, the air of the room blue with toxins. Instantly, without notice, the schedule changed. Nadezhda's "brother" cursed. Mosquitoes rose up out of the cellars at night. Even the person is remont, under reconstruction. (*Leningrad,* 35)

Even without an extensive analysis, we might simply note that while it is easy enough to detect some thematic similarity here, a similar tone of nostalgia and anomie, and even some semantic similarity (In particular, Silliman's last sentence might *mean* the same thing as Hejinian's whole sentence), it is quite difficult to locate any surface *grammatical* regularity. Where Hejinian's sentence is relentlessly hypotactic, Silliman's are equally relentlessly paratactic. If hers is virtually unreadable, his would appear to be eminently acceptable in many imaginable contexts.

But where Silliman's earlier reluctance to specify the content of verse culture seemed like a covert argument for the value of an institution, the substance of which was determined only by opposition, here his lack of specificity about how different sentences could possibly be said to resemble one another if not in their meaning or surface structure points in the direction of universal grammar. And not just toward its highly abstract account of linguistic rules—rules that generate every sentence in any language insofar as it is a sentence in a language—but at the highly abstract concept of person that the universal grammar specifies. This is why, for Silliman, not just poems, but poets are more like one another during collaborations than they are like themselves: not, that is, because the universal grammar does not generate equally the sentences written by one person alone and the sentences written by several people together, but rather because collaboration makes it possible to separate the universal grammar from the merely idiosyncratic habits of a single person, habits that make an individual poet's sentences look like they are specifying a *character*. On this account, the "reappearance" or "reconstruction" of the person is a "theme" that Silliman and Hejinian share, not because they both thematize it by referring to it in their sentences (although they do), but because both exemplify it by making sentences in the first place. "Collaboration," then, in the context of this analysis, looks less like a social form than like a research strategy.[31] That is, if collaborative poetry makes nothing happen, it does make something visible. But what it makes visible is not the poem; for the redirection of the task of "poetic culture" away from the work of making poems and toward the manifestation of the capacity to make poems creates a profound ambiguity about the *unit* of poetry.

Despite appearances, the page shown in figure 4.5 is not from an experimental poem. It is, rather, my attempt to convey to the uninitiated some small sense of the massive productivity, generational spread, and exogamous influence of Language poetry and to illustrate the importance of the sentence—however obscure its reference, whatever form it takes on the page—to that productivity, spread,

A page dramatically estranged, nor lacking
    bombardment out of sync
with the event that
    annihilated into sudden pianissimo
a few songs.

        —Marjorie Welish, "Casting Sequences"

Among the women who came in to eat at the restaurant every day—they had much time at their disposal—was a huge woman always dressed elaborately

She talked to herself having conversations in different voices—I waited on her; the store detective having lunch seated nearby in order to keep an eye on her—her saying I was an ass and referring to other people's asses

  that—some-
    thing
  as able
  to occur only in
  one way in
  the present

        —Leslie Scalapino, Way

First sentence: her cheap perfume
Caused cancer in the White House last night.
With afford, agree and arrange, use the infinitive.
I can't agree to die. With practice,
Imagine and resist, use the gerund. I practice to live
is wrong. Specify: "We've got to nuke 'em Henry"
Second sentence: Inside the box is plutonium.
The concept degrades, explodes,
Goes all the way, in legal parlance.

        —Bob Perelman, "Seduced by Analogy"

Let me try to repeat all the things we tried to say today,
  but for some reason weren't able to
Alright. But we still won't be able to.
That's okay. Let's see what we say.

        —Steve Benson, Blue Book

Crime teething hero God inhabits us all indifferently—
    especially
you!, adumbrates—so thin, so light, so crisp;
fur stops a drain
as Jesus taught, excuse my parole.

        —Bruce Andrews, I Don't Have any Paper, So Shut Up, or, Social Romanticism

The matrix of your hamstrung home-life
is undercutting all my generous gifts.
The current temper is such that soon
even the most bedlamite among us
will be threatened by marriage.

        —Jennifer Moxley, Imagination Verses

Say This. There is a sentence in my moth there is a chariot in my mouth. There is a lamp whose light fills empty space and a space which swallows light.

        —Michael Palmer, "Sun"

Then from a great disturbance

The most delicate message accumulates

But you must know why you write a novel, said Vodonoy

It's not to displace anything

It has context and metronome

By insisting on a comprehension of every word I am free to signify place though not to represent it.

So I must oppose the opposition of poetry to prose

Just as we can only momentarily oppose control to

discontinuity, sex to organization, disorientation to

domestic time and space, and glasnost (information) to the hunt

        —Lyn Hejinian, Oxota

Given the distance of communication, I hope the words aren't idling on the map on my fingertips, but igniting wild acres within the probabilities of spelling. As a hawk describes circles whose inner emptiness bespeaks the power of gravity, where the lever catches on a cog of the world.

        —Rosmarie Waldrop, The Reproduction of Profiles

I intend to speak this sentence against its will

His footnote to doubt fulfills an ideological need

In time for a symphony to play Ode to Joy in Berlin . . .

Non Sequiturs,

    invisibly to dream

A tactical sequence of one-liners . . .

Until we return to writing the poem

Even you learned to speak. Used up . . .

        —Barrett Watten, Under Erasure

In the Evangelist's mind

It is I absolutely I

Word before name

Resurrection and life are one

it is I

without any real subject

all that I say is I

A predicate nominative

not subject the I is

the bread the light the door

the way the shepherd the vine

        —Susan Howe, "The Nonconformist's Memorial"

Figure 4.5. A page dramatically estranged: writers in, around, and after Language poetry find poetry in the primacy of syntax.

and influence. There appears to be an overwhelming consensus among poets in and around the Language movement that whatever work remains to be done poetically will be done, not so much by foregrounding the materiality of the poem (Language poetry's early emphasis), but by foregrounding its syntacticality. Thus the picture of the movement I present here, while obviously not inclusive, does aspire to be representative. Like any device of representation, but particularly like the sort we call *the anthology,* this one is vulnerable to a number of serious objections. Perhaps to one especially: by removing sentences from their poems, poems from their books, books from their careers, I have imposed the mere image of a unified movement upon the diversity of its voicings and foreclosed any substantive consideration of the complex and particular ways in which a poet's projects respond to their contexts, the ways in which the poems enlist and anticipate the interests of their audiences. I do so, such an objection might continue, not in order to give you a *real* sense of the poetry, but to give you *my* sense of it, to reproduce in my audience my experience, whether of fascination or of boredom.[32]

But while my picture does represent *something*, it is precisely not my experience. I am not interested in arguing for my sense of the poetry over anyone else's; I do not argue that no one is or can be interested in Language poetry, or that no one does or can find it beautiful, or amusing, or exciting, or any of the many attitudes that one could strike in relation to the phenomenon of a Language poem. What I am trying to demonstrate in a variety of ways is that what is portrayed here—a large collective enterprise devoted to the production of grammatical sentences *without regard to any particular use to which they might be put by an author or a reader*—is not the phenomenology of the Language poetry project at all, but rather an index to its linguistic ontology. Like all ontological claims, this one is extremely difficult for an observer to arrive at by means of an inference from empirical instances. A poetic culture will always look like it is made up of poems, and poems will always seem to solicit our responses and experiences. It is this epistemological difficulty that motivates Language poetry's dual imperative—its theoretical emphasis on linguistic invention on the one hand, and its institutional emphasis on poetic multiplicity on the other—in much the same way as it motivates the scientist to seek refinements in experimental design and to increase the number of experiments performed. What the Hejinian sentence accomplishes by multiplying internal complexities to the point where its grammaticality could be conceptually separated from its acceptability, the movement as a whole does by multiplying the number of sentences far in excess of even the most enthusiastic reader's capacity to accept them. Taken together as mutually reinforcing strategies, Language poetry theory and practice make authorial intention and readerly attention look incidental to the project of *manifestation*—the difficult work of indicating a universal competence that can be neither produced nor received, but which makes both production and reception possible.

This solicitation of reception as a means to disclose its irrelevance structures Language poetry's productivity all the way down—on the local scale as well as on the global. It can be found, for example, even in the work of a Language poet interested in reintroducing into Language poetry a more traditional lyric sensibility (a poet whose work, incidentally, I find quite beautiful):

> Say this. There is a sentence in my mouth, there is a chariot in
> my mouth. There is a ladder. There is a lamp whose light
> fills empty space and a space which swallows light

This stanza from Michael Palmer's poem "Sun"[33] commands the reader to speak a series of sentences in a language that looks quite ordinary, with extraordinary results. "There is a sentence in my mouth" is as close as you might hope to come to a sentence that could *only* be intended as the literal truth, because saying it makes it so. By the same token, "There is a chariot in my mouth" is difficult to dissociate from its literal falsity, because if it were so, one could not say. While this sentence certainly *could* be meant as a metaphor—perhaps even a metaphorical assertion of magisterial rhetorical power—it is so obviously and comically compromised by its literal meaning that even if I were to intend its metaphorical meaning you would be justified in calling me not just mistaken but a liar. The final sentence, on the other hand, seems impossible to imagine meaning in anything *but* a metaphorical sense: not only because it invokes traditional Romantic images for imaginative power associated with the use of metaphor (interior illumination and infinite space) but also because it couches those images in the form of a logical contradiction, a version of the philosophical chestnut of irresistible forces and immovable objects.[34] Each of these sentences, in other words, seems so bound to ascriptions of particular forms of intentionality—literal truth-telling, lying, metaphorizing—that it is hard to conceive of uttering them for any other purpose. While it is perhaps the case that any sentence could be intended to mean anything given a determinedly perverse speaker, the point of commanding the reader to utter *these* sentences appears to be to insist that she have the experience of sentence meaning *determining* intention, and thus to force the reader to have a number of incompatible intentions in quick succession.

Putting it this way, however, makes it seem as though the point of the poem was to force the reader to have the experience of being in Watten's "total human situation." For we can and do speak all manner of sentences—truths, lies, metaphors—in quick succession and experience no difficulty intending all of them, just insofar as we are in situations that call for them. But the effect of presenting a series of necessarily conflictual intentional acts as components of a *single* utterance ("say *this*") and even more strongly, a single *lyric* utterance (which carries with it the strong presumption of a single intentional act, however complex) is to make it difficult to imagine that *meaning* "this" could be the point of saying "this" at all; saying "this" looks instead like it means to stage a competition between what *can* be said and what one *should* say, between capacity, which is independent of context, and intentionality, which is always contextual. The speaker of these sentences belongs to no situation; or if, as Chomsky insists, "human language, in its normal use, is free from the control of independently identifiable external stimuli or internal states and is not restricted to any practical communicative function" (*Cartesian Linguistics*, 29), then the result of obeying Palmer's command is to have an extraordinary experience of ordinary human freedom—an experience unique for not being an experience of subjectivity.

III. Poets as Persons

On Chomsky's account, it is language's unique status that provides "[t]he explanation for the central position of poetry" in traditional thought about art. "Poetry is unique," he writes, "in that its medium is unbounded and free; that is, its medium, language, is a system with unbounded potentialities for the formation and expression of ideas" (*Cartesian Linguistics,* 17–18). This is, it seems to me, the definition of "poetry" that accounts for the peculiar an-aesthetic of so much Language poetry. What initially appears to be a rather severe reduction of the lyric's traditional resources for representing complexly individuated psychological states or for provoking complex and individual psychological responses is actually a reorientation of poetry toward the sort of performance suitable to a theory of the mind that preexists purposes. From the perspective of the universal grammar, Watten is correct: there *are* no languages in the commonsense sense of the term. What we ordinarily call languages are epiphenomenal, derivative, and otherwise without significance. But Watten is wrong to imagine that the alternative is a "total syntax" defined only by contingency. For what is *real* (in the ontological sense) is grammar, hard as it is to focus on with all the sentences getting in the way. Language poetry's reinvestment of the resources of lyric in grammaticality suggests an empiricist updating of Shelley's idealist defense of poetry, to which poems are, as I have already suggested, irrelevant: "the copiousness of lexicography and the distinctions of grammar are the works of a later age, and are merely the catalogue and the form of the creations of Poetry."[35]

While the various strategies I have outlined here—internal complexity, numerousness, the de-situating of the lyric speaker—do not get rid of intention and attention (do not get rid of poems), they do represent an extremely energetic effort to refocus the claim of the poetic so that it does not denote but rather indicates, or, to use Shelley's term, "catalogues" the real.

Language poets are not *saying* that a community of poets exists or reporting on its views by saying (writing) all the sentences that make up *Leningrad*—it is not meaningful in this way. Still less are they bringing a community into existence by writing all the sentences that make up *Leningrad*—it is not performative in that way. Language poets are *Language* poets in just this sense—they intend their poems not as sentences representing propositions, but as exemplifications of the species-specific creative competence to freely produce and to recognize new sentences as sentences in a language.[36]

This emphasis on speciation provides another way to think about Language poetry's bearing on the social world, and suggests why the end of poetry might be particularly appropriate to the end of history. The liberation of the language from standards is frequently taken to liberate language from restrictive conventions in order to make way for other, equally valid conventions—as in my initial reading of Silliman, for example, or as in defenses of dialect poetry. In contrast, a practice that posits the priority of language to communication posits a freedom from the obligation to represent any *form* of human interest altogether—it has all the interest of the human itself. If the universal grammar were to become manifest, not just as a theoretical representation of an innate capacity, but as an actual speaker, it might indeed look like a *movement*; it might look a great deal like the "uncommunity" of Language poets: neither a culture nor a school, but an endlessly productive faculty generating a potentially endless array of "New Sentences," and not for use or instruction, but as bare proof of its existence and tokens of its nature.

Finally, though, the particular interest of the Language poetry project will lie in the rigor with which it can adhere to the fact that the universal grammar is not a speaker, but rather a competence to speak. In its strong form, which is perhaps to say, its notional form, Language poetry neither embodies nor inculcates disinterest, it is uninteresting, and not just to the uninitiated but on principle. Only insofar as it was really appealing to no one could it succeed in exemplifying everyone.

Identifying "personhood" with linguistic competence might be impressive and suggestive. But it must be acknowledged that the mere species-fact of "personhood" does not specify what the rights of the person are, nor what our obligations toward the person should be; strictly speaking, it does not even guarantee that the person is valuable. As John Rawls is only among the latest to point out, "Human nature and its natural psychology are permissive: they may limit the viable conceptions of persons and ideals of citizenship, and the moral psychologies that support them, but do not dictate the ones we must adopt."[37] This is why, on his account, a theory of justice must be political, rather than metaphysical or psychological.

But if the Language poetry project is in this sense "permissive," or *pre*-political, it also suggests why pre-political accounts of persons are important to the radical poetry of the twentieth century, in which it has seemed all too easy for experience-based accounts of personhood, no matter how reasonable, rational, or minimal their stipulations, to fail to attribute personhood to all persons. The central interest of the "radical" poetry of the tradition of which Language poetry is a part is not social justice but the truth, or the ontological basis of the social; it means neither to represent particular interests in order to create opportunities for sympathetic identification, nor to create the social structures that allow for adjudication between interests, but rather to offer an approach to the profound problem of determining in virtue of what it can be said that persons are there to begin with. The Language poets' appeal to grammaticality is particularly ingenious in that grammaticality regrounds personhood in such a way that it can make *itself* manifest, and does so in such a way that we know it when we see it. And this, as Joseph Graham has suggested, is no job for actual poems. "For literature," he writes, "we have no special competence. We have but our wits, our pains, and if they fail, our tears. Grammar is then a consolation; at least we are good at something."[38] And, the Language poet might add, at least "we" are something. For if poetic competence is synonymous with universal linguistic competence, then "poet" is synonymous with person.

CHAPTER **FIVE**

We Are Reading

So We must meet apart—
You there—I—here—

I. "We understand, then, do we not?"

—*Walt Whitman*

A MIDST THE TRANSLATIONS, mistranslations, hybrids, and fictions that make up Jack Spicer's 1957 book *After Lorca,* we find a series of letters from the living American poet to the dead Spanish one:

Dear Lorca,

When I translate one of your poems and I come across words I do not understand, I always guess at their meanings. I am inevitably right. A really perfect poem (no one yet has written one) could be perfectly translated by a person who did not know one word of the language it was written in. A really perfect poem has an infinitely small vocabulary.[1]

This, from the volume's second letter to Lorca, precedes one rather lumpish Englishing of an actual Lorca poem ("The Ballad of Weeping"); one complete mangle— "Song of the Poor," a quarter of which is left untranslated, half of which (including the title, "*Es Verdad*") is arrant mistranslation, and a quarter of which is interpolation; and two poems, presented as translations, that are actually wholesale inventions ("Ballad of the Dead Woodcutter" and "Alba"). These in turn are followed by

Spicer's well-known reinvention of Lorca's "Ode For Walt Whitman"—a "translation" whose aggressively enlarged and amplified vocabulary renders "stains" as "wet dreams," and *maricas* (a derivation from Mary that has something of the import of girly-man or fairy) as "cocksucker."

The ramped-up intensity that Spicer's translation brings to his relation to Whitman is very much to the point; for by insisting on the inevitable "rightness" of his motley assortment of guesses and guises, Spicer is returning us to a distinctly Whitmanian sense of poetics and linguistics: one that conflates the idea of a "perfect" poem with the idea of perfect translatability; and one that defines translation, not just as the ability to decode some particular person's words within a particular communicative context, or to decode and then recode the particular expressive intentions manifest in a work of verbal art, but as the possibility of entering into perfected and non-agonistic sociability with persons altogether. Whitman's fullest imagination of these compounded perfections appears in his "Song of the Answerer":

> Every existence has its idiom, every thing has an idiom and
> tongue,
> He resolves all tongues into his own and bestows it upon
> men, and any man translates, and any man translates him-
> self also,
> One part does not counteract another part, he is the joiner, he
> sees how they join.
> He says indifferently and alike How are you friend? to the
> President at his levee,
> And he says Good-day my brother, to Cudge that hoes in the
> sugar-field,
> And both understand him and know that his speech is right.

I've just claimed that this notion of translation involves *more* than the decoding of language; but it might be more precise to say that it may not involve the decoding of language at all. Though he appears sometimes as a universal translator, sometimes as an embodied Esperanto, Whitman's Answerer has the ability to transcend differences of all kinds—of national vernacular, professional jargon, and class idiolect; but also of religious doctrine, temperament, or worldview. Such "universal welcome" makes it difficult to imagine that perfect comprehension of another could be a function of the practical mastery of many languages, or, conversely that there could be one language—whether conlang or Cratylan—that would do the work of intersubjective "joining" that he envisions.

As extreme as Whitman's imagination of relation by translation may be, Spicer's is even more so. For Spicer, a perfect translation spans not just the difference between Cudge and Congressman, German and Spaniard, Jew and "Russ," soldier and sailor, insulter, angry person, or beggar, but something altogether more intractable: the difference between the living poet and the companion who stands at the discourteous remove of death. In Homer, the dead have no language—only an inarticulate batlike squeaking. In Spicer, mortal loss cannot stop correspondence; the dead are our brothers and lovers; they answer and ask, cajole and comprehend.

Whitman's manifest interest in manifest words—his praise of the lexicographer and comparative philologist in "Song of Myself"; his delighted recitation of Native American tribal names in "Starting from Paumanok"—will sometimes give way, as in "Song of the Rolling Earth," to the strange imagination of perfected "words" that repel both audition and print:

> I swear I begin to see little or nothing in audible words,
> All merges toward the presentation of the unspoken meanings
>   of the earth,
> Toward him who sings the songs of the body and of the truths
>   of the earth,
> Toward him who makes the dictionaries of words that print
>   cannot touch.

Spicer too begins by celebrating the inevitable rightness of his understanding of Lorca's words—and perhaps his skill as translator for finding equivalent native ones—but in the end he justifies his declaration that the "perfect poem" could be understood by a person who didn't understand "one word" of the language with the proposition that the perfect poem would not even *have* one word, but rather, an "infinitely small" number of them. Spicer's choice of term for that which the poem refuses—"vocabulary"—is not merely a rejection of the brute denotations of the lexicon. He means to reject every imaginable sort of meaning that enthusiasts of the poem can muster in relation to language.

> Most of my friends like words too well. They set them under the blinding light of the poem and try to extract every possible connotation from each of them, every temporary pun, every direct or indirect connection—as if a word could become an object by mere addition of consequences. Others pick up words from the streets, from their bars, from their offices and display them proudly in their poems as if they were shouting, "See what I have collected from the American language. Look at my butterflies, my stamps, my old shoes!" What does one do with all this crap?

This crap would *include* denotation, certainly, but also the more obliquely inferential "connotation," the "pun"—so dependent on the groaning similitude of word sounds. It would include music and its impact upon the listener, and indeed "every direct or indirect connection" that the creative mind can fathom or invent as a "consequence" of words. If words are—as Spicer declared in the first of his Vancouver lectures—like memories or mental furniture, "things which just happen to be in your head instead of someone else's head,"[2] then the poem of "infinitely small vocabulary" aims to sweep out the detritus that separates one head from another, to reject every axis of difference and individuation. The elimination of all the imaginable species of consequence suggests the degree to which translation, as Spicer intends it, cannot be intended to facilitate intersubjective *understanding* at all. Spicer understands himself to stand with Lorca, not in understanding him, but on some ground of relation that does not wait upon the labors or hazards of understanding.

As was the case for Whitman, the language Spicer seeks is, in some crucial sense, not a language in any ordinary sense of the word. Vocabulary, bound to the particulars of person, time, and place, is, for Spicer, a kind of death ("My vocabulary did this to me," he is supposed to have declared with his dying breath). "Correspondence" across the limits of particular experiences, idioms, or languages, across the complete and mortal divide between person and person, occurs not through any commensuration of vocabularies but through a deeper relation that Spicer can only point to: "This is how we dead men write to each other" (34).

This book has tried to unfold the tradition that would make legible Spicer's description of the poet as a "dead man" whose particular form of death promises a particular account of life together with others (of being numerous) that circumvents the problems of understanding. The birdsong of Yeats's dead shrouds in "Cuchulain Comforted," Oppen's "ontologic man," O'Hara's "great rolls of celluloid" where the even the extra becomes luminously visible, the generative grammar of Language poetry—all figure or theorize the perfected relations that come at the price of the individuating work that makes up a vocabulary or a life.

Spicer's life was not led in a perfecting idiom.[3] Nor is Spicer's book of one mind about the perfectibility of relations, nor about the elimination of vocabulary that such perfection would entail. Whitman stands between Spicer and Lorca as a common text, but Lorca's posthumous "response" to Spicer's importuning letters, and indeed to the whole project of "translation," is, as the dead poet frankly declares, "fundamentally unsympathetic." In his preface to the volume, Spicer's Lorca takes an oddly conservative stand, insisting on the poet's right to his own words and on the integrity and intentions of his own work. He sounds at once like Spicer rebuking his own poetic contemporaries—who substitute their own vision of "consequences" in the place of a poet's singular cause—and like the Puritan who rebukes the poetic imagination for making, not poems, but monsters of the imagination:

> In even the most literal of them Mr. Spicer seems to derive pleasure in inserting or substituting one or two words which completely change the mood and often the meaning of the poem as I had written it. More often he takes one of my

poems and adjoins to half of it another half of his own, giving rather the effect of an unwilling centaur. (Modesty forbids me to speculate which end of the animal is mine.) (107)[4]

One possible consequence of setting oneself the task of understanding the work of living poets (as opposed to dead ones) is that they may resist even more forcefully your claims to inevitable rightness, and they may view any departure from their own self-description as monstrous. Through his work of ventriloquism, Spicer is able to have it both ways: his willingness to grant himself license for a "translation" of Lorca's poems that veers completely away from the actual objects that that poet made is contingent both upon his masochistic imagination of Lorca's rebuke and his subsequent imagination of Lorca's charitable concession that "the dead are notoriously hard to satisfy" (108).

The living may take a harder line. In the last chapter, I argued that in order to get what it wants—an account of poetry as an enterprise deeply involved in manifesting the possibility of social life, or in producing confidence in the ground of social life—Language poetry has, in important ways, given itself up to a kind of death. The same might be said of any poet considered as having a "vocabulary," in the sense of a language, idiom, or project that makes *this one*'s work distinct and apprehensible; that sets *that one* apart as having a name:

> The singers of successive hours of centuries may have ostensible names, but the name of each of them is one of the singers,
> The name of each is, eye-singer, ear-singer, head-singer, sweet-singer, night-singer, parlor-singer, love-singer, weird-singer, or something else.
> (Whitman, "Song of the Answerer")

Poets and poems go about their businesses, whether that business is beauty, or some other business equally solicitous of the particularizing attentions of eye, ear, and mind. And there can be no question that poets are often invested in the distinctiveness of their particular projects and in the distinction that accrues to a unique name. The singer who stands behind her songs is as unlikely as Lorca to assent happily to Spicer's claim that her words are so many butterflies, stamps, and old shoes; to wholeheartedly embrace Whitman's idea that "the words of true poems" lie elsewhere than in the words a poet makes; or to concede to my argument that it is only by viewing poems in their representative sweep that they can be seen to disclose or indicate their true significance. In the case of Language poets, for example, I have described the thwarting of particularity not as a problem but as a solution; nevertheless, there is no denying that such solutions are not consistent with the poets' every desire.

I would like to register the force of one aspect of this line of objection. Previous chapters of this book have not shied away from presenting themselves as revisionary readings of particular poets' intentions with respect to poetry, even as I have argued that one must make the occasional leap from the artifact of the poem (and the constructive intentions behind it) to a universalizing intention that the specificity of the poem both indicates and frustrates. The living resistance that Language poets present to the abstraction involved in my account of Language poetry, however, challenges the idea of such leaping, and contests the existence of what I have called Language poetry's "functional motive"—an account that *would* make sense of a complex ensemble of practices, discourses, institutions, and affects. Mine is a formulation that oscillates uncertainly between interpretation and speculation, constructing an object of analysis by adding consequences.

I am thus rebuked by resistance to my ascriptions of motive on the ground of what one might call "responsibility." I hear in this term two senses: first, while it might seem legitimate to hold a poet responsible for a project or intention, it is less obvious that poets can be held individually responsible for work conceived as if by a plural subject or group mind. Even in the case of the Language poets, who evince a more-than-casual interest in constituting and presenting themselves as a community of like minds and shared affections, it could be a mistake to ascribe to a group of poets a set of collective *intentions* or *meanings.*

Second, one could well suggest that the critic has a greater responsibility to treat his objects of analysis with particularizing care. In some sense the only way to offer the account of Language poetry that I do is to fail to read the poems as they present themselves for reading. On this view, what it means to *read* is to invest oneself wholly in a working through of the unassimilable particularity of the poem; to fail to do so is perceived, not just as a failure of understanding, but as a kind of bad faith—a failure of sympathy and care.

I had initially imagined ending this book with something that could be definitively called a reading. I had hoped, that is, to discover in the poetic present the next evolution of the tradition I have been describing here: the poet who could show what it might mean to undertake the work of disclosing the real of personhood as the starting point of an affirmative poetic project, rather than to discover this vocation belatedly or unconsciously as a compensation for a failed grasping after worldly engagement and "consequences." Certainly we find ourselves no less in a state of emergency than the poets I have looked at in this book; our present crises of value and human dignity are not different in kind from those in 1919, 1939, 1969, or 1989. Arjun Appadurai has recently accounted for the global violence of our present moment as the result of two interlocking problems. The first is the persistence of the idea of an "ethnic genius" behind even the most enlightened of modern nations. The second is the large-scale "social uncertainty" attendant upon an age of rapid and near-uncontrollable mobility of persons and ideologies.

When an ineradicable ethnonationalism meets a radical uncertainty about the boundaries between "them" and us, Appadurai argues, violence can become a sort of "folk-discovery procedure" for determining or producing the distinctions that have been lost or obscured. Under such conditions, there might be some profit in looking to see whether a new Answerer has arrived, where the "words of true poems" might be found that could offer an alternative to the risks of even the most capacious forms of sympathy, and what model of personhood that figure has to offer to a reader.

Instead, instructed by this example of disagreement and conflict that can arise precisely through the work of reading and interpreting poetry, I will end it with a sort of experiment in imagining my argument about the history of poetry as a prescription, not for writing, but rather for *reading*. In so doing, I set out to address both of the concerns I have raised here—to think about the nature or structure of collective intentions, and to offer a defense of a kind of intense and deliberated *inattention* to poems.

As the provocation for this line of thought arises, in a sense, out of my argument's biography, my method here will be in part autobiographical, taking my own use and abuse of poetry as a case study. I will argue by example that by paying attention to some of the things we *do* with poems—uses that are not answerable to the heroic accounts of agency or epistemology that underwrite what we mean by "competence" in reading, nor to any criterion of professional responsibility; uses that are *ordinarily* idiosyncratic or merely personal, that adhere to and propose no methods; uses that are experiments in living as much as they are experiments in reading—we may come closer to observing something both noncontingent and shared about our ordinary intentions and mental actions.

John Ashbery speculates about the costs and benefits of this sort of defense in "The One Thing That Can Save America":

> I know that I braid too much on my own
> Snapped-off perceptions of things as they come to me.
> They are private and always will be.
> Where then are the private turns of event
> Destined to bloom later like golden chimes
> Released over a city from a highest tower?
> The quirky things that happen to me, and I tell you,
> And you know instantly what I mean?
> What remote orchard reached by winding roads
> Hides them? Where are these roots?

Ashbery's resolution upon the "roots" that connect one person to another with more certainty than the acts of telling and understanding suggests the direction my thinking will follow. If there is something general or collective about the relations between poems and persons, it might well be found to reside in a general or "root" account of persons, rather than in the particularity of poems. My own snapped-off perceptions of poetry, itself so variable, might then be considered to be a place where thinking about invariance might take place—where the mind, given rather than made, can be approached through the made thing.

One thing we do with poems is read them together.

II. "I cannot live with you"

—Emily Dickinson

In December of 1995, I sent a book to a woman I loved but could no longer live with. The book was A. R. Ammons's *Tape for the Turn of the Year,* a long poem in the form of a journal that runs from Dec 6, 1963 to Jan 10, 1964.[5] The conceit of the poem (perhaps it is true) is that each of its sections was composed over the course of a single day, and takes in, "plain as / day, exact and bright," the talk and thoughts of the poet in real time and *in propria persona.* Accordingly, the sections are variable in content and in length as they would be if the reflectiveness of even the most reflective man sometimes had to give way to action: the shortest day (Friday, December 13) is twenty-seven lines; on that day, the poet receives a book of his poems (almost certainly *Expressions of Sea Level*) from his publisher, goes Christmas shopping, and goes out to dinner. The longest entries stretch on for a dozen pages or more and travel greater representational distances, taking up mythic figurations of the poet's own writing task (the voyage of Ulysses, the labor of Sisyphus); addresses to his Muse in moods of supplication, gratitude, or rebuke; speculations on the sciences (physics, geology, biology) and on the economics of Christmas trees. In its fits and starts of attention, its rhetorical range from high to low (and not eschewing middle flight), the poem makes a more than usually literal attempt to represent a mind in action.

To say even this much is already to say more than I knew about the poem; I hadn't yet read it. In the letter that I sent along with the book, I proposed that we would read it together—one "day" at a time—from December of 1995 to January of 1996.

What did I think we were doing? Reading poems together ("precedents out of beautiful old books") is not an unusual thing for lovers—successful or unsuccessful—to do. But the way of reading together I proposed was different than what one does when one takes a poem into one's own mouth as one's own speech, or offers it as a stand-in or replacement for speech that is inadequate or blocked. That sort of self-ventriloquism is abetted by certain formal features of poems: live and in person, by a prosody that originates in (and thus makes fit matter for) performance; at a distance, by poetry's heavy conventional dependence on pure indexicals—*I, you, here, now*. And this way of communicating by means of poems is predicated on the act of interpretation, or it is directed toward interpretation. In order for me to hope to say something to you by means of the poem, I must have or develop some account of the way it can be understood as speaking for me. This may involve interpreting the poem in light of my situation, or it may involve interpreting our situation in the light of the poem; quite often it involves both.[6]

The poem I chose, though, turns out not to be particularly amenable to that kind of substitution, nor to the modes of interpretation that it licenses. Ammons periodically worries about the various ways in which individual perspectives, otherwise at odds, might be synchronized by means of what he calls (117)

> Drives, motions.
> intellections, symbologies,
> myths

But the poem is much more conspicuously built around multiple indices of particularity. Ammons's insistence on dating his entries (tying them to the passing) is one of these—albeit one that we managed to defeat somewhat by the timing of our reading so that we shared his dates. Another, harder to game, is the speaker's maddening—or perhaps just deadening—preoccupation with the weather, notice and description of which opens and closes almost every entry:

> today
> is dim
> again:
>
> the sun makes diffuse
> shadows
> that go
> in & out
> of focus:
>
>> (just now, the
> thorns
> are black
> against the wall)
>
> maybe it's gonna clear off:
> not very cold

Calendrical time and weather are both (differently) sharable things; the former is a way of talking that makes a sharable world; talk about the latter registers the world we are in together. But the tying of one to the other, social fact to brute fact, makes these different ways of creating or experiencing the common world into something uncommon. The poem's insistence upon narrating to the moment ("just now") the flux of such minute and specific sensory data as the blurring and sharpening contours of shadows highlights the degree to which "now" clocks a moment I do not occupy (now, it is bright, not dim), and "here" picks out a place I do not see (here there are no thorns, no shadows); the catalogue of differences seems to exceed the common sentiments that might rebuke my ability to use these words as my own.[7] And even when the poem rises from observation into registers of sublime rhetoric or conceptual generality, the perspectivalism implied by this speaker's insistently demotic voice blocks my inclination to do so.[8]

If there was an aspect of the poem that made it seem peculiarly, even constitutively shareable (both in the prospect and retrospect of my own case), it was its central formal innovation—what Ammons terms its "serious novelty" (3). The dimensions of the poem—both its extravagant length and its meager breadth—were determined entirely by the surface onto which it was composed: a roll of adding machine tape fed through a typewriter. This choice of support frames the problem of poetic closure by conceding in advance to an end that is at once certain and (unlike the closural demands of a sestina, say, which are far off but still in view) unpredictable. Ammons initially tasks himself with the tape, stumbled over in the House & Garden store two weeks prior (1):

> today I
> decided to write
> a long
> thin
> poem

But after this first decision, the poem unspools as a continual submission to and negotiation with its own givens. It begins self-consciously by naming and cataloguing the conventions of beginning: "this / part is called the pro- / logue: it has to do with / the business of / getting started"; it worries along the way about whether order and value are emerging as the diameter of the roll shrinks and the tangled knot accumulating in the trashcan into which it feeds grows; and it ends by announcing that it knows how tall it is and placing its own hand atop its head as a form of self-measure and a gesture of farewell: "so long." That the tape itself is "thin" as well as "long" also sets the terms of other, more proximate endings. Ammons's lines are constrained by character rather than by beat; the tape, as it happens, is twenty-six characters across, suggesting perhaps that the language of the poem might be viewed as a species of the same sort of limit as the material support on which language is inscribed.

I would like to say, with the matter of the poem in mind, that what made it particularly apt as a gift was its givenness. But though the term rings portentous, it won't bear the same kind of metaphysical burden as Heidegger's "thrownness";[9]

nor do I mean for it to do the theoretical work often associated with the idea of materiality.[10] What I want instead is a term that acknowledges that much of what we do in relation to poems has only marginal relation to the projects that our modes of criticism (traditional, avant-garde) admit. I want to suggest, for example, that taking a poem (as this poem asks to be taken) as a *given* thing pries it loose from the project of evaluation. Is the poem a good poem or a bad one? In whole or in parts? Answer: *Today I decided to give a long, thin poem.* But perhaps more importantly for this discussion, I want to claim that by taking up a poem as given, we can pry the work we do as readers from the critical task understood as interpretation. For it turns out that in this instance of reading a poem together, I am much less interested in understanding what A. R. Ammons means in and by his poem than in understanding what I imagine another person is making of it. The construal of sentences plays a role in our making things of poems (or of my imagining what another makes of them) but not the decisive one. The poem, rather, becomes a place in which our intentions meet (or, as I hope to explain, an occasion on which my intentions *for us* are realized).

I've been speaking as though givenness is a function of form, but it might be truer to say it is function of attitude. Reading this way (whatever way that should turn out to be) is a relinquishing of theory and justification, a contingent and entirely irresponsible embrace of my interest in the poem over the meaning of the poem.[11] Adopting this kind of attitude toward poems is always possible (though Ammons may make it easy). As Steve Knapp declares in *Literary Interest:* "I see no reason why the activity triggered by a poetic metaphor—or indeed by any literary representation—should take the form of an attempt to *interpret* the representation."[12] My interest in literature is variable and deeply dependent on context as multifarious as the kinds of poems I take up and the reasons I have for doing so. But is there anything to be *learned* by this embrace of my interest? What is it that I am interested in when I am interested in *that*? Perhaps more to the point, why should anyone else be interested in it?

One possible answer is that we are interested in what structures my interest. In his well-known essay "Communities of Readers," Roger Chartier describes the difficulty of laying hold of reading as something that can be attended to. Reading is something "that only rarely leaves traces, that is scattered in an infinity of singular acts, and that easily shakes off all constraints."[13] Chartier's intention here is to make a preliminary, and not a final, diagnosis; he means to identify not a mystery but a research program. This suggests another way in which I might think about my reading: as a piece of hard-won evidence toward a history or ethnography of reading practices. I could view my interest in and experiment with this poem in the same spirit as we view the marginalia, commonplace books, periodicals, and correspondence of past readers—as part of an archive of the ways in which persons take up texts as part of larger cultural agendas: as indices of our *interestedness,* whether those interests are progressive or reactionary, disciplinary or revolutionary.

In paying attention to my own acts, I might, for example, understand my reading as scholia of a very peculiar kind—peculiar, since my reading consists in large measure of speculations about what another person is making of moments in a poem, and so of imagining another reader's scholia.[14]

Thus, when I read Ammons on December 7 (6):

> this is that & that is this
> & on and on: why can't
> every thing just be itself?
> what's the use of the
> vast mental burden
> of correspondence? doesn't
> contribute to the things
> resembled:
>
> except in the mind: except
> in the mind: there's
> the reality that needs to
> hold:

I hear in the poem's argument with the conventional practices of its own genre (asserting likenesses, finding correspondences) an argument that my fellow reader and I have had many times about the conventional habits of our respective minds. As I read it, I know that she too has noted it, *must* have noted that Ammons's plaintive call for the irreplaceable specificity of each person or thing ("why can't everything just be itself?") echoes her own deepest investments; and now my reading is of her noticing. I follow her reading as it proceeds in my own mind— from the first shock of recognizing her own position in the poem, through annoyance at the implied rebuke of mine. I imagine her imagination of my satisfaction that, in the poem, the side of correspondence gets the last word. And the unnameable feeling that sets in when her reading of me extends to take in the fact that this is almost certainly my uncharitable imagination of her: I imagine that too. If I go on long enough, what I arrive at is not a reading of the poem: it is not a vindication of one position or another on offer in the poem, not some dialectical resolution or ironic rhetorical suspension between them; what I achieve is a life together, hers and mine, produced as a function of my own intention.

The ethnography of reading practices is only one of the various lenses through which recent literary criticism has tried to recover the putative privacy of reading on behalf of an expanded account of sociality. Another is the less methodologically developed notion that Michael Warner has recently termed "uncritical reading": a set of less disciplined practices that might include "identify[ing] with characters" "fall[ing] in love with authors" "warm[ing] with pride over national heritage," and "cultivat[ing] reverence and piety."[15] Such uncritically affective relations to poems, as Joan Shelley Rubin has argued, may indeed arise from a thoroughgoing encounter with the poets' "message, theme, or style"—but they need not: "Poetry evokes feelings, in other words, because of the needs and purposes with which readers imbue poems at the site of reading, uses which can intersect with, but also obviate or transcend, the lines on the page."[16]

But what of a use like this one, where no conversation was ever intended to take place, where readers—if they meet at all—must "meet apart"? This kind of reading does not take place within the confines of a readily locatable "site" or institution of reading: school, church, family, or nation. It issues no judgments and it establishes no protocols. It is not a discourse; it circulates no images or models of itself, and it manifests no signs that can be interpreted or exchanged. Such "reading," taking place in my head (and just perhaps some equivalent version of it in hers), lacks the public-making consequence that Rubin attributes to the circulation of poetic reading. It falls short, too, of the implied promise of resistance embedded within the Warner account of "alternative practices." What I want to suggest, however, is that cutting reading loose from its institutional contexts and social consequences in this way is not a suspect act of ideological sequestration; insisting upon its real rather than merely notional privacy is not a mystification and a resistance to analysis. It is, instead, the enabling condition of a different kind of analysis—a way of focusing attention on another level at which community formation takes place. For before reading together can be considered as an action, I must first possess it as an *intention*. And before tracing out the consequences of our acts, we might first reflect upon their possibility.

III. *"I want you to be"*

—Augustine

What is it that we do when we dance elaborate or simple dances, push a car together in the snow, read a poem together? Reframed in this admittedly abstract way, the problem of reading together can be seen as an instance of the more general problem of collective action—a problem that lies at the center of current debates in social philosophy. The questions that the philosophy of society has traditionally sought to answer are normative ones: How is it that social contracts and conventions can give rise to rights or obligations, or vice versa? How can social groups be organized to produce good and just outcomes? But in the last half-century, philosophical inquiry into social life has increasingly come to seem less exclusively the property of political and ethical philosophy, and more a subset of the philosophy of action and of mind.[17] This relocation of the problem of the social has had the effect of pushing philosophical accounts in the direction of conceptual analysis and speculation about the ontology of social reality. Before determining the justice of our acting together, the thinking goes, we must establish what it is to act collectively: not just in ways that are traditionally understood to count (rituals, contracts, movements, revolutions) but in any ways; not just in familiar social categories of togetherness (families, classes, nations, or "identities") but altogether. How is it that "we" can intend to do anything? Or, just what is it that I am doing when I intend "we"?[18]

We know some poetic answers to the question:

> But we by a love so much refined,
> That ourselves know not what it is,
> Inter-assurèd of the mind,
> Care less, eyes, lips and hands to miss.[19]

But rather than adopting this view of "inter-assurance"—Donne's "two souls therefore, which are one"—or any of its larger-scale philosophical cousins such as Hegel's *Geist*,—the contemporary philosophy of society begins with a different premise. If work on the history of reading practices has proceeded by discovering either the public scene of a putatively private act or the collective determinations of individual life, then work on social-action concepts like collective intention has aimed to recover the individual basis of collective life. Such work tends to adopt the foundational premise that all intentions—including those that underwrite collective actions—are had by individual persons.[20] The question is, then: How is it possible that individuals, with their single minds (minds that must be understood in some relation to individual brains and bodies), are nonetheless capable of formulating collective intentions and undertaking cooperative actions? This formulation of the question seems deeply relevant to the case of my experiment in reading poems with another person; for our reading was a collective action that took place (if it could be said to take place at all) not in some transpersonal cultural no-place, nor in a group mind that can be accorded intentions of its own, but in minds and bodies that were (to paraphrase the Dickinson of my epigraph) "together apart."

One standard account of collective action has been called "summative," because it argues that collective intentions consist exclusively of individual intentions *plus* something else. Thus, according to the influential summative account put forward by Raimo Tuomela and Kaarlo Miller, what it means to say that *we intend* to act together is that *I* intend to do something, that I *believe* that it can be done (that it is logically and empirically possible), that I believe that *you* intend to do it, *and* that I believe that you have a set of beliefs equivalent to mine (that is to say, that that you also believe both that I will do it and that it can be done).

In Tuomela and Miller's more technical vocabulary, a "we-intention" takes the following form:

(i) A_i intends to do his part of X;

(ii) A_i has a belief to the effect that the joint action opportunities for X will obtain, especially that at least a sufficient number of the full-fledged and adequately informed members of G, as required for the performance of X, will (or at least probably will) do their parts of X;

(iii) A_i believes that there is (or will be) a mutual belief among the participants of G to the effect that the joint action opportunities for X will obtain.[21]

This account, however unpoetic its notation, does have a certain resonance in the context of this discussion; for in bringing together the exercise of the will, a reflective optimism about the willingness of the world to afford opportunities for action, and a believing reach toward the mental states of other persons, it does seem to capture some epistemological and rhetorical stances familiar to readers of poems. Here is a poetic account of collective intention:

> Others will enter the gates of the ferry, and cross from shore
>   to shore;
> Others will watch the run of the flood-tide;
> Others will see the shipping of Manhattan north and west,
>   and the heights of Brooklyn to the south and east;
> Others will see the islands large and small;
> Fifty years hence, others will see them as they cross, the sun
>   half an hour high;
> A hundred years hence, or ever so many hundred years
>   hence, others will see them,
> Will enjoy the sunset, the pouring in of the flood-tide, the fall-
>   ing back to the sea of the ebb-tide.
>
> **3**
> It avails not, neither time or place—distance avails not;
> I am with you, you men and women of a generation, or ever
>   so many generations hence;
> I project myself—also I return—I am with you, and know how
>   it is.[22]

The actions Whitman describes here (entering, crossing, watching) could well be undertaken singly and alone; indeed, the fact that Whitman might appear (especially to himself) to be performing these actions alone (perhaps in the midst of others but still without any real connection to others) is precisely the problem that the poem exists to address, and, by means of address, to solve. Whitman anticipates the order of Tuomela and Miller's definition, though what he offers is less a logical analysis of what collective intention consists in than a narrative of how collective intentions are formed. In order to reconceptualize his individual actions as collective (through the imaginative work he calls "projecting" and "returning"), Whitman first notes the persistence of the world—the immortal shipping of Manhattan, the ferry as both a conveyance and the space across which it travels, the heights of Brooklyn and of the sun—as the condition of possibility for collectivity. This world may initially appear to be occupied with its own purposes and intentions and in need of arresting confrontation ("FLOOD-TIDE below me! I watch you face to face!" [line 1]) but Whitman wills a relation to it as something dimensional, crossable, open to and permissive of action. He describes the ferry and its environs, I want again to say, as something *given*—as a place where our intentions (or, more properly, his intentions for "us") land. Whitman's will to act jointly, *plus* his confidence that the world will permit it, license his belief in other people and their motives, even when those other people are at the greatest imaginable distance away (the distance between the actual present and the notional future). On this account, Whitman achieves something real in his great conclusion:

> We use you, and do not cast you aside—we plant you permanently within us;
> We fathom you not—we love you—there is perfection in you also;
> You furnish your parts toward eternity;
> Great or small, you furnish your parts toward the soul.

This is not just the consolation of a rhetorical fiat, or the conviction of the theological fiat. Whitman does not mean by "soul" merely the fondest wish of the self, nor does he mean to invoke something mystical beyond selves; rather, in bringing himself to the point where he can say "we," he has achieved the real satisfaction at having met the conditions for a form of collective intentionality within the single self.

Though it might seem counterintuitive, Ammons seems to be thinking specifically of Whitman as the model for his own frequent addresses to readers in *Tape for the Turn of the Year* (195):

> And you, O supposed
> (& actual maybe)
> reader: how
> weary you are!
> I've bludgeoned you
> with every form of
> emptiness: you've
> endured my wrestling need:
> may something accrue
> to satisfy you:

Or perhaps Ammons entertains a Whitmanian relation to readers precisely in order to negate the predecessor-poet's optimistic vision with his own chastened one. But I suggest that the obvious formal differences between Whitman's breadth and Ammons's narrowness, like the tonal differences between Whitman's elevated declarations and Ammons's plaintive hypotheticals, are not signs that they have different accounts of what it is to achieve solidarity with another person. Both, that is, understand collective intention to be constituted of their own will to act together, plus a belief in the existence and good will of other persons. But summative accounts of collective intention and action can be represented in different *moods*. One might say of Tuomela and Miller's account that in aspiring to collective action my intending is done in a spirit of believing; but such belief is entirely consistent with the epistemic modesty of the skeptical outlook. It would be equally true to say that my intending is done in the spirit of doubting.

If I take the examples of Ammons and Whitman as explanatory (if I credit the philosophical account of collective intention that parallels the terms of these poetic accounts), then I take myself to stand in relation to my fellow reader in the same epistemic relation as the poet stands to me—the relation of care, need, and wish. On this account, to say "we are reading" is to say that I am reading and that I believe that you too are reading and believing. Perhaps we will find that the reading of another is always imaginary, and that what it means to take reading or aesthetic response as the model for communal relations is that my pleasures and satisfactions are only the bittersweet pleasures involved in fantasy and self-deception.

To Fanny Brawne, 4 July (?) 1820:

Tuesday Af[tn]

My dearest Fanny,

For this Week past I have been employed in marking the most beatutiful [*for* beautiful] passages in Spenser, intending it for you, and comforting myself in being somehow occupied to give you however small a pleasure. It has lightened my time very much. I am much better. God bless you.

Your affectionate,
J. Keats[23]

IV. "And yet I am and live"

—*John Clare*

There is, however, another account of collective action worth considering in relation to poems, though it may not be an account that we will find *represented* in poems. "We-intentions," John Searle declares, "cannot be analyzed into sets of I-intentions, even I-intentions supplemented with beliefs, including mutual beliefs, about the intentions of other members of a group."[24] Rather, Searle takes we-intentions to be *sui generis,* a form of intentionality, had by individuals, that is complete in its own right: "The thought in the agent's mind is simply of the form 'we are doing so and so'" (407). On this nonsummative account, I can acknowledge the imaginary nature of the other parties to my action without its affecting my capacity to form a "we-intention." For though the existence of a cooperative action depends on whether others are in fact engaged in it with me, the existence of a collective intention does not. We might call this the optimism of internalism. I can intend "we" independently of any beliefs about the other's mental states; indeed, I can intend "we" in the radical absence of the existence of anyone else to have mental states. Collective intention is what Searle calls a "primitive"— an irreducible psychological (and, finally, biological) fact.

But if this is to be plausible, then Searle must address two further questions: First, what is the structure of collective intentions? How is it that my having a collective intention relates to my individual action, which can only be a component of the collective action, and not its whole? When, for example, I am engaged in a dance, or helping to push a stranger's car out of the snow, I am engaged in a series of individual movements and acts; but while my movements and acts may be dancing, they are not (*pace* Yeats) the dance; nor is my pushing the cooperative act of our pushing. If it is the case that I can "we-intend" the dance, I must understand how that intention bears on my particular action, an action that has its own intentional content and conditions of satisfaction.

Searle resolves this problem by means of the "by means of" relation. A single intention, he argues, can encompass a series of causally related actions. If I intend to fire a gun, I intend to do so by means of my pulling the trigger, which causes the gun to be fired. In the same way, a collective intention encompasses a series of causally related actions, which includes my individual action as the (individual) means to (collective) ends. My intention that we dance and my intention to move my body in particular ways are not two separate intentions, one collective and one singular; rather, my intention is that we are dancing by means of my moving. The intentional actions I perform as part of pushing a car from the snow is included in my intention that we push by means of my pushing.

The second question is in some ways less technical, but more profound: What sort of creatures are we such that we are capable of formulating intentions that have this structure? Here Searle's account waxes admittedly speculative. For he understands the capacity to form "we-intentions" to derive from what he calls the "Background": "the set of nonintentional or preintentional capacities that enable intentional states to function."[25]

The manifestation of any particular form of collective intentionality will require particular Background skills. . . . But are there any features of the Background that are general or pervasive (even if perhaps not universal) for collective be-havior? I think there are, but they are not easy to characterize. They are the sorts of things that old-time philosophers were driving at when they said things like "Man is a social animal" or "Man is a political animal." In addition to the biological capacity to recognize other people as importantly like us in a way that waterfalls, trees and stones are not like us, it seems to me that the capac-ity to engage in collective behavior requires something like a pre-intentional sense of "the other" as an actual or potential agent like oneself in cooperative activities.[26]

One does not have to find Searle's rather minimalist account of background capacities—with its disparaging evocation of "old-time" philosophy, whether of Aristotle or Marx or Husserl—entirely satisfying. But whether or not Searle is cor-rect (or close enough to correct) in his formulation of the matter, I want to suggest that if the summative account captures the poetic phenomenology of intersubjec-tivity (represented in poetry as a problem of communication or understanding between poets and readers), the Searlean account captures something consis-tent with the need with which I undertook my experiment in reading; an experi-ment in which, as I have suggested earlier, the goal was not mutual understand-ing, but something else, a form of consolation appropriate to the particular conditions of loss that gave rise to it. But what is that consolation?

Suppose for a moment we consider that we-intentions are an irreducible aspect of the background—our Background. Then my reading "together apart" presents an interesting problem. Note that on Searle's account of the "by means of" rela-tion, the content of my individual action is derived from the content of the collec-tive action. This makes good sense in the case of actions in which the individual and collective actions have manifestly different content, as in the case of a dance. Absent the framing context of stage or site, my singular intention is to perform a sequence of moves that are unlikely to seem like much of an action in their own right. In their excess or stylization, the movements direct us to consider them as a means to accomplishing a collective action. Even in the less choreographed case of pushing a car (which I could certainly do singly as well as collectively, even if someone else happened to be pushing), the fact that my individual action is a means to an end will certainly be manifest in the innumerable ways that I *adjust* my own actions to my sense of its role in accomplishing that end. The nature of my action will show in my timing, in my adaptations to the presence and actions of my fellow agents.

But how does my collective intention to read manifest itself in my reading? The problem is not, or not only, that there might be barriers to *seeing* how it is manifest (because the readers are far apart, because there is no material realization of our reading in interpretation or conversation). It is, rather, as I suggested in my earlier hypothetical reconstruction of a moment of reading, that the intended collective action was not exactly to share a reading. It was, rather, to be in a certain state—the state that might now be understood as a preparedness for others. The goal of reading "together apart" was not to have an experience of reading in (believing) relation to another; it was to realize a capacity for relation to another in ourselves. Another way of putting this would be to say that by reading together apart, the collective action I sought to accomplish was precisely the capacity for "we-intentions." I wanted to be we, and feel it.

Can one feel, in the first person, the state of being we? Can I know a feature of the background experientially rather than merely theoretically? Or to reframe the question in the context of this particular collective intention, how can I know my background capacity for collective intention *in reading,* or *as reading?*

> There's unity
> But objects don't
> Describe it:
> Nor do words:
>
> If you go west on an
> east-west highway
>   this time of year
> you will find dirty
> snow
> on the right (by woods)
> and a sunny bank (by
> woods) on the left:
>   the reason is,
> with the sun low south
> the trees
> turn their shadows
> on one side:
>   that's a fact:
>   caught up
> in an abstract
>   configuration:
>
> a further reason is, the
> highway's wider
> than the length
>   of the shadows:
>   wouldn't work with
> footpaths or woods roads:

the proposition is:
when the width of the
highway exceeds the length
of the tree shadows (depends
    on the kind of
    forest—sequoias
    would require a
    vast
thoroughfare) then one
roadbank will be
sunny
(providing it isn't cloudy)
  · · · ·

    now, predict
yourself some things with
high probability:

Ammons here (167–68) provides an image that suggests why, though we exercise our capacities in making poems, or in reading them, we do not quite read our capacities in reading poems. Objects, like actions, don't bear on their surfaces the background unity of conditions (laws, potentialities) that make them possible. The road has its dimensions—more or less long, more or less wide—that suit its functions: to get from here to there, to be sufficient to carry this or that burden. One might say that if a road could experience the purposes for which it is built as its own intentions, and if it could describe those intentions in words, neither its intentions nor its words would make reference to the "configuration" that Ammons describes. Though the background of the world (the laws that govern sun and shadow, heat and melt) underwrites the road's work, and (under the right conditions) can be observed in its going, that "configuration" plays no part in its going.

    Imagining the road's functions as intentions allows us to see just what it means to say that capacities are "pre-intentional." Capacities are not representations (descriptions or words) but rather the basis on which our intentional practices (describing, signifying, intending singly or collectively) become possible. Ammons's address to us here—"now, predict / yourself some things"—marks the difference between an experiential and a theoretical stance. From a theoretical perspective, we might ascertain background capacities through a configuration of facts that have their own phenomenologies, and on the basis of that knowledge predict other facts with high degrees of confidence. This is a form of ontological confidence that we can come to know as theoreticians, but which we (engaged, like the road, in our going) do not feel as readers.

Perhaps. But in the case of reading together apart (as perhaps nowhere else) the idea of collective intentionality allows for a strange and unsettling form of error. For let us say that in reading together apart (quite unlike pushing a car or dancing a dance) one can discover that one's partners were illusory without concluding that one has been in the grip of hallucination or delusion. If the ability to intend "we" is irreducible and primitive, part of the background set of capacities that constitute our mental lives, then there is an important difference between the story in which *I* intend to read a poem and, at the same time, believe that *you* are reading it only to discover that my belief was wrong; and the story in which *we* read a poem (by means of my reading it) only for me to discover that there was no we.

In the first case, I am wrong in my beliefs about the world—but this is often the case, and no cause for special alarm. In the second case, I am still wrong in my beliefs, but I am additionally wrong about something that we do not ordinarily understand that one can be wrong about: the nature my own mental action.[27]

There are, obviously, ways in which we are often wrong or just ignorant about the causes of our intentional actions. The inevitability of such mistakes is often the driving fact behind our fictions: *Lord Jim* is the story of the inability either to discover or to live with the causes of an action. ("'I had jumped . . .' He checked himself, averted his gaze. . . . 'It seems,' he added").[28] Likewise, it is an entirely normal tragedy to be wrong about the consequences of our intentional actions: Oedipus is terribly underinformed about the consequences of his actions, and as a result he comes to suffer them.[29] But in the present case, I am not wrong about either cause or consequence—I am wrong about what my intentional action was. I had thought that "we were reading" (that my reading was a means by which our reading was happening), but it turns out it was I that was reading.

It is difficult to capture the reorientation required by this anti-Cartesian realization that one's account of one's own mental action is incorrect. It is not the same as a failure of my belief to be true; it is an invalidation of the form of my intention by the content of the world. Such an apparent violation of the requirements of internalism is deeply unsettling; it is as if I believed that I intended to read a poem, only to discover that there had been no I. But if there is something both dizzying about the experience of such radical error and the reorientation toward my own mind that it requires, I want to suggest that there is also something heartening about it. For it is precisely in learning that they are not present that I come to *experience* my capacity for we-intentions; experience it, that is, as more than a theoretical claim or an analytical necessity, but as the felt loss of a capacity that I must, because I can lose it, possess.

Why should we long for this ontological confidence? Particularly when it requires such abstractions from everyday experience of living or reading as these detours through the estranging notations of analytic philosophy? Wallace Stevens, in "A Collect of Philosophy," set out to identify certain concepts in philosophy that he views as "inherently poetic." But the poeticity of philosophical concepts seems to stand in inverse relation to their accessibility to experience: "The sun rises and sets every day," writes Stevens, "and yet it brings to few men and to those men only infrequently a sense of the universe of space."[30] Similarly, my claim at the outset of this chapter that one "must possess" collectivity as a form of intentionality before pursuing it as a cooperative action conflates a logical point (intention comes before action, or defines just what the action is and determines its conditions of satisfaction) with a practical claim—that I must *possess* my intention as a matter of consciousness or will. From a certain philosophical perspective—call it that of the ordinary—and from a certain existential perspective—call it the perspective of living a life—this is a misguided account of the enterprise of knowing—and an implausible account of reading. The satisfactions achieved by receding or retreating into a background of possible actions could look something like Yeats's end-of-life vision in "Cuchulain Comforted"—a kind of comfort, perhaps, but not, exactly, a life.

But poetry, as I have been suggesting throughout this book, does not always name the ordinary case. There are, I propose, situations in which the capacity to act is (strangely) not adequate, does not provide the confidence in self and world that one seeks. At such moments, the estranged and estranging form of "reading" I propose here is *not* an estrangement from the heart, but a route to self-possession.

The fact that this poem became the occasion for my experience and consideration of collective intentionality was most certainly an accident; but the fact that *a* poem became the occasion for my consideration of collective intention is not an accident—though it is a configuration of contingencies. The former fact, that is, was a contingency of my own existence: of my history and my character, my experiences and my tastes; it was an expression of my circumstances, my class, and much else besides. But the latter fact is a contingency of the tradition of poetic uses I have been explaining throughout—part of the continuing history of intending poetry as the project of discovering the foundations of personhood.

Paul de Man, in arguing that "poetic writing is the most advanced and refined mode of deconstruction," defined poetry as the genre that knows better; in which our will to know the self is undercut by the poem's self-conscious strategies and structures of deferral.[31] But perhaps this "poetry" might be better understood, not as a form of *writing*, not as a practice at all, but rather as the problematic of coming to know the something real about persons and their capacities *through* their contingent intentions and actions. Stevens captures something of this sense when he writes: "Essentially what I intend is that it shall be as if the philosophers had no knowledge of poetry and suddenly discovered it in their search for whatever it is that they are searching for and gave the name of poetry to that which they had discovered" (856).

The particular account I have given here suggests that poetry is the genre that knows only by knowing worse. If the capacity for collective intentionality becomes most acutely felt, not in instances of its exercise, but in the experience of its failure, then it is by producing occasions for its exercise—in reading, as reading—that poems give to us, as longing and loss, such powers as we have.

.   .   .

> 7 Jan
> two jays in the sumac
>   grove: they make
>   no patterns:
> as would three or four:
> from branch to ground
> to cherry tree
>   to lawn: always two
>   poles
> of an invisible world,
> shrinking, enlarging,
> dipping, twisting its
>   axis:
> two points of radiation:
>   two sources
> with magnetic field:
> close in
> and the emotions rise—
>   anger
>   or affection—
> and then one jay flies
> away:

On January 6th, the Blizzard of 1996 began. Between the 6th and the 8th, twenty-two and a half inches of snow would fall on Baltimore. On January 7th, I finished reading my daily section of Ammons's poem, and went outside. Typically, for Baltimore, plows hadn't come yet; when they did, they would clear only the narrowest track from even the widest streets—a straitening of travel that would last for weeks. Almost no one was out. The stores had been cleared of the most needful things (milk and toilet paper) in anticipation of the storm. Certainly nothing would stay open for long. In a small act of rebellion, I walked down the center of St. Paul Street, forcing the one car that I could see to steer a wide arc around. It briefly lost traction, and I paused for a minute to see if I would need to help the driver push— but the wheels caught and the car went on. Everyone had someplace to be; everyone wanted to get home.

A few days later, I'd learn that she had stopped reading around December 22nd. Life got in the way; she'd finish another time, she thought.

NOTES

Introduction: Poems, Poetry, Personhood

1. For an incisive history of the various ways in which the distinguishing feature of poetry has been identified with particular uses and powers of language, see Gerald Bruns, *Modern Poetry and the Idea of Language: A Critical and Historical Study* (Champaign, IL: Dalkey Archive Press, 2001). For a study that discovers all modern conceptions of the literary—its aestheticism, its autonomy, its formalism—to be nascent in antiquity, see Adrian Marino, *The Biography of "The Idea of Literature": From Antiquity to the Baroque,* trans. Virgil Stanciu and Charles M. Carlton (Albany: State University of New York Press, 1996).

2. For a collection of recent defenses of the idea that an account of aesthetic experience ought to be central to the ontology of art, see Richard Shusterman and Adele Tomlin, eds., *Aesthetic Experience* (New York: Routledge, 2007).

3. In a series of "Excurses," Ernst Robert Curtius defines a "history of the theory of poetry" as the study of "the concept of the nature and function of the poet and of poetry, in distinction from poetics, which has to do with the technique of poetical composition" (468). Curtius's distinction between poetry's "nature" and "function" and its "technique" will be important to this study, as will some elements of Curtius's fragmentary history: poetry's traditional connection to metaphysics, for example ("The Poet's Divine Frenzy" [474–75]), or its role in establishing and preserving the value of persons ("Poetry as Perpetuation" [476–78]). Other elements of his discussion, like the poet's "mode of existence," (by which Curtius means his way of earning a living), or the conception of poetry as "entertainment," point toward a sociological reading of poetic function that I will be concerned to resist. Ernst Robert Curtius, *European Literature and the Latin Middle Ages* (Princeton: Princeton University Press, 1973).

4. "[Man] is only fully a human being when he plays." Friedrich Schiller, *On the Aesthetic Education of Man*, ed. and trans. Elizabeth M Wilkinson and L. A. Willoughby (Oxford: Clarendon Press, 1967), 107.

5. This is to reject a familiar argument that would take lyric subjectivity as an illusory artifact of ideology; an account clearly (though hardly uniquely) articulated by T. J. Clark: "By 'lyric' I mean the illusion in an artwork of a singular voice or viewpoint, uninterrupted, absolute, laying claim to a world of its own" (*Farewell to an Idea: Episodes from a History of Modernism* [New Haven, CT: Yale University Press, 1997], 401), and to put in its place an account more like Mutlu Konuk Blasing's recent description of the lyric subject as a formal construction of self for which we (as makers and interpreters) must take full responsibility: "The lyric makes audible a virtual subjectivity in the shape of a given language, a mother tongue, and the historical permutations of the concept and status of an 'individual' are not of help in understanding poetic subjectivity, which will elude methodologies that assume that concept as a given." Mutlu Konuk Blasing, *Lyric Poetry: The Pain and the Pleasure of Words* (Princeton, NJ: Princeton University Press, 2007), 5.

6. Hannah Arendt, *The Life of the Mind*, ed. Mary McCarthy (New York: Harcourt Brace Jovanovich, 1978), vol. 1: *Thinking*, 19.

7. Sappho, *The Poetry of Sappho*, trans. Jim Powell (New York: Oxford University Press, 2007), 18. For contemporary reflections on the relation between mourning and personhood, see Judith Butler: "The question that preoccupies me in the light of recent global violence is, Who counts as human? Whose lives count as lives? And, finally, *What makes for a grievable life?*" *Precarious Life* (London: Verso, 2004), 20.

8. Oliver Wendell Holmes, *The Autocrat of the Breakfast-Table* (Boston: Houghton Mifflin, 1916), 254.

9. Friedrich Schiller, *"Naïve and Sentimental Poetry" and "On the Sublime": Two Essays,* trans. J. Elias (New York: Ungar, 1966).

10. Holmes, *Autocrat*, 254.

11. On the continuity of Modernism with Romanticism, see Frank Kermode, *The Romantic Image* (London: Routledge and Kegan Paul, 1957), and Richard Eldridge, *The Persistence of Romanticism: Essays in Philosophy and Literature* (Cambridge: Cambridge University Press, 2001).

12. Thomas Travisano has argued for the historical and conceptual aptness of the label "postmodern" for these formative mid-century poets. See Thomas Travisano, *Mid-Century Quartet: Bishop, Lowell, Jarrell, Berryman and the Making of a Postmodern Aesthetic* (Charlottesville: University Press of Virginia, 1999). See also James Longenbach, *Modern Poetry after Modernism* (Oxford: Oxford University Press, 1991).

13. Robert Lowell, "Epilogue," in *Day by Day* (New York: Farrar, Straus & Giroux, 1977), 127.

14. Frank Bidart, "Lament for the Makers," in *Star Dust* (New York: FSG, 2005), 22.

15. Gertrude Stein, "Composition as Explanation," in *Writings 1903–32* (New York: Library of America, 1998), 522.

16. William Carlos Williams, *Spring and All,* in *The Collected Poems of William Carlos Williams: Volume I, 1909–1939* (New York: New Directions, 1991), 183. *Spring and All* consists of twenty-seven untitled poems interleaved with polemical and exploratory prose; thus I cite all passages from the volume by page number in *The Collected Poems.*

17. Rae Armantrout, "Seconds," in *Up to Speed* (Middletown, CT: Wesleyan University Press, 2004), 23–24.

18. Joseph Conte makes this point in a martial idiom that captures the representative tone in which such intuitive perceptions are offered: "For the veteran of the 'poetry wars' of the middle decades of this century, many estimations flicker through the synapses before the poem has even been read. Thus poetic form is truly an advance guard, the initial point of contact between opposing forms." *Unending Design: The Forms of Post-Modern Poetry* (Ithaca, NY: Cornell University Press, 1991), 13.

19. Marjorie Perloff, *21st-Century Modernism: The "New" Poetics* (Malden, MA: Blackwell, 2002), 8. This is a revision (and perhaps a softening) of earlier formulations that pitted the poetry of "indeterminacy" (in which words or images have "no definable referents" [*The Poetics of Indeterminacy: Rimbaud to Cage,* Princeton: Princeton University Press, 1981, 13]) against a "symbolist" aesthetic invested in "organic unity, coherence, indirection, multiplicity of meanings" (27).

20. Harold Bloom, *Where Shall Wisdom Be Found?* (New York: Riverhead/Penguin, 2004), 1. The distinction between poetry and non-poetry, though inferable throughout Bloom's work, is preserved as an explicit judgment only in a conversation recollected in David Antin, *What It Means to Be Avant-Garde* (New York: New Directions, 1993), 46.

21. For examples, see Andrew Ross, "The New Sentence and the Commodity Form: Recent American Writing," in *Marxism and the Interpretation of Culture* (Urbana: University of Illinois Press, 1988), 361–80; and Hank Lazer, *Opposing Poetries: Volume One—Issues and Institutions* (Evanston, IL: Northwestern University Press, 1996). For a recent history of the reactionary (and sometimes counterfactual) association of modernist experimentation with leftist politics, see Alan Filreis, *Counter-Revolution of the Word: The Conservative Attack on Modern Poetry, 1945–1960* (Chapel Hill: University of North Carolina Press, 2008).

22. Introduction to *The Selected Letters of George Oppen,* ed. Rachel Blau DuPlessis (Durham, NC: Duke University Press, 1990)*,* ix.

23. Not *no* signs, however. Cole Swensen's introduction to the Norton anthology *American Hybrid,* for example, declares an end to hostilities and discovers that "the model of binary opposition is no longer the most accurate one" to describe the uncategorizeable writing of her poetic peers (*American Hybrid: A Norton Anthology of New Poetry* [New York and London: Norton, 2009], xvii). "Instead, we find a thriving center of alterity, of writing and writers that have inherited and adapted traits developed by everyone from the Romantics through the Modernists to the various avant-gardes, the Confessionalists, [the New American Poetry's] margins, and finally to Language poetry and the New Formalists. The product of contradictory traditions, today's writers often take aspects from two or more to create poetry that is truly postmodern in that it's an unpredictable and unprecedented mix" (xx–xxi).

It seems to me, however, that Swensen's description of a magpie relation to "contradictory traditions" is in fact an argument for the ascendancy of the avant-garde tradition under a different name. To treat some poetic possibilities as moves or gestures free for redeployment and resignification is to sever them from their most fundamental commitments. A poetry that stakes claims to revelatory truth, for example—whether that poet is a "traditionalist" like Yeats or an avant-gardist like Duncan—is not merely one style among others, but a bid for wisdom. To transcend the opposition implicit in such a demanding style is not to adapt it but to refuse it.

24. One might, for example, note the generational and institutional shifts that have taken place between Marjorie Perloff's seminal arguments on behalf of a "Poetics of Indeterminacy" as yet unacknowledged (in 1981) in our literary history, and the establishment (in 1996) of the Northwestern University Press series "Avant-Garde and Modernism Studies" edited by Marjorie Perloff and Rainer Rumold; likewise between the early anti-institutional polemics of the Language poets and the founding of an Alabama University Press series devoted to "Modern and Contemporary Poetics" edited by Charles Bernstein and Hank Lazer. Both series are built on the foundations of the division I describe here, and continue to develop and maintain it.

25. Perhaps not enough time has passed for the farrago of anecdote and literary-cultural gossip that would substantiate this point to attain the respectable status of literary sociology. A book like Christopher Beach's *Poetic Culture: Contemporary American Poetry between Community and Institution* (Chicago: Northwestern University Press, 1999) is a first attempt to formalize these distinctions and transactions in a quasi-sociological idiom; a collection like *Telling It Slant: Avant Garde Poetics of the 1990s* (Tuscaloosa: University of Alabama Press, 2001) presents it as an assemblage of poetic testimonies. Perhaps the clearest signs of the dominance of the two-tradition model is the ongoing project of its anthologization one the one hand (e.g., Hoover's *Norton's Anthology of Postmodern Poetry*, Messerli's *From the Other Side of the Century: "A New American Poetry, 1960–1990"*) and on the other hand, the emergence of critical challenges to the conceptual frames by which these histories are told: see for example Jennifer Ashton, *From Modernism to Postmodernism: American Poetry in the Twentieth Century* (New York: Cambridge University Press, 2005), and Brian Reed, "Grammar Trouble," *Boundary 2* 36.3 (2009): 133–58.

26. The classic text theorizing the need for this recovery is Sandra Gilbert's *Shakespeare's Sisters: Feminist Essays on Women Poets* (Bloomington: Indiana University Press, 1979). For a small sampling of the energetic work of recovery, see also Jane Stevenson and Peter Davidson, *Early Modern Women Poets (1520–1700): An Anthology* (Oxford: Oxford University Press, 2001); Mary Loefflholz, *From School to Salon: Reading Nineteenth-Century American Women's Poetry* (Princeton: Princeton University Press, 2004); Jane Dowsen, *Women's Poetry of the 1930s: A Critical Anthology* (New York: Routledge, 1995); Diane Wood Middlebrook and Marilyn Yalom, *Coming to Light: American Women Poets in the Twentieth Century* (Ann Arbor: University of Michigan Press, 1985); Cristanne Miller, *Cultures of Modernism: Marianne Moore, Mina Loy, and Else Lasker-Schuler;* and Claudia Rankine, *American Women Poets in the 21st Century: Where Lyric Meets Language* (Wesleyan University Press, 2002).

For an interesting exchange on the meaning of the tendency of the feminist avant-garde to emphasize the gendered body as a crucial feature of women's poetic production, see Jennifer Ashton's "Our Bodies, Our Poems," and Jennifer Scappettone's response, "Bachelorettes, Even: Strategic Embodiment in Contemporary Experimentalism by Women," in *Modern Philology* 105.1 (August 2007).

27. Mark Sanders describes the way that Sterling A. Brown uses the dialects and rhythms of oral balladry to frame a modernist "contingent subjectivity." See "Sterling A. Brown's Master

Metaphor: *Southern Road* and the Sign of Black Modernity," *Callaloo* 21.4 (1998): 920. Relevant also is the pioneering work on black postmodernity by Aldon Lynn Nielson (*Black Chant: Languages of African American Postmodernism* [Cambridge: Cambridge University Press, 1997] and *Integral Music: Languages of African-American Innovation* (Tuscaloosa: University of Alabama Press, 2004]): "If American postmodernity is to be comprehended in its transracial plenitude, critical readings will have to follow black poets as they read and transform the texts of whites" (*Black Chant*, 36). The converse point is made by Michael North's exploration of High Modernists' mimicry of black dialect in *The Dialect of Modernism: Race, Language and Twentieth-Century Literature* (Oxford: Oxford University Press, 1994).

On the tensions and intersections between Asian American poetry and avant-gardism, See especially Timothy Yu, *Race and the Avant-Garde: Experimental and Asian American Poetry since 1965* (Palo Alto, CA: Stanford University Press, 2009), and Yunte Huang, *Transpacific Imaginations History, Literature, Counterpoetics* (Cambridge, MA: Harvard University Press, 2008).

28. Geoffrey O'Brien, editor-in-chief of the Library of America, describes the principle of selection as a refusal of likeness, suggesting that "each poem included would earn its place by striking a note or evoking an attitude not replicated elsewhere" (Charles Bernstein, "A Conversation with Geoffrey O'Brien," *Boundary 2* 28.1 [Summer 2001]: 2).

29. Sidney Bernard, "A Reading and a Mourning," *New York Times,* April 24, 1977.

30. Jennifer Moxley, *Imagination Verses* (New York: Tender Buttons, 1996), x.

31. W. B. Yeats, *A Vision* (1937; rpt. New York: Collier, 1966), 5. For reasons that will become clear in chapter 1, Yeats was particularly confounded by Pound's insistence that there are events that do not recur. Such singular occurrences would certainly have no role to play in Yeats's conception of history or of art. Thus the dedication of *A Vision,* with its endlessly cycling gyres, to "Ezra Pound, whose art is the opposite of mine, whose criticism commends what I most condemn, a man with whom I should quarrel more than with anyone else if we were not united by affection." The affection is fully reciprocated in Pound's evocation of Yeats in *The Pisan Cantos*, but Pound's comprehension of the stakes of the older poet's art is no greater. On the Yeats-Pound connection more generally, see James Longenbach, *Stone Cottage: Pound, Yeats and Modernism* (Oxford: Oxford University Press, 1991).

32. Stevens did *own* some of Pound's poetry—*Hugh Selwyn Mauberley, Pavannes and Divisions,* and *Cathay* at the least—though some of what he owned was clearly part of a completist impulse in collecting fine press editions. Stevens appears to have owned only one section of the Cantos, *Cantos LII–LXXI.* Perhaps more directly to the point, when Stevens refused to support Pound for the Bollingen Prize in 1949, he claimed to do so not so much on ideological grounds but on the grounds that he had not the time to read the poet carefully.

The Pound/Stevens divide is another name by which the two-tradition model has been forwarded in the history of criticism. See "Pound/Stevens: Whose Era?" in Marjorie Perloff, *The Dance of the Intellect: Studies in the Poetry of the Pound Tradition* (Chicago: Northwestern University Press, 1996). Perloff's argument is revisited by a number of critics in a special issue of the *Wallace Stevens Journal* (26.2, Fall 2002).

33. There are thousands of pages of Oppen's uncollected and unpublished writing in the Archive for New Poetry at Mandeville Special Collections Library, University of California, San Diego. Six substantial excerpts have been published in journals, and a further selection has

appeared as an edited volume. The journal publications include "An Adequate Vision: From the Daybooks," ed. Michael Davidson, *Ironwood* 25 (1985): 5–31; "Meaning Is to Be Here: A Selection from the Daybook," ed. Cynthia Anderson, *Conjunctions* 10 (1987): 186–208; "Selections from George Oppen's Daybook," ed. Dennis Young, *Iowa Review* 18.3 (Fall 1988): 1–17; "The Circumstances," ed. Rachel Blau DuPlessis, *Sulfur* 25 (Fall 1989): 10–43; "Anthropologist of Myself," ed. Rachel Blau DuPlessis, *Sulfur* 26 (Spring 1990): 135–64; "Philosophy of the Astonished," ed. Rachel Blau DuPlessis, *Sulfur* 27 (Fall 1990): 202–20; and "A Selection from 'Daybook One', 'Daybook Two', and 'Daybook Three' from The Working Papers of George Oppen," ed. Stephen Cope, *Germ* 3 (Spring1999): 192–253. The volume is George Oppen, *Selected Prose, Daybooks and Papers*, ed. Stephen Cope (Berkeley and Los Angeles: University of California Press, 2007).

34. Oppen, "An Adequate Vision," 14.

35. Oppen, "A Selection from 'Daybook One'. . . ," 200.

36. There is at least one other mention of Bishop in Oppen's *Selected Letters* which extends Oppen's rejection still further: "on the other hand such non young poets as Eliz[abeth] Bishop, a good deal more infuriating. But fury isn't debilitating: I have a feeling the being furious at E Bishop may be good for us Or makes us young again." See also Elizabeth Bishop, *One Art,* ed. Robert Giroux (New York: Farrar Strauss and Giroux, 1994).

Strikingly, both Oppen and Bishop have recently and separately been declared to be absolutely central to postwar poetry and to an understanding of the contemporary scene. Ron Silliman, for example, has identified Language poetry and its successors—the tradition he calls "post-avant"—as belonging to what he calls "Third Phase Objectivism," as though to locate Oppen's circle at the conceptual core of his own ("Third Phase Objectivism," *Paideuma* 10.1 [Spring 1981]: 85–89). Even more explicitly, Peter Nicholls ties the legacy of the poet to the legacy of poetic and philosophical modernism, in his recent *George Oppen and the Fate of Modernism* (New York: Oxford University Press, 2007), while Henry Weinfield judges Oppen simply the finest poet (along with William Bronk) in his generation (*The Music of Thought in the Poetry of George Oppen and William Bronk* [Iowa City: University of Iowa Press, 2009]). David Orr, on the other hand, in his review of *Edgar Allan Poe and the Jukebox* ("Rough Gems," *New York Times,* 2 April 2006), proclaims without qualification: "You are living in a world created by Elizabeth Bishop . . . . in the second half of the 20th century, no American artist in any medium was greater." Without taking away from the greatness of either poet, I suggest that such sweeping claims for centrality can be made about such deliberately modest (and deliberately decentralizing) work precisely because of the clarity with which the poets manifest the divide between poetic kinds.

37. Jed Rasula, in *The American Poetry Wax Museum: Reality Effects, 1940–1990* (Urbana, IL.: National Council of Teachers of English, 1996), argues exactly this point: "The seemingly autonomous 'voices and visions' of poets themselves have been underwritten by custodial sponsors who have surreptitiously turned down the volume on certain voices, and simulated a voice-over for certain others" (33).

38. Harold Bloom, *Yeats* (New York: Oxford University Press, 1970), v. Bloom's negative evaluation of Eliot would be substantially qualified, though not wholly withdrawn, in his later "Reflections on T. S. Eliot," *Raritan* 8.2 (1988), which declared his poetry to be "securely in the canon" (76).

39. Christopher Nealon has recently written on what he terms the trope of "unrealizability" in the history of poetry, following it through some of the same pretexts that I consider here. Nealon is determined to recruit that trope as part of the history of what he calls "left aesthetics," a politicized hermeneutic that culminates in Frankfurt School Marxism (Christopher Nealon, "The Poetic Case," *Critical Inquiry* 33.4): 865–86. In contrast, I will argue that poetry's unrealizeability has a relation to politics much more difficult to label or chart—indeed, its ontological orientation makes it difficult to describe as political at all.

40. W. K. Wimsatt, *The Verbal Icon* (Lexington: University of Kentucky Press, 1954), 263. On the persistence of New Critical objectification, see Douglas Mao, "The New Criticism and the Text Object," ELH 63.1 (1996): 227–54, and, in a very different vein, Walter Benn Michaels*, The Shape of the Signifier* (Princeton: Princeton University Press, 2004).

41. Theodor Adorno, "On Lyric Poetry and Society," in *Notes to Literature,* ed. Rold Tiedemann, trans. Sherry Weber Nicholson (New York: Columbia University Press, 1991), 1: 37, 38.

42. Theodor Adorno, *Aesthetic Theory*, trans. C. Lenhardt (London: Routledge, 1984), 214.

43. Adorno, "On Lyric Poetry and Society," 39. Adorno's conception of the dialectical relation between the poem and the society it resists—a resistance that is in large part a function of its materiality—was deeply appealing to the New Critical temper, even though Adorno's politics were not. On John Crowe Ransom's relation to Adorno, see Mark Jancovitch, *The Cultural Politics of the New Criticism* (Cambridge: Cambridge University Press, 1993), 111–13.

44. In her 2007 PMLA essay "What Is New Formalism?" (PMLA 122.2 [2007]: 558–69) Marjorie Levinson gives a slightly different taxonomy of "New Formalists," sorting between "(a) those who want to restore to today's reductive re-inscription of historical reading its original focus on form (traced by these critics to sources foundational for materialist critique—e.g., Hegel, Marx, Freud, Adorno, Althusser, Jameson) and (b) those who campaign to bring back a sharp demarcation between history and art, discourse and literature, in which form (regarded as the condition of aesthetic experience as traced to Kant, i.e., disinterested, autotelic, playful, pleasurable, consensus generating, and therefore both individually liberating and conducive to affective social cohesion) is the prerogative of art. In short, we have a new formalism that makes a continuum with new historicism and a backlash new formalism" (559). For examples of the former, see particularly Richard Strier, *Resistant Structures: Particularity, Radicalism and Renaissance Texts* (Berkeley and Los Angeles, CA: University of California Press, 1995) and "How Formalism Became a Dirty Word, and Why We Can't Do Without It," in *Renaissance Literature and Its Formal Engagements*, ed. Mark Rasmussen (New York: Palgrave, 2002), 207–15.

45. When what counts as poetry is determined by purposes or origins rather than results, there is no obvious way a poem could cease to be a poem by failing to possess some *quality*: "I believe it is possible, even essential, that when poetry fails it does not become prose but bad poetry. The test of Marianne Moore would be that she writes sometimes good and sometimes bad poetry but always—with a single purpose out of a single fountain which is of the sort—." By the same logic, since all poems just insofar as they are poems derive from the "single fountain" of origin, no particular moment in a poem best illustrates or typifies what is poetic about it: "Her work puzzles me. It is not easy to quote convincingly" (Williams, *Spring and All,* 231).

46. Allen Grossman, *How to Do Things with Tears* (New York: New Directions, 2001), 95.

47. Percy Bysshe Shelley, *Shelley's Poetry and Prose,* ed. Donald H. Reiman and Sharon B. Powers (New York and London: Norton, 1977), 480–83.

48. Maureen McLane, *Romanticism and the Human Sciences* (Cambridge: Cambridge University Press, 2000), 32.

49. A more complete consideration of the history of intuitionism from Moore and Bergson, to Ross and Maritain, and on to contemporary ethical rationalists like Robert Audi, might show how the progression of intuitionist ethical thought relates to and informs the history of poetry as I will tell it. Such a history lies beyond my present capabilities, and certainly beyond the scope of this book, which is trying to keep literary problems front and center. I will suggest, though, that the problems of induction, example, evidence, and principle in intuitionist philosophy have important parallels to the problem of poetic reading that I will be describing. See Candace Vogler's "Some Remarks on Robert Audi's *The Good in the Right*" in *Rationality and the Good: Critical Essays on the Ethics and Epistemology of Robert Audi,* ed. Mark Timmons, John Greco, and Alfred R. Mele (Oxford: Oxford University Press, 1997).

50. This is to think about "intention" in a special sense, similar to the one used by Sartre to describe the emotions in *The Emotions: A Sketch of a Theory.* According to Sartre, an emotion, rather than merely taking some state of affairs in the world as its object (the sense in which a perception or a belief is intentional), additionally intends "a transformation of the world." Thus (to cite one of his examples) Aesop's fox, unable to reach the bunch of grapes above him, feels the world into a place in which grapes are repulsive, not worth having. These are transformations whose agent (in the case of emotions, the perturbations of the feeling body) is not in any actual sense empowered to alter the world: "Its end is not really to act upon the object as such through the agency of particular means. It seeks by itself to confer upon the object, and without modifying it in its actual structure, another quality." Sartre likens the intentionality of the emotions to a kind of magic, as though the body's feelings could make manifest a world that—despite all appearances to the contrary—conformed to our desires. In the sense of "poetry" I am describing, the poet's work on the poem, like the emotion's work on the body, intends to confer on the world another quality—the quality that I will describe as "being numerous." But work on the poem does not intend its transformations by means of the poem, and it does not exactly hope to modify the world by acting upon or within it, by undertaking some practical mediation. To put it slightly differently, to intend poetry is to intend the world into possessing the quality it should have.

Of course, for Sartre, the magical thinking of the emotions was precisely the hallmark of their bad faith, rather than a valid form of intention.

51. Sharon Cameron, *Impersonality: Seven Essays* (Chicago: University of Chicago Press, 2007), viii.

52. This account of personhood may seem intuitive with respect to the personhood of others, which is always epistemically distant. Perhaps less intuitively, it is also meant to revise our intuitions about ourselves. Thus Rom Harré: "[A] human being does not learn that he or she is a person by the empirical disclosure of an experiential fact. Personal identity is symbolic of social practices, not of empirical experiences. It has the status of a theory." Rom Harré, *Personal Being: A Theory for Individual Psychology* (Cambridge, MA: Harvard

University Press, 1984), 212. Personhood may be contingent on recognition of the correctly constituted being's undergoing a process of development, schooling and socialization before being regarded as a person by others—or even by the self. See also Axel Honneth's appropriation of G. H. Mead's developmental theories in order to explain the emergence of full personhood through recognition: "The only way in which individuals are constituted as persons is by learning to refer to themselves, from the perspective of an approving or encouraging other, as beings with certain positive traits and abilities." *The Struggle for Recognition: The Moral Grammar of Social Conflicts* trans. Joel Anderson (Cambridge: Polity Press, 1995), 173. See also Kelly Oliver's critique of Honneth in *Witnessing: Beyond Recognition.* (Minneapolis: University of Minnesota Press, 2001).

53. Daniel Dennett, "Conditions of Personhood," in A. O. Rorty, ed., *The Identities of Persons* (Berkeley and Los Angeles: University of California Press, 1976), 175–96.

54. Immanuel Kant, *Grounding for the Metaphysics of Morals,* trans. James W. Ellington (Indianapolis, IN: Hackett Publishing Co., Inc., 1981), 36.

55. This is doubtless what makes the constructivist account of personhood attractive to certain styles of cultural analysis. The determining force of convention makes it seem as though the substance of personhood could not matter, or as though assertions of the normative are merely masks for power. This has the advantage of making personhood seem as though it could have a future different than its present—and the disadvantage of making it seem infinitely alterable, and therefore an inadequate basis for hope.

There has, however, been a resurgence of interest in accounts of personhood that are both substantively descriptive and morally demanding. Michael Tooley's argument for the time-limited permissibility of infanticide in the period prior to the child's acquisition of the right kind of self-concept is perhaps among the most notorious for its unabashed derivation of moral standing from psychological capacities. Other arguments lie closer to traditionally *literary*-philosophical concerns: Slavoj Žižek's resurrection of the Cartesian subject (in an intensely negational but still substantive form, as argued in *The Ticklish Subject: The Absent Center of Political Ontology*), Giorgio Agamben's conception of "whatever being," Alain Badiou's revisions of Pauline universalism, all wrestle in their various ways with the Kantian heritage that founds moral personhood in the unassailable dignity of reason.

56. Stanley Cavell, *The Claim of Reason: Wittgenstein, Morality, and Tragedy* (New York: Oxford University Press, 1979).

57. For important recent work on the institution of slavery and the production and regulation of personhood, see Joan Dayan, "Legal Slaves and Civil Bodies," in *Materializing Democracy: Toward a Revitalized Cultural Politics,* ed. Russ Castronovo and Dana D Nelson (Durham, NC: Duke University Press, 2002), 53–92; and Stephen Best, *The Fugitive's Properties: Law and the Poetics of Possession* (Chicago: University of Chicago Press, 2004).

58. Ludwig Wittgenstein, *Philosophical Investigations,* trans. G.E.M. Anscombe (Oxford: Basil Blackwell, 1958).

59. Ira Katznelson, *Desolation and Enlightenment: Political Knowledge after Total War, Totalitarianism, and the Holocaust* (New York: Columbia University Press, 2003), 155. Of course, the solutions to these criticisms offered by the intellectuals who made up the political studies enlightenment of the '30s and '40s differ dramatically from those of the poets I describe, the former being altogether more pragmatic and concerned with the mechanics of toleration.

60. Markham L. Peacock, Jr., *The Critical Opinions of William Wordsworth* (New York: Octagon, 1969), 340. Saintsbury concurs, finding in Shelley "the most perfect products yet of emancipated prosody. . . . the variety is innumerable without a single failure to produce beauty."

61. Ezra Pound, *Literary Essays of Ezra Pound,* ed. T. S. Eliot (New York: New Directions, 1968), 51.

62. A number of critics have recently given powerful accounts of the way that Shelley's poetic idealism may be reconciled with more secular or practical mechanisms of political change. James Chandler argues that Shelley's highly self-conscious figures of figuration and mediation reveal him as a sophisticated thinker about the way history is made by acts of interpretation and reflection (*England in 1819: The Politics of Literary Culture and the Case of Romantic Historicism* [Chicago: University of Chicago Press, 1998], 525–49). Andrew Franta, in a related vein, takes Shelley's outscale imagination of poetry's effects to offer "a myth of transmission rather than transcendence," an investment in the political potential that inheres in the ungovernability of reception in an expanding reading public ("Shelley and the Poetics of Political Indirection," *Poetics Today* 22.4 [Winter 2001]: 765–93).

I think that these accounts sacrifice some of Shelley's strangeness in order to bring him closer to our concerns. Still, if these accounts are correct, then in retrenching upon the gap between poetry as cause and world-transformation as desired effect, it may be that I am not so much describing Shelley, as taking "Shelley" as the name for a problem traditionally associated with him. As we shall soon see, one might call this avatar of perfect justice miraculously achieved through the work of poetry *Yeats's* Shelley. As Yeats explained in his 1900 essay, "The Philosophy of Shelley's Poetry":

> I have re-read *Prometheus Unbound*, which I had hoped my fellow-students would have studied as a sacred book, and it seems to me to have an even more certain place than I had thought among the sacred books of the world. I remember going to a learned scholar to ask about its deep meanings, which I felt more than understood, and his telling me that it was Godwin's *Political Justice* put into rhyme, and that Shelley was a crude revolutionist, and believed that the overturning of kings and priests would regenerate mankind. . . . [O]ne soon comes to understand that his liberty was so much more than the liberty of *Political Justice* that it was one with Intellectual Beauty, and that the regeneration he foresaw was so much more than the regeneration many political dreamers have foreseen, that it could not come in its perfection till the Hours bore "Time to his tomb in eternity." (*Essays and Introductions* [New York: Macmillan, 1961], 67)

For the poets I consider here, the problem as Franta frames it—"Why did a writer committed to many of the tenets of radical political reform choose poetry as his vehicle? In short, if your aim is to change the world, why choose a form of expression with a severely limited and in many ways radically inappropriate audience?"—might be reframed in the following way: What vehicle should the poet committed not to the reform of the world but to its perfection choose? As I shall show, poetry's difficulty in this regard arises, not from the fact that its audience is too small and its effects too restricted, but from the fact that it has any audience, any effect at all.

63. On the centrality of Celan to American poetry, see Jerome Rothenberg, "Paul Celan: A Memoir and a Poem," in *Paul Celan*, special issue of *Studies in 20th Century Literature* 8.1

(Fall 1983): 110–14. Matthew Hofer explores the roots of Donald Hall's conviction that *"every American poet knew Paul Celan"* by the 1960s in "'Between Worlds': W. S. Merwin and Paul Celan," *New German Critique* 91 (Winter, 2004): 101–15. Celan's influence is directly attested in work by Michael Palmer, Anne Carson, Susan Stewart, and Rachel Blau DuPlessis—to name a very few.

64. Paul Celan, *Poems of Paul Celan,* trans. Michael Hamburger (New York: Persea Books, 1989), 238.

65. As Hamburger argues in his translator's preface to the *Poems*:

> "Mein-gedicht" could mean "my-poem" but it could also mean "false poem" or "pseudo-poem" by analogy with the German word "Meineid", a false oath. Probably Celan had both senses in mind when he coined the word. In this case translation had to resolve the ambiguity, and after much pondering I decided in favour of "pseudo-poem", although "Meineid" is the only modern German word that retains this sense of "mein". Paul Celan was a learned poet with an outstandingly rich vocabulary derived more from reading than practice in the vernacular—inevitably, considering how little time he spent in German-speaking countries. The retention of that root in a single modern word is the kind of thing that would have struck and intrigued him no less than the ambiguity of "my" and "false" in that syllable. (26)

Pierre Joris emphasizes the connection between self-representation and misrepresentation still further by translating *Mein- / Gedicht* as "perjury poem."

66. Paul Celan, *Collected Prose,* trans. Rosemarie Waldrop (New York: Routledge, 2003), 26.

67. Anne Carson, *Economy of the Unlost* (Princeton, NJ: Princeton University Press, 1999), 113.

68. Felstiner decides this question, prematurely (and in my view mistakenly), by translating *Genicht* as "lie-noem," a coinage that places the "noem" firmly on the side of misrepresentation. In *Selected Poems and Prose of Paul Celan*, trans. John Felstiner (New York: Norton, 2001), 218.

69. Ibid., 409.

70. Susan Stewart, "Notes on 'Weggebeizt'" *Field* (Oberlin, OH: Oberlin College Press) 71 (2004): 33.

71. See also Edmund Husserl, *Experience and Judgment: Investigations in a Genealogy of Logic,* trans. James S. Churchill and Karl Ameriks, ed. Ludwig Landgrebe (Evanston, IL: Northwestern University Press, 1973).

72. Celan imagines crematorium smoke as a terrible synthesis between the smoke that indexes fire and the sign that tells that a value-bearing thing has been present in his "Death Fugue": "you'll rise up as smoke to the sky / you'll then have a grave in the clouds where you won't lie too cramped" (*Selected Poems and Prose,* 33).

73. Walt Whitman gives a dramatically different account of seeing in his 1855 preface to *Leaves of Grass*, one that will prove much closer to the mysterious accounts of mediation that this book will encounter: "What the eyesight does to the rest he does to the rest. Who knows the curious mystery of the eyesight? The other senses corroborate themselves, but this is removed from any proof but its own and foreruns the identities of the spiritual world.

A single glance of it mocks all the investigations of man and all the instruments and books of the earth and all reasoning."

74. Rainer Maria Rilke, *New Poems [1907],* trans. Edward Snow (New York: North Point Press, 1984), 177.

75. Yopie Prins, "Historical Poetics, Dysprosody, and *The Science of English Verse,*" *PMLA* 123.1 (January 2008): 229–34.

76. "The riddles, papyrae, epigrams, songs, sonnets, *blasons*, *Lieder*, elegies, dialogues, conceits, ballads, hymns and odes considered lyrical in the Western tradition before the early nineteenth century were lyric in a very different sense than was or will be the poetry that the mediating hands of editors, reviewers, critics, teachers, and poets have rendered as lyric in the last century and a half. . . . The various modes of poetic circulation—scrolls, manuscript books, song cycles, miscellanies, broadsides, hornbooks, libretti, quartos, chapbooks, recitation manuals, annuals, gift books, newspapers, anthologies—tended to disappear behind an idealized scene of reading progressively identified with an idealized moment of expression. While other modes—dramatic genres, the essay, the novel—may have been seen to be historically contingent, the lyric emerged as the one genre indisputably literary and independent of social contingency, perhaps not intended for public reading at all." Virginia Jackson, *Dickinson's Miseries: A Theory of Lyric Reading* (Princeton, NJ: Princeton University Press, 2005), 7.

77. Wai Chee Dimock, for example, has been exploring the ways in which reading poems (Mandelstam reading Dante, Thoreau reading the Bhagavad Gita) enables the imagining of modes of association that are global rather than national in scope: "My own conclusion is that literary studies requires the largest possible scale, that its appropriate context or unit of analysis is nothing less than the full length and width of our human history and habitat. I make this claim from the standpoint of literature as a linguistic form with agency in the world, a linguistic form compelling action. This action gives rise to a jurisdictional order whose boundaries, while not always supranational, are nonetheless not dictated in advance by the chronology and territory of the nationstate." Wai Chee Dimock, "Planetary Time and Global Translation: 'Context' in Literary Studies," *Common Knowledge* 9 (2003): 489.

Chapter One: White Thin Bone: Yeatsian Personhood

1. Daniel O'Hara, "*Yeats in Theory,*" in *Post-Structuralist Readings of English Poetry*, ed. Richard Machin and Christopher Norris (Cambridge: Cambridge University Press, 1987), 350.

2. Richard P. Blackmur, *The Double Agent: Essays in Craft and Elucidation* (New York: Arrow, 1935; rpt. Gloucester: Peter Smith, 1962), 186.

3. See John Ayre, "Frye's Geometry of Thought: Building the Great Wheel," *University of Toronto Quarterly* 70.4 (Fall 2001): 825–38.

4. Harold Bloom, *Yeats* (New York: Oxford University Press, 1970), 4.

5. The early work appears as "Image and Emblem in Yeats" in *The Rhetoric of Romanticism* (New York: Columbia University Press, 1984), pp. 145–238. The fully developed deconstructive theory is on display in "Semiology and Rhetoric," *Diacritics* 3.3 (Autumn 1973): 27–33.

6. William Butler Yeats, "Under Ben Bulben," *The Variorum Edition of the Poems of W. B. Yeats,* ed. Peter Allt and Russell K. Alspach (New York: Macmillan, 1965), 357. Unless otherwise specifiied, all quotations from Yeats's poetry are from this volume.

7. O'Hara, "*Yeats in Theory*," 349–50.

8. Ibid.

9. W. B. Yeats, "The Symbolism of Poetry," *Essays and Introductions* (London: Macmillan, 1961), 157–58.

10. Other important or predictive first books include Frank Kermode's *Romantic Image* (New York: MacMillan, 1957); Allen Grossman's *Poetic Knowledge in the Early Yeats: A Study of The Wind among the Reeds* (Charlottesville: The University of Virginia Press, 1969); and Gayatri Spivak's *Myself I Must Remake: The Life and Poetry of W. B. Yeats* (New York: Crowell, 1974). Like Bloom, some important critics come to Yeats later, but with important consequences for their thought and method: strong examples include Edward Said in *Culture and Imperialism* (New York: Vintage, 1994) and Jerome McGann in *Black Riders: The Visible Language of Modernism* (Princeton, NJ: Princeton University Press, 1993).

11. Marjorie Perloff, *Rhyme and Meaning in the Poetry of Yeats* (The Hague: Mouton & Co., 1970).

12. Helen Hennessy Vendler, *Yeats's Vision and the Later Plays* (Cambridge, MA: Harvard University Press, 1969). Vendler argues that Yeatsian numerologies, though "seemingly theoretical and abstract," were "in truth only another statement of the human experiences we find embodies in Yeats's work; . . . we must translate Yeats's esoteric metaphors into the human terms from which they originated, an undertaking sometimes easy, and sometimes almost impossible" (5).

13. Marjorie Perloff, *Poetic License: Essays on Modernist and Postmodernist Lyric* (Evanston, IL: Northwestern University Press, 1990), 95.

14. Helen Vendler, *Our Secret Discipline: Yeats and Lyric Form* (Cambridge, MA: Harvard University Press, 2007), xiii–xiv.

15. The legacy of Orpheus is complex. But for the distinction between Orpheus as a maker of masterful forms and Amphion as a causer of effects, we might compare Shelley's Orpheus, in the poem by that name:

> Thus the tempestuous torrent of his grief
> Is clothed in sweetest sounds and varying words
> Of poesy. Unlike all human works,
> It never slackens, and through every change
> Wisdom and beauty and the power divine
> Of mighty poesy together dwell,
> Mingling in sweet accord

to his Amphion, in the Chorus to *Hellas:*

> If Greece must be
> A wreck, yet shall its fragments reassemble,
> And build themselves again impregnably

> In a diviner clime,
> To Amphionic music on some Cape sublime,
> Which frowns above the idle foam of Time.

16. The literature on Yeats and postcolonialism is ever growing, and full of internal debate. Particularly important contributions include David Lloyd, *Anomalous States, Irish Writing and the Post-Colonial Moment* (Dublin: Lilliput, 1993); Declan Kiberd, *Inventing Ireland: The Literature of the Modern Nation* (London: Vintage, 1996); *Yeats's Political Identities: Selected Essays,* ed. Jonathan Allison (Ann Arbor: University of Michigan Press, 1996); and Jahan Ramazani, "Is Yeats a Postcolonial Poet?" in *W. B. Yeats Critical Assessments,* ed. David Pierce, vol. 4 (Mountfield, East Sussex: Helm Information, 2000), 794–813. For an extremely judicious assessment of the state and stakes of postcolonial readings of Yeats, see Marjorie Howes, "Postcolonial Yeats: Culture, Enlightenment, and the Public Sphere," *Field Day Review* 2 (2006): 55–74. Some of these scholars have noted connections between Yeats's political desires and his metaphysical investments, and I have learned from their arguments, whether they take the connection to be a simple intellectual-historical fact or the basis of a political critique of Yeats's retrograde thinking. My argument, however, is that *any* account that takes cultural production seriously enough to care whether it is part of a colonizing process or a decolonizing process has already given over much to Yeatsian theories of poetic agency.

17. W. B. Yeats, "If I Were Four-and-Twenty," in *Explorations* (New York: Macmillan Publishing Company, 1962), 274.

18. "Education," in this context, must be understood quite expansively to include the whole range of experience, competencies, and limitations that can, under ideal conditions, be acquired by any person. In practice, of course, there are many more barriers to the educability of persons or classes of persons than the geographic, and thus there are many limits to the transferability of national identity—some of which will be discussed later in this chapter.

19. Seamus Deane attributes the Yeatsian vision of the Ascendency to willful ignorance: "Yeats's account of the Anglo-Irish tradition blurs an important distinction between the terms 'aristocracy' and 'Ascendency'. Had he known a little more about the eighteenth century, he would have recognized that the Protestant Ascendency was, then and since, a predominantly bourgeois social phenomenon." *Celtic Revivals: Essays in Modern Irish Literature* (South Bend, IN: University of Notre Dame Press, 1986), 3. I believe that no amount of knowledge about the eighteenth century would have "corrected" Yeats's investment in his view of an aristocracy that is not the opposite of the bourgeoisie, but the negation of the whole hierarchy of which it is a part. For a description of the competing conceptions of aristocracy in a developing capitalist economy, see Jerome Christensen, *Lord Byron's Strength: Romantic Writing and Commercial Society* (Baltimore: Johns Hopkins, 1993): "As a resistance to the mutuality of interest shared by peerage and gentry, aristocratic contempt . . . may be described not as consciousness of class but as resistance to class consciousness" (13).

20. "The Later Poetry of W. B. Yeats," in *Selected Essays of R. P. Blackmur,* ed. Denis Donoghue (New York: Ecco Press, 1986), 159.

21. Denis Donoghue, "Orality, Literacy, and Their Discontents," *New Literary History* 27.1 (1996): 145–59. The truculence of the syntax is quite deliberate; the final version of the poem published in *The Wild Swans at Coole* eliminated a comma that had followed "Others" in *The Little Review*. This revision is a reversion to the original draft manuscript, produced with un-characteristic perfection in 1915. W. B. Yeats, *The Wild Swans at Coole: Manuscript Materials*, ed. Stephen Parrish (Ithaca, NY: Cornell University Press, 1994), 202.

22. Marjorie Perloff proposed that "[e]piphora has almost no significance in Yeats's poems, except in the late period" when Yeats's work in ballad form dramatically increased its frequency in refrains. Perloff, *Rhyme and Meaning,* 25. (Though she does grant that "A Deep Sworn Vow" is an exception to the general insignificance.)

But even in Yeats's middle period the rarity of repetition is a mark of importance rather than triviality. "The Collar-bone of a Hare," for example, opens with an oddly compressed subjunctive phrase. The compression of the more common "would *that* I could" introduces the poem with a rhetorical flourish of archaism, diction appropriate to a speaker whose most immediate association with water and sail is a lost world of kings and idealized romance. While the omission of the expected "that" helps us to characterize the speaker as a roman-tic, it also helps us to identify something about the formal character of the poem. By bringing "would" and "could" closer together, the poem emphasizes the internal rhyme that has al-ways been part of the conventional phrase (though rarely so clearly audible as here), as though to introduce sound similarity as the poem's central feature.

The erasure of difference—first by rhyme, and then, increasingly as the poem goes on, through repetition—is not only the dominant formal feature of the poem, but its central the-matic concern as well. Yeats's poem gives formal expression an unusual desire: the desire to reduce or even eliminate the difference between things and persons—one "kiss" and another "kiss," one lover and another lover. By reducing the difference of rhyme to the iden-tity of repetition, Yeats offers a critique of our conventional understanding of love as a kind of rhyme, as the special fit of one individual self to another. In its place, the poem offers an uncompromising idea: that "the best thing" might be a perfectly *indifferent* love—one that is not just unselfish, but opposed to the idea of individual selves altogether.

23. See also the fourth elegy in Rainer Maria Rilke's *Duino Elegies and the Sonnets to Orpheus,* trans. A. Poulin Jr. (Boston: Houghton Mifflin, 1977): "Look, we don't love flowers / with only one season behind us; when we love / a sap older than memory rises in our arms" (23).

24. R. F. Foster, *W. B. Yeats: A Life*, vol. 1: *The Apprentice Mage 1865–1914* (Oxford: Oxford University Press, 1997), 201–2.

25. Bloom, *Yeats,* 444.

26. Patrick Pearse, *Collected Works of Padraic H. Pearse: Political Writings and Speeches* (Dublin and London: Phoenix, 1922), 221.

27. Michael Hopkinson, *The Irish War of Independence* (Montreal: McGill-Queen's University Press, 2002), 204.

28. Edward Said, *Culture and Imperialism* (New York: Vintage, 1994).

29. See especially the materials collected in the "Celtic Twilight" section of W. B. Yeats, *Mythologies* (New York: Macmillan, 1989).

30. For a thorough account of the consonance between Yeats's folkloric interests, activities, and anthropological methods and the ethnographic project of the Irish Revival, see Gregory Castle, *Modernism and the Celtic Revival* (Cambridge: Cambridge University Press, 2001).

31. Michael North, *The Political Aesthetic of Yeats, Eliot, and Pound* (Cambridge: Cambridge University Press, 1991).

32. Others, of course, have filled the void: notably, George Mills Harper, *Yeats's Golden Dawn: The Influence of the Hermetic Order of the Golden Dawn on the Life and Art of W. B. Yeats* (London: Macmillan, 1974); Kathleen Raine, *Yeats, the Tarot and the Golden Dawn*, 2nd ed. (Dublin: Dolmen Press, 1976); Mary Catherine Flannery, *Yeats and Magic: The Earlier Works* (Gerrards Cross: Smythe, 1977); Frank Kinahan, *Yeats, Folklore, and Occultism: Contexts of the Early Work and Thought* (London: Unwin Hyman, 1988); Graham Goulden Hough, *The Mystery Religion of W. B. Yeats* (Sussex: Harvester, 1984), Kathleen Raine, *Yeats the Initiate: Essays on Certain Themes in the Work of W. B. Yeats* (Portlaoise: Dolmen, 1986); and William T. Gorski, *Yeats and Alchemy* (Albany: State University of New York Press, 1996). For a brilliant and comprehensive account of the role of occultism in the formation of the British avant-garde (including substantial consideration of Yeats), see Alex Owen, *The Place of Enchantment: British Occultism and the Culture of the Modern* (Chicago: University of Chicago Press, 2004).

33. See especially North's reading of "The Lake Isle of Innisfree" (22–27).

34. John Hutchinson, *The Dynamics of Cultural Nationalism: The Gaelic Revival and the Creation of the Nation State* (London: Allen & Unwin, 1987), 21.

35. The most important consideration of the complexity of racialist thinking in Yeats's thought is still John Kelly, "The Fifth Bell: Race and Class in Yeats's Political Thought" (in *Irish Writers and Politics*, ed. Okifumi Komesu and Masaru Sekine [Gerrards Cross: Colin Smythe, 1989]).

36. Douglas Hyde, "The Necessity of De-Anglicizing Ireland," in Charles Gavan Duffy, George Sigerson, and Douglas Hyde, *The Revival of Irish Literature* (London: T.F. Unwin, 1894), 161.

37. D. George Boyce, *Nationalism in Ireland,* 2nd ed. (London: Routledge, 1991), 240. See also Philip O'Leary, *The Prose Literature of the Gaelic Revival, 1881–1921: Ideology and Innovation* (University Park: Pennsylvania State University Press, 1994).

38. Hyde, *Necessity*, 127.

39. There were, of course, more orthodox proponents of a purely racialist doctrine in Ireland during the Gaelic Revival. The prevailing myth of Irish descent—from Milesian invaders a thousand years before the birth of Jesus—was much less forgiving even than Hyde's assimilative ethnicity, and much less credible than MacNeill's scholarship. It has, nevertheless, proved remarkable durable. For an astonishingly credulous recapitulation of this myth reprinted as recently as 1972, see Seamus MacManus, *The Story of the Irish Race: A Popular History of Ireland* (New York: The Devin Adair Company, 1921).

40. Eoin MacNeill, *Phases of Irish History* (Dublin: M. H. Gill and Son, Ltd., 1919), 97.

41. Boyce, *Nationalism in Ireland,* 242.

42. George Bernard Shaw, *The Matter with Ireland,* ed. David H. Grene and Dan H. Laurence (London: Hart-Davis, 1962), 294.

43. Boyce, *Nationalism in Ireland,* 161. For Davis's own justifications, see his "The National Library of Ireland," originally printed in *The Nation* in June of 1845:

> *Hugh O'Neill*—he found himself an English tributary, his clan beaten, his country despairing. He organised his clan into an army, defeated by arms and policy the best generals and statesmen of Elizabeth, and gave Ireland a pride and a hope which never deserted her since. Yet the only written history of him lies in an Irish MS. in the Vatican, unprinted, untranslated, uncopied; and the Irishman who would know his life must grope through *Moryson*, and *Ware*, and *O'Sullivan* in unwilling libraries, and in books whose price would support a student for two winters.
>
> . . . .
>
> The rebellion of 1641—a mystery and a lie—is it not time to let every man look it in the face? The Irish Brigade—a marvellous reality to few, a proud phantom to most of us— shall we not all, rich and poor, learn in good truth how the Berserk Irish bore up in the winter streets of Cremona, or the gorgeous Brigade followed Clare's flashing plumes right through the great column of Fontenoy?
>
> . . . .
>
> This country of ours is no sand bank, thrown up by some recent caprice of earth. It is an ancient land, honoured in the archives of civilisation, traceable into antiquity by its piety, its valour, and its sufferings. Every great European race has sent its stream to the river of Irish mind. Long wars, vast organisations, subtle codes, beacon crimes, leading virtues, and self-mighty men were here. If we live influenced by wind and sun and tree, and not by the passions and deeds of the past, we are a thriftless and a hopeless People.

Charles Gavan Duffy reiterated this pragmatic emphasis, proclaiming that "ideas are the root of action, and books are the cabinet of ideas." "What Irishmen May Do for Irish Literature," in *The Revival of Irish Literature*, ed. Charles Gavan Duffy (London: T. Fisher Unwin, 1894), 19. The struggle between Gavan Duffy and Yeats over the revival of the National Library project is documented in Foster, *W. B. Yeats,* vol. 1, 120–24.

44. In the draft text of "The Fisherman" transcribed from the Maude Gonne Notebook, this line originally read "I shall have made him one"; "made him" was subsequently canceled and replaced with the final "written him." For Yeats "imagining a man," "making him," and "writing him one / Poem" lie close together in the space of the imagination. W. B. Yeats, *The Wild Swans at Coole: Manuscript Materials,* ed. Stephen Parrish (Ithaca and London: Cornell University Press, 1994), 141.

45. After completing this chapter, I read Michael Golston's *Rhythm and Race in Modernist Poetry and Science* (New York: Columbia University Press, 2008). Readers of Golston's book and mine will be struck, as I was, by our shared perception of the fundamental problems Yeats encountered in thinking about how poems might contribute to the work of cultural construction, consolidation, and transmission in a culture of degeneration. Golston focuses, quite compellingly, on Yeats's account of *rhythm* as the "machine" that links the primordial national ideal with the individual body: "More than simply a formal means to hypnotize a reader and render him or her susceptible to the force of unconscious symbols,

rhythm carries with it an 'indefinable' trace of the national metabolism and is thus that gear in the 'machinery' of poetry most critical for the process of nation-forming" (167). Without contesting Golston's account of the mystic (and pseudo-scientific) instrumentality of Yeatsian rhythm, I show that Yeats's imagination of the role artifacts play in forming persons after ideal types is not limited to poetry. The eugenic machine of meter, then, is just one phantasmatic solution (albeit one that played a powerful role in Yeats's practice) for what he would eventually perceive as a metaphysical problem to which *no* form of practical mastery—metrical, magical, imagistic, conceptual, or pedagogical—was adequate.

46. Edwin John Ellis and William Butler Yeats, "The Necessity of Symbolism," in *The Works of William Blake, Poetic, Symbolic and Critical* (London: Bernard Quaritch, 1893, 3 vols.), vol. 1, 235–45. Although the collaborative nature of the Yeats-Ellis *Blake* makes definitive attribution of the essay difficult, the positions espoused here are fully consistent with those Yeats articulates elsewhere.

47. As Yeats would put it much later, in his published diary of 1930: "I think that two conceptions, that of reality as a congeries of beings, that of reality as a single being, alternate in our emotions and in history, and must always remain something that human reason, because always subject to one or the other, cannot reconcile. I am always, in all that I do, driven to a moment which is the realization of myself as unique and free, or to a moment which is the surrender to God of all that I am. . . . Could these two impulses, one as much a part of truth as the other, be reconciled, or if one or the other could prevail, all life would cease" (*Explorations,* 305).

48. Ellis and Yeats, *The Works of William Blake*, 236.

49. See Allen Grossman, *Poetic Knowledge and the Early Yeats* (Charlottesville: University Press of Virginia, 1969): "Just as Yeats, in embracing the cosmic psychology of the Moods, disavows true nationality, so also he disavows true identity. Archetypalism, like nonrational psychology, bypasses identity by locating value above or below consciousness. Personal identity was the abstract unity which Yeats felt it necessary to abolish, and the style of *The Wind Among the Reeds* is exactly oriented to convey the sense of the extinction of personality in the process of transformation" (73).

50. In this it might be usefully contrasted with the Noh drama of Japan, which Yeats understood as a genuinely aristocratic form, possible only in a culture that was continuous with itself in a way that Irish culture could not be. "Some of the old noble families are to-day very poor, their men, it may be, but servants and labourers, but they still frequent these theatres. 'Accomplishment' the word Noh means, and it is their accomplishment and that of a few cultivated people who understand the literary and mythological allusions and the ancient lyrics quoted in speech or chorus, their discipline, a part of their breeding. The players themselves, unlike the despised players of the popular theatre, have passed on proudly from father to son an elaborate art, and even now a player will publish a family tree to prove his skill" ("Certain Noble Plays of Japan," *Essays and Introductions,* 230).

51. Elizabeth Cullingford, *Yeats, Ireland and Fascism* (London: Macmillan: 1981), 229.

52. For a detailed account of Yeats's involvement with the eugenics movement, see David Bradshaw, "The Eugenics Movement in the 1930's and the Emergence of *On the Boiler,*" in *Yeats Annual* 9 (1992): 189–215; and Marjorie Elizabeth Howes, "The Rule of Kindred: Eugenics, *Purgatory*, and Yeats's Race Philosophy," in *Yeats's Nations: Gender, Class, and*

Irishness (Cambridge: Cambridge University Press, 1996), 160–85. For a broader survey of eugenic thinking in Yeats's work, see Paul Scott Stansfield, *Yeats and Politics in the 1930's* (London: Macmillan, 1988), and Donald J. Childs, *Modernism and Eugenics: Woolf, Eliot, Yeats, and the Culture of Degeneration* (Cambridge: Cambridge University Press, 2001).

53. Bradshaw, "The Eugenics Movement," 192.

54. W. B. Yeats, *On the Boiler* (Dublin: The Cuala Press, 1939), 423.

55. *The Variorum Edition of the Plays of W. B. Yeats,* ed. Russell K. Alspach (London and New York: Macmillan, 1966), 486.

56. Note that in both "Long-Legged Fly" and "Under Ben Bulben," Yeats claims a similar function for the image of Adam on the ceiling of the Sistine Chapel.

57. Stansfield, *Yeats and Politics*, 177.

58. W. B. Yeats, *The Senate Speeches of W. B. Yeats,* ed. Donald R. Pierce (Bloomington: Indiana University Press, 1960), 166.

59. For an extremely partisan account of the entire controversy (as well as the source of the plates reproduced from Lane's collection), see Thomas Bodkin, *Hugh Lane and His Pictures* (Dublin: Pegasus Press, 1932). The book was commissioned from Bodkin, director of the National Gallery of Ireland, by the executive council of Saorstat Eireann.

60. Roger Fry, "The Sir Hugh Lane Pictures at the National Gallery," *Burlington Magazine for Connoisseurs*, April 1917, pp. 147–53.

61. Thus Said's persistent interest in the figure of the literary exile: if there *are* no homes, no identities, there *can* be no exiles. The exile *knows* he has a home, and knows too that he is forbidden to enter it. Edward Said, *The World, The Text, and the Critic* (Cambridge, MA: Harvard University Press, 1983).

62. Walter Benjamin, *Gesammelte Schriften,* ed. Rolf Tiedmann and Hermann Schweppenhauser (Frankfurt am Main: Suhrkamp, 1974–89), vol. 1, pt. 3, 1239, cited in Giorgio Agamben*, Potentialities*: *Collected Essays in Philosophy*, ed., trans., and with intro by Daniel Heller-Roazen (Stanford, CA: Stanford University Press, 1999), 48.

Chapter Two: Oppen's Silence, Crusoe's Silence, and the Silence of Other Minds

1. Mary Oppen, *Meaning a Life: An Autobiography* (Santa Barbara, CA: Black Sparrow Press, 1978), 146.

2. Quoted in Daniel Aaron, *Writers on the Left: Episodes in American Literary Communism* (New York: Columbia University Press, 1992), 208.

3. This excerpt from Specter's review of Charles Reznikoff in a 1934 issue of *Dynamo* is quoted by Eric Homberger, "George Oppen and the Culture of the American Left," in *George Oppen: Man and Poet,* ed. Burton Hatlen (Orono, ME: National Poetry Foundation, 1980), 190.

4. Sherwood Anderson, "When I Left Business for Literature," *Century*, August 1924, 489–96.

5. Sherwood Anderson, "A Writer's Notes," *New Masses* 8 (1932): 14.

6. A case in point is the story of Harold Harwell Lewis, "the red-starred laureate," as reconstructed in Cary Nelson, *Repression and Recovery: Modern American Poetry and the*

Politics of Cultural Memory, 1910–1945 (Madison: University of Wisconsin Press, 1989). Though Lewis and Oppen are very different poets, there are some parallels between their careers: Lewis, like Oppen, was a committed leftist whose work was extremely well received by William Carlos Williams in the '30s. Unlike Oppen, however, Lewis spent the end of his life in obscurity and silence. Nelson's argument has less to do with the incompatibility of poetry and politics than with the institution of literary criticism privileging a *kind* of poetry that made Lewis's proletarian and anti-experimental aesthetic invisible. For more details about the Lewis-Williams relationship, see Douglas Wixson, "In Search of the Low-Down Americano: H. H. Lewis, William Carlos Williams, and the Politics of Literary Reception, 1930–1950," *William Carlos Williams Review* 26.1 (2006): 75–100.

7. Nicholls persuasively reads this altered epigraph as a "tacit" part of Oppen's otherwise explicit rejection of canonical high Modernism (37–38). But even though Oppen did repeatedly lump Yeats together with Eliot and Pound (and Joyce and Lawrence and Proust) as negative exemplars of an art "reactionary to the point of insanity," his relation to Yeats seems to have been somewhat more complex than such rhetoric suggests. Oppen never called Yeats's greatness as a poet into question; and he made something of a habit of citing Yeats on the subject of the relation between imaginative work, truth, and human value: "I don't think life should be valued only when it can be sentimentalized (this remark derived from Yeats)" (*Selected Prose, Daybooks and Papers*, 56). Or, in a 1962 letter to Steven Schneider, "There is a sentence of Yeats', by the way: 'Those who are concerned with truth have no Pity.' And, misquoting the rest a little; therefore the threshold of sanctity is blood-stained, and haunted by murder" (ibid., 68). Oppen's appropriations and pointed misquotations have the effect of allying him—albeit in a conflicted way—with Yeats's wisdom about the aspirations and costs of his own art. Perhaps this sideways sympathy lay behind Oppen's backing and forthing about the inclusion of the accusatory epigraph to *The Materials*—omitting it in the 1972 Fulcrum Press edition of the *Collected Poems*, reinstating it in the New Directions edition of 1975.

8. Hugh Kenner, *A Homemade World: The Modernist American Writers* (Baltimore: Johns Hopkins University Press, 1989), 169.

9. Burton Hatlen and Tom Mandel, "Poetry and Politics: A Conversation with George and Mary Oppen," in Hatlen, *Man and Poet,* 25.

10. Edward J. Drea, "Recognizing the Liberators: U.S. Army Divisions Enter the Concentration Camps," *Army History* 24 (Fall/Winter 1992/1993): 1–5.

11. Erich Ludendorff's *Der totale Krieg* was published in 1935.

12. George Oppen, *Collected Poems* (New York: New Directions, 1975), 49. All subsequent quotations from Oppen's poetry are from this edition.

13. Michael Heller, *Speaking the Estranged: Essays on the Work of George Oppen* (Cambridge: Salt Publishing, 2008), 6.

14. Heller does acknowledge what he calls "superficial" resemblances "in appearance" between the "shortened lines and isolated phrases" of the late work and the poems of *Discrete Series.* But, he goes on to argue, "it is hard to imagine finding lines in the later work like these: 'Her ankles are watches / (Her arm-pits are causeways for water)' (Oppen 2002, 9), lines that suggest surrealism, archness or a kind of sophisticated, even superior knowingness?" (*Speaking the Estranged*, 7). I find inflections of surrealism less difficult to imagine finding in

the late poems than Heller suggests. And though such things are hard to adjudicate, I find the arch knowingness Heller hears in these lines to be more the result of the critic's attentive but determined ear straining for difference then an objective report on the lines.

15. For the definitive account of Oppen's relation to communism, see Eric Hoffman, "A Poetry of Action: George Oppen and Communism," *American Communist History* 6.1 (June 2007): 1–28.

16. Nevertheless, Oppen was certainly familiar with first of these sources, and very probably with the second as well. In his "Interview with Mary Oppen" (*Iowa Review* 18.3 [Fall 1988]: 19–47), Mary Oppen asserts that Oppen's interest in the philosophical problem of numerousness led him to read both Heidegger and Wittgenstein. Oppen's refractions of Heidegger have been explored by Peter Nicholls and Henry Weinfield; see also Burt Kimmelman, "George Oppen and Martin Heidegger: The Philosophy and Poetry of *Gelassenheit*, and the Language of Faith," *Jacket* 37 (2009), http://jacketmagazine.com/37/kimmelman-oppen-heidegger.shtml; Susan Thackrey, *George Oppen: A Radical Practice* (San Francisco, CA: O Books, 2001); and Paul Naylor, "The Pre-Position 'Of': Being, Seeing and Knowing in George Oppen's Poetry," *Contemporary Literature* 32.1 (1991): 100–115. Oppen's connections to Wittgenstein's thought have received less attention, but see Heller, *Speaking the Estranged*, 64–81.

17. Henry Weinfield also comments on the possible relation of Oppen's Crusoe to Marx's, in "'Of Being Numerous' by George Oppen" (in Hatlen, *Man and Poet*, 376). He revisits and revises his views in *The Music of Thought*, 48–49.

18. Karl Marx, *Capital: A Critique of Political Economy*, vol. 1, ed. Friedrich Engels, trans. Samuel Moore and Edward Aveling (New York: Modern Library, 1906), 81.

19. Karl Marx, *Grundrisse: Foundations of the Critique of Political Economy* (*Rough Draft*), trans. Martin Nicolaus (Harmondsworth: Penguin Books, 1973), 83.

20. All citations of Bishop's poems are from Elizabeth Bishop, *The Complete Poems: 1927–1979* (New York: Farrar Straus Giroux, 1979).

21. For a dramatically different contextualization of Bishop's concern with social agreement in this poem, see Frances Dickey, "Bishop, Dewey, Darwin: What Other People Know," *Contemporary Literature* 44.2 (Summer 2003): pp. 301–31.

22. Helen Vendler and Dan Chiasson have each pointed out the many ways in which Bishop's Crusoe serves as a proxy for Bishop herself. Taking up such elaborate personae is, on the one hand, a method of concealment—of mystifying oneself with the estranging mask of another. At the same time, this kind of indirect autobiography emphasizes the ways in which one person's experience, no matter how unusual, may speak to, or for, another's. The more baroque the persona, the more strict the injunction to sympathize. See Dan Chiasson, *One Kind of Everything: Poem and Person in Contemporary America* (Chicago: University of Chicago Press, 2007).

23. Properly speaking, the difference between congenital and structural is not just a difference between political economy and philosophy; it is a difference within philosophy as well. In 1949, Gilbert Ryle described the "official theory" about the absolute separateness of persons with reference to the Crusoe story: "the mind is its own place and in his inner life each of us lives the life of a ghostly Robinson Crusoe" (*The Concept of Mind* [Chicago: University of Chicago Press, 1949], 13). But it was an exchange between A. J. Ayer and Rush Rhees

that first took up Robinson Crusoe as the paradigm of a private *language* user (A. J. Ayer and Rush Rhees, "Can There Be a Private Language?" *Proceedings of the Aristotelian Society,* supplementary vol. 28 [1954]: 63–94, reprinted in *Wittgenstein: The Philosophical Investigations*, ed. George Pitcher [Notre Dame, IN: University of Notre Dame Press, 1968], 251–85. As Ayer explains it, the question concerns what we might call a "congenital Crusoe": "Imagine a Robinson Crusoe left alone on his island while still an infant, having not yet learned to speak. Let him, like Romulus and Remus, be nurtured by a wolf, or some other animal, until he can fend for himself; and so let him grow to manhood" (259). Kripke, as I will shortly explain, intensifies the Crusoe scenario by regarding him not as the subject of suppositional history but as a structural problem.

24. Saul Kripke, *Wittgenstein on Rules and Private Language: An Elementary Exposition* (Cambridge, MA: Harvard University Press, 1982).

25. There is a nontrivial disagreement about whether Kripke's Wittgenstein is a good account of Wittgenstein's "private language argument." Again, for my purposes, what Wittgenstein thought will ultimately be less important than the degree to which the account sheds light on what Oppen thought.

26. Though the definitive version of his interpretation of the Wittgenstein problem was not published until well after the poem appeared, Kripke's had formulated his account as early as 1962 and was lecturing publicly on it by 1964. Although it hardly provides evidence for the influence on Oppen of Kripke's Wittgenstein, it might nonetheless be worth noting that while the earlier sequence entitled "A Language of New York" (1965) contained a number of the sections that would later be reincorporated into "Of Being Numerous," the Crusoe passage is not one of them.

27. The history of the statue in question is a fascinating study in the way icons become fodder for ideological conflict. See Vivien Green Fryd, *Art and Empire: The Politics of Ethnicity in the U.S. Capitol, 1815–1865* (New Haven and London: Yale University Press, 1992), 105:

> The United States Capitol dome and its colossal bronze statue are frequently seen on the nightly television news and in political cartoons as signifiers of the U.S. government. Neither photographs of the Capitol nor cartoons, however, provide clear details of the statue on the dome, which is often misidentified in the media and by the general public as an Indian. Thomas Crawford's *Statue of Freedom* is in fact a difficult monument to discern, in part because of its location, far above the viewer's eye, but also because the artist was forced to make a number of compositional and iconographic changes to satisfy his patron, the U.S. government, represented by two men, Captain Montgomery Meigs (1816–1889), from the U.S. Army Corps of Engineers and the financial and engineering supervisor of the Capitol extension between 1853 and 1859, and his boss, Secretary of War Jefferson Davis (1808–1889). . . . Thomas Crawford allowed his statue to fall victim to southern suppression of potentially threatening symbols. As a result, he created a monument of compromise manifest even in the title; the work is identified by government publications as *Statue of Freedom* rather than its more appropriate title, *Armed Liberty*. Politics eroded the work's meaning, and, with each concession made by the artist, the work's iconography became more obscured.

What is ironic is that during the Civil War Crawford's *Statue of Freedom* resonated with additional meaning that applied directly to the division between the North and the South. In particular, President Lincoln had the monument hoisted onto the Capitol dome in 1863, to symbolize the nation's reunification under northern hegemony, a meaning that Jefferson Davis, now president of the Confederacy, obviously had never intended.

28. On curiosity and valuing, see Hans Blumenberg, "The Trial of Curiosity," in *The Legitimacy of the Modern Age,* trans. Robert M. Wallace (Cambridge, MA: MIT Press, 1983): 229–456.

29. Oppen, "A Selection from 'Daybook One' . . . ," 206.

30. Ibid.

31. William Rose Benét, "The Phoenix Nest," in *The Saturday Review of Literature,* March 24, 1934, 580. This view has been most recently revived by William Logan, who in his review of the *New Collected Poems* characterizes Oppen as "a Zen master with a migraine."

32. Peter Nicholls, "On Being Ethical: Reflections on George Oppen," in *The Objectivist Nexus*, ed. Rachel Blau DuPlessis and Peter Quartermain (Tuscaloosa: University of Alabama Press, 1999), 250.

33. Michael Davidson, *Ghostlier Demarcations: Modern Poetry and the Material Word* (Berkeley: University of California Press, 1997), 71.

34. For a critical account of the practical politics that accompany a theoretical commitment to the materiality of the text (as well as examples of the many forms such a commitment can take), see Michaels, *The Shape of the Signifier,* 19–66.

35. Jerome McGann, *Black Riders*, 112.

36. Quoted in Nicholls, *George Oppen and the Fate of Modernism*, 56. In March of 2006, Farrar Strauss and Giroux published a book of "new" poems with Elizabeth Bishop's name on the cover. Titled *Edgar Allan Poe and the Juke Box: Uncollected Poems, Drafts and Fragments,* the volume set off a literary scandal of the sort rarely seen in relation to poetry in the last fifty years. The book's offense, as described by Helen Vendler, whose merciless attack in *The New Republic* caught the attention even of the nonliterary press, was not so much with the publication of "drafts and fragments" (though she certainly objected to this too, on the grounds that Bishop herself would not have wished them to appear), as with the rubric of "uncollected poems" under which the volume was presented. "It should have been called "Repudiated Poems," Vendler countered, resting her case on a claim to which any attentive reader is sure to assent—that Bishop was, by all accounts, an unusually exacting judge of her own work. The "eighty-odd poems" she chose to publish, Vendler argued, "are Elizabeth Bishop as a poet." Helen Vendler, "The Art of Losing," *New Republic*, 3 April 2006, 33–37. The odd qualifier intensifies and elevates the term "poet" into an identity claim; if the published work is what constitutes the identity of the poet "as a poet," then to publish the unpublished work can only be construed as a form of violation. Thus, Vendler writes, "It seems to me a betrayal of Elizabeth Bishop as a poet to print items from the archive in magazines and journals as if they were 'real poems' and not attempts that were withheld by the poet from just such public appearances" (34).

Four years earlier, the University of California Press published George Oppen's *New Collected Poems*. If Bishop's volume received the widest notices imaginable for a book of its kind, Oppen's *New Collected* attracted only the ordinary fanfare—little of it outside of a sphere of initiates—and certainly no scandal. Yet much like the Bishop volume, *New Collected* contains—along with published poetry that Oppen could not have included in his self-assembled *Collected Poems* (his final volume, *Primitive,* was published only some years later)—a section of what editor Michael Davidson chose to call "selected unpublished poems." As in Bishop's case too, these are more than simply poems that Oppen chose not to publish; they include as well some unspecified number of texts which are not with any certainty poems at all. Here is one such text, which though it seems fully consistent with the poet's concerns, hovers uncertainly between poem, fragment, and undigested *pensée,* self-reflexively raising questions about identity and completeness:

> There are many of us,
> There are very many,
> Are they all us? (335)

The generic uncertainty here troubles our sense of just what it is that an editor does. Alice Quinn eliminated from consideration those bits of Bishop that she found "restrictively fragmentary"; but for Davidson it seems that there may be no fragment too restricted to consider. Davidson justifies his editorial decision to cull from the poet's correspondence and his notebooks "poems" that could just as easily be considered drafts, parts of letters, notes, or scrap, by pointing to what he calls "the peculiar quality of Oppen's compositional method" (xx), by which he means to evoke Oppen's valorization of fragmentation and his predilection for unconventional poetic surfaces. Like Emily Dickinson, Oppen wrote short; like her, he wrote in particulate sequences. Like Dickinson too, Oppen composed on random bits of paper—envelopes or laundry lists—mixing literary laboring with more ordinary labors, and composing work without the obvious guidance of a generic frame that could be definitively called lyric. As a result, Davidson notes, "it is often difficult to determine where the poem ends and where the 'rubble' begins" (xiv).

The difference between the reception of an expanded Bishop and that of an expanded Oppen, then, is not just an index of the attention paid to a traditional or mainstream poet or the general indifference to an innovative and "alternative" one. Rather, the difference in the critical response—both in volume and in kind—is a way of registering the presence of two quite different conceptions of poetry (though without quite elucidating the difference). The heat of the Bishop "scandal" depended on a fundamental agreement about the nature of Elizabeth Bishop's poems among all parties to the conflict. Whether we characterize the poems of *Edgar Allan Poe and the Jukebox* (with Quinn) as merely "uncollected" or (with Vendler) as "stunted and maimed," the fundamental point is that they are not, as Vendler terms them, "real poems." For Elizabeth Bishop, as even Quinn would come to agree, publication followed only upon perfection; and perfection is a triumph of realization: "Naturally most of the drafts can't compete with her finished work on an artistic level. Part of Bishop's genius was in recognizing when something was perfected and not publishing work that *hadn't* reached that level" (Tess Taylor, "Paper Trail," *Atlantic,* 20 January 2006). Once that principle is established, the only remaining question is whether the service to the scholar done by the publication of the unreal outweighs the betrayal of the poet "as a poet."

For Oppen, though he is without question a scrupulous craftsman and an equally obsessive reviser of his own work, no such distinctions hold. The border between "rubble" and poem is this case is not merely "difficult to discern"; rather, such borders do not define the nature of poetry as Oppen conceived of it. In his introduction to the new volume, Eliot Weinberger takes this borderless quality to explain the odd underdetermination of Oppen's poetic sequences:

> He wrote short poems and series of short poems, and what is remarkable is that nearly any of the short poems could have been placed in one of the series, any of the series poems could have been a separate short poem, and almost none of them can stand alone as self-contained "anthology pieces." (xi)

But as Davidson's editorial decisions suggest, "borderlesness," or at least a lack of self-distinction or assertion, can be seen to structure even the "short poems" themselves. To view Bishop's fragments as unreal poems, and Oppen's fragments as real ones, raises the question of where poets locate "reality" with respect to poems—or, to put it slightly differently, it raises the question of whether the "reality" that matters is the reality of *poems*. The difference in how we have counted these poets' poems reflects a difference in their understanding of what it means for poetry to count.

37. Philip Fisher, speaking of the rainbow, argues the Bishop point: "the aesthetics of wonder and the poetics of thought are two sides of the same coin" (*Wonder, the Rainbow, and the Aesthetics of Rare Experiences* [Cambridge MA: Harvard University Press, 1998], 45).

38. Compare this to Rush Rhees in "Can There Be a Private Language?": "He may understand the Language that I speak, but he will not understand what I understand" (274).

39. And yet, such intuitionism, inherited from Maritain, was not entirely foreign to Oppen's way of thinking, as evidenced by this passage from his Daybooks: "Thus the primordial intuition of being is the intuition of the solidity and inexorability of existence; and second, of the death and nothingness to which MY existence is liable. And third, in the same flash of intuition, which is but my becoming aware of the intelligible value of being, I realize that this solid and inexorable existence, perceived in anything whatsoever, implies—I do not yet know in what form, perhaps in the things themselves, perhaps separately from them—some absolute, irrefragable existence, completely free from nothingness and death. these three leaps." George Oppen, cited in Nicholls, *George Oppen and the Fate of Modernism*, 33.

Chapter Three: The Justice of My Feelings for Frank O'Hara

1. Frank O'Hara, *Poems Retrieved,* ed. Donald Allen (New York: Knopf, 1974).

2. See Bill Berkson's note on the poem entitled "F.Y.I." in *The Collected Poems of Frank O'Hara,* ed. Donald Allen (New York: Knopf, 1971): "'F.Y.I.' comes from the typical heading for office memorandums—'For Your Information'—which was also the title of *Newsweek* magazine's 'house organ,' a little offset journal of employee gossip distributed weekly. I had worked at *Newsweek* the summers 1956–57 and told Frank about it & he picked up on 'F.Y.I.' He was also inspired to ring a lot of changes on the original titles like 'F.M.I.' ('For My Information'), etc." (501).

3. The little magazines that involved O'Hara most directly (*Kulchur,* for which he wrote most of his "Art Chronicles," Don Allen's *Evergreen Review,* and *Locus Solus,* the magazine most closely associated with the New York School Poets proper) tended to be avant-garde

in the "high" European fashion; but the more aggressive *Fuck You: A Magazine of the Arts* is perhaps more typical of the explosion that would largely follow after O'Hara's death.

4. Allen Ginsberg, "City Midnight Junk Strains," in *Homage to Frank O'Hara,* ed. Bill Berkson and Joe LeSeur, 3rd ed. (Bolinas, CA: Big Sky, 1988), 149.

5. Cited from the unpublished notes for a talk on "The Image in Poetry and Painting" in Marjorie Perloff, *Frank O'Hara, Poet among Painters, with a New Introduction* (Chicago: University of Chicago Press, 1997), 9.

6. *The Collected Poems of Frank O'Hara,* ed. Donald Allen (New York: Knopf, 1971), 17.

7. Frank O'Hara, *Early Writing,* ed. Donald Allen (Bolinas, CA: Grey Fox Press, 1977).

8. The references are, of course, to Wordsworth's definition and Eliot's respectively. See "Tradition and the Individual Talent": "There are many people who appreciate the expression of sincere emotion in verse, and there is a smaller number of people who can appreciate technical excellence. But very few know when there is an expression of *significant* emotion, emotion which has its life in the poem and not in the history of the poet. The emotion of art is impersonal. And the poet cannot reach this impersonality without surrendering himself wholly to the work to be done" (*Selected Prose of T. S. Eliot*, ed. Frank Kermode [New York: Harcourt, 1988], 44).

9. For the list of courses O'Hara took at Harvard, see *Early Writing,* 149–51. Syllabi for English 1b are located in the Harvard University Archives, as are the James Buell Munn Papers containing Munn's lecture notes and class assignments.

10. Jim Elledge has collected early reviews in *Frank O'Hara: To Be True to a City* (Ann Arbor: University of Michigan Press, 1990); Bell's is reproduced on p. 39.

11. Ronald De Sousa, "Fetishism and Objectivity in Aesthetic Emotion," in *Emotion and the Arts,* ed. Mette Hjort and Sue Laver (New York: Oxford University Press, 1997), 177–89.

12. The essay appears as the introduction to *The Collected Poems,* vii–xi.

13. Ron Padgett and David Shapiro, eds., *An Anthology of New York Poets* (New York: Random House, 1970).

14. Ron Padgett, "Strawberries in Mexico," in *An Anthology of New York Poets*, ed. Ron Padgett and David Shapiro (New York: Random House, 1970), 466.

15. See, for example, O'Hara's remarkable "Naphtha":

> Ah Jean Dubuffet
> when you think of him
> doing his military service in the Eiffel Tower
> as a meteorologist
> in 1922
> you know how wonderful the 20th Century
> can be

16. Perloff, *Poet among Painters*, xvi. Mutlu Konuk Blasing, *Politics and Form in Postmodern Poetry: O'Hara, Bishop, Ashbery, and Merrill* (Cambridge: Cambridge University Press, 1995) attempts a similar recuperation.

17. Reva Wolf, *Andy Warhol, Poetry, and Gossip in the 1960's* (Chicago: University of Chicago Press, 1997), 15.

18. David Lehman, *The Last Avant-Garde: The Making of the New York School of Poets* (New York: Doubleday, 1998), 190–93. O'Hara's "On looking at *La grande jatte,* the czar wept anew" appeared in *Partisan Review* 19.2 (March/April, 1952): 183–84.

19. O'Hara and Matthiessen had a warm correspondence about a speech the latter gave in support of the Progressive candidate for President, Henry Wallace, in 1946. Following Wolf's account of "gossip," Matthiessen's suicide (as a result of having been "outed" as both a fellow traveler [in *Life* Magazine] and a homosexual) could easily have given O'Hara sufficient grounds to cast judgment against one of Matthiessen's literary, ideological, and identitarian opponents. For details of the O'Hara-Matthiessen connection, see Brad Gooch, *City Poet* (New York: Knopf, 1993), 129–30.

20. For a more thorough thinking through of the question of what it might mean to "choose" Melville at an earlier moment in American literary history, see Langdon Hammer, *Hart Crane and Allen Tate: Janus-Faced Modernism* (Princeton, NJ: Princeton University Press, 1993), 146–54.

21. Michael Clune asks a set of related questions in his "'Everything We Want': Frank O'Hara and the Aesthetics of Free Choice," *PMLA* 120.1 (January 2005): 181–196. For Clune, O'Hara's insistence on collective choice suggests that choice is a phenomenon best understood in external (sociological) rather than internal (psychological) terms. "Personal poetry" maps out "the coordinates of [O'Hara's] position relative to space, time, and companions" but does not "account [for] the reasons for his choices. Choice is determined by an instant response to the immediate environment rather than by the speaker's fixed values, desires, or beliefs" (183).

22. Pierre Bourdieu, "Flaubert's Point of View," *Critical Inquiry* 14 (Spring 1988): 544. For a greatly expanded version of this argument, see Bourdieu, *The Rules of Art: Genesis and Structure of the Literary Field,* trans. Susan Emanuel (Stanford: Stanford University Press, 1992).

23. Vendler in Elledge, *To Be True to a City,* 234; Mutlu Konuk Blasing in *Politics and Form,* 31.

24. Pierre Bourdieu, *Practical Reason* (Stanford, CA: Stanford Univ. Press, 1998), 78.

25. *Germ* 1 (Fall 1997): 1–11.

26. Oscar Wilde, *The Complete Oscar Wilde* (New York: Crescent Books, 1995), 11.

27.

> The notion of interest is opposed to that of disinterestedness, but also to that of indifference. One can be interested in a game (in the sense of not indifferent), while at the same time being disinterested. The indifferent person 'does not see why they are playing,' it's all the same to them; they are in the position of Buridan's ass, not making a distinction. Such a person is someone who, not having the principles of vision and division necessary to make distinctions, finds everything the same, is neither moved not affected. (*Practical Reason,* 77)

28. O'Hara, "Personism: A Manifesto," in *Collected Poems,* 498.

29. See T. S. Eliot, "The Possibility of a Poetic Drama," in *The Dial* 69.5 (November 1920): "The Elizabethan drama was aimed at a public which wanted entertainment of a crude sort, but would stand a good deal of poetry; our problem should be to take a form of entertainment,

and subject it to the process which would leave it a form of art. Perhaps the music hall comedian is the best material" (447).

30. Ronald de Sousa, *The Rationality of Emotion* (Cambridge, MA: MIT Press, 1997), 8.

31. My discussion of the *Symposium* is indebted to Martha Nussbaum's *Love's Knowledge: Essays on Philosophy and Literature* (Oxford: Oxford University Press, 1990). Quotations from Plato are from Nussbaum, with reference to her page numbering.

32. *The Jade Mountain: A Chinese Anthology, Being Three Hundred Poems of the T'ang Dynasty 618–906,* trans. Witter Bynner (New York: Alfred A. Knopf, 1929); the volume has gone through at least ten printings since its original publication date. For another interpretation of this "error," see Andrew Epstein, *Beautiful Enemies: Friendship and Postwar American Poetry* (New York: Oxford University Press, 2006), 247–49.

33. Lytle Shaw, *Frank O'Hara: The Poetics of Coterie* (Iowa City: University of Iowa Press, 2006).

Chapter Four: Language Poetry and Collective Life

1. Bob Perelman, *The Marginalization of Poetry: Language Writing and Literary History* (Princeton: Princeton University Press, 1996).

2. The literature on Language poetry is now quite large. For an introduction to the poetry, see *"Language" Poetries: An Anthology*, ed. Douglas Messerli (New York: New Directions, 1987), and *In the American Tree: Language Realism Poetry*, ed. Ron Silliman (Orono, ME: National Poetry Foundation, 1986). For writings that comprise the "theoretical arm" of Language poetry, see the still valuable *L=A=N=G=U=A=G=E Book,* ed. Bruce Andrews and Charles Bernstein (Carbondale: Southern Illinois University Press, 1984*)*. Other useful references (by no means an exhaustive list) include *The Politics of Poetic Form: Poetry and Public Policy*, ed. Charles Bernstein (New York: Roof Books, 1990); Bernstein, *A Poetics* (Cambridge, MA: Harvard University Press, 1992); Hank Lazer, *Opposing Poetries* (Evanston, IL: Northwestern University Press, 1996, 2 vols.); Bruce Andrews, *Paradise and Method: Poetics and Praxis* (Evanston, IL: Northwestern University Press, 1996); *Onward: Contemporary Poetry and Poetics,* ed. Peter Baker (New York: Peter Lang Publishers, 1996), and other works (by Alan Golding, Ron Silliman, and Steve McCaffery) cited elsewhere in this chapter. Useful secondary sources include Perelman himself and the many books of Marjorie Perloff. On the Marxism of the Language poets, see George Hartley, *Textual Politics and the Language Poets* (Bloomington: Indiana University Press, 1989). I am not overly concerned at the outset to provide a single definition for Language poetry, which, as I argue over the course of this chapter, is most interesting as a movement performing evasive maneuvers against self-definition. But for a sense of the complex ensemble of styles, positions, and attitudes the school comprises, Steve McCaffery's account will do very well: "A contrived textual indeterminacy . . . alongside a critique of voice and authenticity, an embrace of artifice, a laying bare of the method of production, a preference for heteroglossia over monoglossia while at the same time rejecting narrative modalities, and a general critique of instrumental language under capitalism, mass mediation, and the consciousness industry—all key elements in its early theorizing"("Autonomy to Indeterminacy," *Twentieth Century Literature* 53.2 [Summer, 2007], 215).

Nor do I address the various terminological debates around Language poetry (L=A=N=G=U=A=G=E poetry, Language writing, Language-oriented poetry, and so on.). Despite protestations to the contrary, I do not see that the term chosen has much of an effect on the descriptions or arguments proffered. For reasons of convenience, I use the term "Language poetry" throughout (with nothing in quotation marks), although I might simply prepare the reader to note that the move from "L=A=N=G=U=A=G=E" (as both a journal title and a sort of declaration of the movement's fundamentally structuralist linguistic orientation) to the currently more popular "Language" anticipates my argument in miniature.

3. For a representative exchange in the mode of critique, see the articles by Jerome Mc-Gann, "Contemporary Poetry, Alternative Routes," and Charles Altieri, "Without Consequences Is No Politics: A Response to Jerome McGann," in *Politics and Poetic Value,* ed. Robert von Hallberg (Chicago: University of Chicago Press, 1987), 253–76, 301–8.

4. Charles Bernstein, "Provisional Institutions: Alternative Presses and Poetic Innovation," *Arizona Quarterly* 51.1 (Spring 1995): 144.

5. Steve McCaffery, in his essay "Diminished Reference and the Model Reader," identifies one version of this impasse. The reader of Language poetry is "closed" on his account, constituted upon a series of prohibitions (you can't consume, you can't reproduce an identical message, you can't subvert a representation). Hence the emancipatory character of the reading becomes a mandatory liberation." Steve McCaffery, *North of Intention: Critical Writings 1973–1986* (New York: Roof Books, 1986), 28.

6. Ron Silliman, *Tjanting* (Great Barrington, MA: The Figures, 1981), 11.

7. Rosetti laments the lack of the former in the poetry of Walt Whitman; Greenberg decries the absence of the latter in the sculpture of Robert Morris. "Letters of D.G. Rosetti" in *Atlantic Monthly,* July 1897, p. 53. Clement Greenberg, "Avant-Garde Attitudes: New Art in the Sixties," *The Collected Essays and Criticism,* ed. John O'Brien, vol. 4: *Modernism with a Vengeance 1957–1969,* 300.

8. Ron Silliman, *The Alphabet* (Tuscaloosa: University of Alabama Press, 2008). Silliman began writing *Universe* in 2005; the book is ongoing.

9. Michael Davidson, Lyn Hejinian, Ron Silliman, and Barrett Watten, *Leningrad: American Writers in the Soviet Union* (San Francisco: Mercury House, 1991), 8.

10. Francis Fukayama, "The End of History?" *The National Interest* 16 (Summer 1989): 3–18. In the essay for *The National Interest*, Fukayama promised an "idealist" analysis of the failure of alternatives to liberalism in the sphere of consciousness and ideology as an alternative to materialist arguments attributing the liberalization of politics to the liberalization of economic policy. That analysis was largely deferred until the publication of *The End of History and the Last Man* (New York: Free Press, 1992).

11. John Rawls, *Political Liberalism* (New York: Columbia University Press, 1993), 146. On "self-respect" as "the most important primary good," see especially *A Theory of Justice* (Cambridge, MA: Harvard University Press, 1972), 440.

12. Timothy Garton Ash, *The Magic Lantern: The Revolution of '89 Witnessed in Warsaw, Budapest, Berlin and Prague* (New York: Random House, 1990).

13. The place to begin such a study is with Frederick J. Hoffman, Charles Allen, and Carolyn F. Ulrich, *The Little Magazine: A History and a Bibliography* (Princeton, NJ: Princeton University Press, 1946). See also Elliot Anderson and Mary Kinzie, eds., *The Little Magazine*

in America: A Modern Documentary History (Stamford, CT: Pushcart Press, 1978). Much work remains to be done on the poetry publishing world after World War II. Alan Golding's work on Cid Corman's *Origin* (*From Outlaw to Classic: Canons in American Poetry,* Madison: University of Wisconsin Press, 1995) is important, as is Daniel Kane, *All Poets Welcome: The Lower East Side Poetry Scene in the 1960's* (Berkeley and Los Angeles: University of California Press, 2003). The New York Public Library's catalogue from its exhibition of little magazines (Steven Clay and Rodney Phillips, eds., *A Secret Location on the Lower East Side*, New York: New York Public Library and Granary Books, 1998) is an invaluable resource.

14. Barrett Watten, *Total Syntax* (Carbondale: Southern Illinois University Press, 1985), ix.

15. Charles Bernstein, "Poetics of the Americas," *Modernism/Modernity* 3 (September 1996): 4.

16. Ron Silliman, "The Task of the Collaborator: Watten's Leningrad," in *Aerial 8*, ed. Rod Smith (Washington, DC: Edge Books, 1995), 142.

17. William Wordsworth and Samuel Taylor Coleridge, *Lyrical Ballads* (1798 ed.), ed. W.J.B. Owen, 2nd ed. (Oxford: Oxford University Press, 1969), 153, 161.

18. Cf. Wordsworth's 1802 preface: "There neither is nor can be any essential distinction between the language of prose and the language of metrical composition" (*Lyrical Ballads,* 163 n46). It would be quite interesting to explore further the relation between Language poetry and Wordsworth as an index to its relation to Romanticism. Language poets frequently advert to Wordsworth as the poet whose poetic project they are determined to undo—note the critique of the "Instant Wordsworth" written by epigones of the New American Poetry who have adopted an unreflective stance about the value of the individual.

Like Wordsworth's *The Prelude*, however, *Leningrad* documents a revision in the form and politics of Language poetry. Wordsworth revisits in poetry his own 1790 visit to the revolutionary moment before the terror when "to be young was very heaven" and revolutionary action was understood to be oriented toward "the very world, which is the world / Of all of us,—the place where, in the end, / We find our happiness, or not at all!" Only after the betrayal of the future by English and French imperial designs, Wordsworth replaces his Republicanism with a different sort of collectivity: a "spiritual community" ("There is / One great society alone on earth:/ The noble Living and the noble Dead." [Wordsworth, *The Prelude,* in *Selected Poems and Prefaces,* ed. Jack Stilliner (Boston, 1965), 11, 108, 142–33, 393–95, 332, 333, 339].) As I shall shortly argue, the parallels between this Wordsworthian narrative and Language poetry's revision of early revolutionary ambitions toward a later conception of the person existing prior to historical attachments is quite striking.

19. See, however, Bertram Bruce and Andee Rubin, "Readability Formulas: Matching Tool and Task," in Alice Davison, ed., *Linguistic Complexity and Text Comprehension: Readability Issues Reconsidered* (Hillsdale, NJ: Lawrence Erlbaum Associates, 1988), 5–22. The designers and users of grammar-checking software are under no illusions about its neutrality: "The ultimate judge of readability is the reader, not a formula. Formulas do not guarantee readable texts, even less do they grant people power or access in educational, medical, or legal information systems. Unfortunately, they have often helped to perpetuate cultural bias and protect existing power relationships" (ibid., 20).

20. Stanley Fish, *Is There a Text in This Class? The Authority of Interpretive Communities* (Cambridge, MA: Harvard University Press, 1980), 322–37.

21. Watten, *Total Syntax,* 65.

22. Juliana Spahr, *Everybody's Autonomy: Connective Reading and Collective Identity* (Tuscaloosa: University of Alabama Press, 2001), 5.

23. The term "unavowable community" is, of course, drawn from Maurice Blanchot, *The Unavowable Community*, trans. Pierre Joris (New York: Station Hill Press, 1988). Language poetry's relation to the thought of '68 (Blanchot, Nancy, Bataille) as well as to the larger problem of "New Social Movements," while directly relevant to this inquiry, lies beyond the scope of this book.

24. Benedict Anderson, *Imagined Communities: Reflections on the Origins and Spread of Nationalism* (London: Verso, 1993).

25. This claim can be stated in many rhetorical registers. Bold assertion: "[W]hat readers of language writing will find out is that there is not a monolithic thing called language writing" (Lazer, *Opposing Poetries,* 1:18). Lyrical effusion: "There is of course no state of American poetry, but states, moods, agitations, dissipations, renunciations, depressions, acquies-cences, elations, angers, ecstasies; no music to our verse but vastly incompatible musics; no single sentiment but clashes of sentience" (Bernstein, *A Poetics,* 1). Autobiographical testimony: "[I]n writing our piece, the six of us had no desire for a rigorously structured and self-defined group and no such absolutist designs on the future" (Perelman, *The Marginal-ization of Poetry,* 36). Scholarly authority: "Movement ethos, itself the stepchild of the post-structuralist critique of authorship, has, for too long now, occluded the critical need to dis-criminate difference, to define the signature of the individual lyric subject in its complex negotiations with its cultural and historical field of operation" (Perloff, "Language Poetry and the Lyric Subject: Ron Silliman's Albany, Susan Howe's Buffalo," *Critical Inquiry* 25 [Spring 1999]: 434). I note with particular interest the way in which these distinct styles demonstrate a consensus—the consensus that distinct styles demonstrate the lack of consensus.

26. For the difference between acceptability as a concept of performance and grammati-cality as a concept of competence, as well as a list of hypotheses about the relation between sentence structure and acceptability, see Noam Chomsky, *Aspects of a Theory of Syntax* (Cambridge, MA: MIT Press, 1965), 10–15.

27. Noam Chomsky, *Cartesian Linguistics: A Chapter in the History of Rationalist Thought* (New York: Harper and Row, 1966), 29. See also *Rules and Representations* (New York: Columbia University Press, 1980) and *Knowledge of Language: Its Nature, Origin and Use* (Westport, CT: Praeger Publishers, 1986).

28. Ron Silliman, *The New Sentence* (New York: Roof Books, 1987), pp. 63–93.

29. This critique represents a common mischaracterization of Chomsky's methods. There is no doubt that Chomsky has little interest in actual poems (experimental or otherwise), but he does not exclude poetry from his analysis because it provides inconvenient data, but because of the difference between sentences and utterances. "We construct the new sentences we hear in novel circumstances, generally bringing much more than our knowledge of language to the performance of these creative acts." Chomsky has always been explicit about the fact that generative linguistics is not an explanation of how people speak, but of how they *can* speak.

> It is important to bear in mind the fundamental conceptual distinction between genera-tion of sentences by the grammar, on the one hand, and production and interpretation of sentences by the speaker, making use of the resources of the grammar and much else, on the other. . . . The study of grammar raises problems that we have some hope

of solving; the creative use of language is a mystery that eludes our intellectual grasp. (Chomsky, *Rules and Representations,* 222)

30. A more capaciously comparative analysis analysis—as Roman Jakobson's account of poetry as "organized violence committed on ordinary speech" sought to incorporate not just Khlebnikov but also Yeats—might result in the identification of some systematic kinds of grammatical difficulty in poetic language; but such findings would only leave Language poets vulnerable to the charge that they are simply interested in reproducing poetic language as a form of cultural distinction—thus defeating their purpose. Cf. John Guillory, *Cultural Capital* (Chicago: University of Chicago Press, 1993): "Style is nothing other than a certain relation to grammar, a relation most visible at the vanishing point of grammar's abrogation" (78).

31. For a defense of "experiment" (in something like the sense I am trying to describe here) from a history-of-science perspective, see Rom Harré, "Recovering the Experiment," *Philosophy* 73.285 (July 1998): 353–78. Note especially p. 376: "To defend the possibility of using experiments and experimental equipment as a source of reliable knowledge I need to defend the ontology within which and only within which experimentation makes sense, namely the depth ontology of real causal powers as opposed to the surface ontology of actual appearances and manifestations."

32. In all fairness, I should note that this objection is not entirely hypothetical. Ron Silliman responded to an earlier version of this chapter by leveling exactly these charges against it:

> The article is full of incommensurate leaps—taking individual sentences out of context from within a poetic text & turning them into over-arching claims that language poetry supposedly is making for itself. (Invariably making every langpo responsible for anything any other associated poet may have put into print.) To which Izenberg adds as evidence quotations from some (but hardly all, and hardly a representative sweep of) other lang-pos, as well as from others who have always been critical of language poetry (such as Leslie Scalapino & Jennifer Moxley), treated here as examples of the problem itself. Not to mention poets who may have felt one way at one time and another at a different time, such as Michael Palmer & Susan Howe. Part of that may just be the problem of trying to shoehorn a complex reality into a streamlined expository narrative, but mostly it's just intellectual dishonesty. Izenberg very carefully avoids poets like Bob Perelman & Rae Armantrout who would simply contradict most of his major claims (Ron Silliman, Ron Silliman's Blog, entry posted July 23, 2004, http://ronsilliman.blogspot.com/2004/07/also-on-jonathan-mayhews-blog-is-plea.html)

I have responded to these specific charges in an online exchange ("Radically Universal," The Valve, 17 April 2006, http://www.thevalve.org/go/valve/article/radically_universal/. I respond to a more general, and I think more compelling, version of the concerns that Silliman raises in his comment in the next chapter.

33. Michael Palmer, "Sun," in *Sun* (San Francisco: North Point Press, 1988), 84.

34. The likely source for the image reinforces its association with the repudiation of logic and the specification of imagination, here associated with its divine origins: Luke 11:35, "Take heed therefore that the light which is in thee be not in darkness."

35. Don H. Reiman and Sharon B. Powers, eds., *Shelley's Poetry and Prose* (New York: Norton, 1977), 480.

36. John McDowell gets at the complex relation between possessing a capacity (in this case, a particular language) on the one hand, and recognizing that others are part of a community defined by that shared possession on the other:

> Being a speaker of a language is not contingently connected with the ability to recognize one's fellow-speakers. It *includes* that ability. It makes no sense to suppose someone might be a speaker of English though people who recognize one another as speakers of English do not recognize her as one, or she does not recognize them as fellow-speakers. This is an *a priori* link between the status and the idea of recognition (*Having the World in View: Essays on Kant, Hegel, and Sellars* [Cambridge, MA: Harvard University Press, 2009], 168)

37. Rawls, *Political Liberalism,* 87.

38. Joseph F. Graham, *Onomatopoetics* (Cambridge: Cambridge University Press, 1992), 256.

Chapter Five: We Are Reading

1. Jack Spicer, *My Vocabulary Did This to Me: The Collected Poetry of Jack Spicer,* ed. Peter Gizzi and Kevin Killian (Middletown, CT: Wesleyan University Press, 2008), 122.

2. Jack Spicer, *The House That Jack Built: The Collected Lectures of Jack Spicer*, ed. Peter Gizzi (Hanover, NH: Wesleyan University Press, 1998), 29.

3. Spicer's tumultuous life, his alcoholism and depression, his competitiveness and his capacity for cruelty to his closest friends are well documented in Lewis Ellingham and Kevin Killian, *Poet, Be Like God: Jack Spicer and the San Franscisco Renaissance* (Hanover, NH: University Press of New England for Wesleyan University Press, 1998).

4. On the complicated relations between Lorca's supposed hermeticism in *Poeta* and his belief in the role of the audience as completion of the work, see Dennis Perri, "Fulfillment and Loss: Lorca's View of Communication in the Twenties," *Hispania* 75.3 (September 1992): 484–91.

5. A. R. Ammons, *Tape for the Turn of the Year* (New York: Norton, 1993).

6. Helen Vendler takes both of these actions to be not just possible attitudes that one might adopt toward lyric, but as definitive of the genre: "[A] lyric is meant to be spoken by its reader as if the reader were the one uttering the words. A lyric poem is a script for performance by its reader. It is, then, the most universal of genres, because it presumes that the reader resembles the writer enough to step into the writer's shoes and speak the lines the writer has written as though they were the reader's own." At the same time, however, "We do not listen to him [the speaker]; we become him" in an "imaginative transformation of self." Vendler, *Poems, Poets Poetry: An Introduction and an Anthology* (Boston: Bedford Books, 1996), xxliv.

7. C.f. Thomas Street Millington, *Straight to the Mark* (London: Religious Tract Society, 1883), 72:

> Tom promised Mr. Grantly that he would do as he required; he had already promised his mother the same thing, and meant to adhere to it strictly. She had drawn up a kind of almanac of short daily readings for him, keeping a duplicate for herself; and they had

agreed together to read the same portion each day. They would have liked to be able to feel that they were both reading the same words and thinking the same thoughts at one and the same moment; but there were difficulties arising from the difference of longitude which would render that almost impracticable.

We might contrast Tom's promise with Kenny Goldsmith's project in *The Weather,* which transcribes a year's worth of (undated) live radio broadcast weather reports between 2002 and 2003. Here is a section from "Winter":

"Well, we are looking at a, uh, cloudy, mild evening, also foggy, uh, especially on Long Island, uh, this is just the mild air coming on a southerly breeze off of the, uh, cold ocean which is, uh, causing, uh, that fog bank actually from the Verrazano Narrows bridge, all the way out to Long Island, and, uh, temperatures tonight will be staying in the forties. It'll be around forty-seven at midnight in Times Square, we may see a shower or two about that time as well, because there is going to be a cold front moving through during the middle of the night. And then tomorrow, uh, a storm on the southern end of that very same front, uh, is going to [be] paying us a visit. So what is just going to be a shower, a bit of drizzle in the morning hours, uh, becomes a steady, cold, rain as we go through the day. Temperatures aren't gonna move much, uh, we'll stay in the lower forties, might even drop a bit in the afternoon. It's gonna get to be windy, the rain heavy at times to-morrow night, uh, even the possibility that we have, uh, some icing problems, uh, before it ends very late tomorrow night, the low temperature of thirty-two. Then on Thursday, cloudy, windy, uh, some leftover drizzle, the high of thirty-six. Right now we have fifty-two and mostly cloudy with a light west wind. Repeating the current temperature fifty-two going down to forty-two in midtown.

Leaving aside Goldsmith's elaborate methodological justification for the "boredom" of his work, we can view the poem's resolute focus on weather as a massive expansion of Oppen's conception of "the world, weather-swept, with which /one shares the century." The history of weather-talk is a history of what counts as a relevant range of reference and concern, a range that is both widened and problematized in this poems as American radio broadcasts from 2003 come to include reports on weather conditions in Iraq.

8. This may seem counterintuitive, since it is frequently asserted that distinctiveness of voice or experience is the *ground* upon which fellow feeling is generated, whether in the form of sympathy or some other register of consciousness (e.g., the complex relation between intense particularity and generality that Adorno describes in "On Lyric Poetry And Society" [*Notes to Literature,* 1: 51]). In Ammons's case, however, I would argue that particularity of voice functions to frustrate these modes of engagement.

9. Martin Heidegger, *Being and Time*, trans. J. Macquarrie and E. Robinson (New York: Harper & Row, 1962), 174.

10. See in particular Paul de Man, "Phenomenality and Materiality in Kant," in *Aesthetic Ideology* (Minneapolis: University of Minnesota Press, 1996).

11. By distinguishing between materiality and givenness, between forms (or, more properly, theoretical accounts of forms) and attitudes, I hope to sidestep the critique offered by Jennifer Ashton in *From Modernism to Postmodernism.* Ashton targets the theoretical

account of form that would replace that act of reading a text with the act of experiencing an object, demanding instead that we observe the logical difference between a representation of experience and experience itself.

12. Steven Knapp, *Literary Interest: The Limits of Anti-Formalism* (Cambridge, MA: Harvard University Press, 1993), 47.

13. "The historian's task is thus to reconstruct the variations that differentiate the *espaces lisibles*—that is, the texts in their discursive and material forms—and those that govern the circumstances of their *effectuation*—that is, the readings, understood as concrete practices and as procedures of interpretation." Roger Chartier, *The Order of Books: Readers, Authors, and Libraries in Europe between the Fourteenth and Eighteenth Centuries*, trans. Lydia G. Cochrane (Stanford, CA: Stanford University Press, 1994), 1–2.

14. Perhaps I ought really to submit this chapter to some future (and American) version of the Reading Experience Database, a collective enterprise which seeks to assemble a corpus of reading experiences: "For our purposes, a 'reading experience' means *a recorded engagement with a written or printed text—beyond the mere fact of possession*. A database containing as much information as possible about what British people read, where and when they read it and what they thought of it will form an invaluable resource for researchers of book history, cultural studies, sociology and family history, to name but a few." (http://www.open.ac.uk/Arts/RED/experience.htm)

15. Michael Warner, "Uncritical Reading," in *Polemic: Critical or Uncritical*, ed. Jane Gallop (New York: Routledge, 2004), 13.

16. Joan Shelley Rubin, *Song of Ourselves: The Uses of Poetry in America* (Cambridge, MA: Harvard University Press, 2007), 245.

17. I date this shift (very roughly) to the publication of Wilfrid Sellars's essay "Imperatives, Intentions, and the Logic of 'Ought'," *Methodos* 8 (1956): 228–68.

18. For useful surveys of the ground, see Frederick F. Schmitt, ed., *Socializing Metaphysics: The Nature of Social Reality* (Lanham, MD: Rowman & Littlefield Publishers, Inc., 2003), and Georg Meggle, ed., *Social Facts and Collective Intentionality* (Frankfurt: Dr. Hänsel-Hohenhausen AG, 2002).

19. John Donne, "A Valediction: Forbidding Mourning," lines 17–20, in *The Complete English Poems*, ed. A. J. Smith (London: Penguin, 1987), 84.

20. This premise of ontological individualism—What Searle calls "an ontology and metaphysics based on the existence of individual human beings as the repositories of all intentionality, whether individual or collective"—is not uncontested (see John R. Searle, "Collective Intentions and Actions," in *Intentions in Communication*, ed. Philip R. Cohen, Jerry L. Morgan, and Martha E. Pollack [Cambridge, MA: Bradford Books/MIT Press, 1990], 407). Margaret Gilbert, for example, has argued for the existence of "plural subjects": social groups to which it makes good sense to ascribe mental states (belief, intention), even when no individual member of the group can be said to share them. One of her central examples, happily enough, is a poetry discussion group—a casual assembly whose affirmed judgments about poems can have the binding force of obligation, *whether or not any individual member of the group would assent to them* (see Margaret Gilbert, *On Social Facts* [Princeton, NJ: Princeton University Press, 1992], 288–314). I do not consider her arguments at length here, largely because even the relatively unstructured groups she discusses (the poetry

discussion group, taking a walk together) still have more initial agreements, normative protocols, and concrete realizations built into them than the kind of reading I am describing here.

21. Raimo Tuomela and Kaarlo Miller, "We-intentions," *Philosophical Studies* 53 (1988):
375.

22. Walt Whitman, "Crossing Brooklyn Ferry," lines 13–22, in *Leaves of Grass*
(Philadelphia:McKay, [c. 1900]), http://bartleby.com/142/.

23. John Keats, *Letters of John Keats*, ed. Robert Gittings (Oxford: Oxford University
Press, 1975), 383. In the last letter Keats wrote to Brawne, he finds himself unable to read
what he wishes to, and unable to write the alternative. Instead, he gives himself over to a
wish to believe in another that would not be fulfilled: "I enclose a passage from one of your
letters which I want you to alter a little. I want (if you will have it so) the matter express'd less
coldly to me. If my health would bear it, I could write a poem which I have in my head, which
would be a consolation for people in such a situation as mine" (386).

24. John R. Searle, "Collective Intentions and Actions," 403.

25. John Searle, *The Construction of Social Reality* (New York: Free Press, 1995), 129.

26. Searle, "Collective Intentions and Actions," 410.

27. Here is how Searle puts it:

> The assumption is that if I am mistaken it can only be because one of my beliefs is false.
> But on my account, it turns out that I can not only be mistaken about how the world is,
> but that I am even mistaken about what I am in fact doing. If I am having a hallucination
> in supposing that someone else is helping me push the car, that I am only pushing as
> part of our pushing, then I am mistaken not only in my belief that there is somebody else
> there pushing as well, but I am mistaken about what it is that I am doing. I thought I was
> pushing as part of our pushing, but that is not in fact what I was doing. ("Collective Inten-
> tions and Actions," 408)

For a critique that takes this as Searle's admission that his analysis of collective intentionality
is not ultimately consistent with internalism, see Elisabeth. Pacherie, "Is Collective Intentionality Really Primitive?" in *Explaining the Mental: Naturalist and Non-Naturalist Approaches to
Mental Acts and Processes,* ed. M. Beaney, C. Penco, and M. Vignolo (Cambridge: Cambridge Scholars Press, 2007).

28. Joseph Conrad, *Lord Jim* (New York: Penguin Book, 2000), 125.

29. See Bernard Williams's brilliant formulation of the relation between action and consequence in Oedipus: "The terrible thing that happened to him, through no fault of his own,
was that he did those things." *Shame and Necessity* (Berkeley and Los Angeles: University
of California Press, 1994), 70.

30. Wallace Stevens, "A Collect of Philosophy," in *Collected Poetry and Prose*, ed Frank
Kermode and Joan Richardson (New York: Library of America, 1997), 851.

31. Paul de Man, *Allegories of Reading: Figural Language in Rousseau, Nietzsche, Rilke,
and Proust* (New Haven and London: Yale University Press, 1979), 17.

INDEX

acknowledgment, 20, 21, 49, 95, 98

Adorno, Theodor, 26, 195n43; *Aesthetic Theory,* 13; "On Lyric Poetry and Society," 13

Aerial, 144

aesthetics, 1; and Anderson, 79; and Bourdieu, 125; and Language poetry, 142; and non-poetry, 11; and O'Hara, 37, 112, 113, 125, 126, 130, 133; and Oppen, 79–80, 84, 105, 106; political, 45; sensual pleasures of, 26; and Silliman, 141; and Yeats, 36. *See also* beauty

Afro-Modernism, 8

Agamben, Giorgio, 197n55

agency, 42, 43, 75, 170; and Language poetry, 142, 151; and Yeats, 50, 68

Alcmene's Problem, 130–31

Allen, Donald, 116, 119, 125, 128; *The New American Poetry 1945–1960,* 6, 123, 124

Ammons, A. R.: *Expressions of Sea Level,* 171; *Tape for the Turn of the Year,* 171, 172–74, 175, 179–80, 183–84, 187

Amphion, 43

an-aesthesis, 140, 141, 161

anamnetic structure, 59

anamnetic technique, 49

Anderson, Benedict, 154

Anderson, Sherwood, 79

Andrews, Bruce, *I Don't Have any Paper, So Shut Up, or, Social Romanticism,* 158

Anglo-Irish Ascendancy, 46, 55, 57, 202n19

Anglo-Irish Protestants, 57

Anzeichen, 30

Apollinaire, Guillaume, 117

Appadurai, Arjun, 169–70

Aquinas, Thomas, 99

archetype, 44, 63

Arendt, Hannah, *The Life of the Mind,* 3

aristocracy, 46, 57, 60, 65, 73

Aristotle, 182

Armantrout, Rae, 6–7

art, 3; and Anderson, 79; and Bishop, 104; and Chomsky, 161; and Oppen, 36, 81, 98, 106; and Padgett, 117; perfection of work of, 35; and person, 2–3; and transformation, 36; and Yeats, 36, 62, 70, 73

art-for-art's-sake, 127

Ash, Timothy Garton, 144

Ashbery, John, 9, 115; "Daffy Duck in Hollywood," 3; "The One Thing That Can Save America," 170–71; "Self-Portrait in a Convex Mirror," 2–3

Ashton, Jennifer, 222n11

Asian American poetry, 8

Auden, W. H., 77, 81, 112

Augustine, 176

authenticity, 8

autonomy, 3, 13, 81, 110, 153, 154, 155